CW01086240

RAFAEL MONEO

BUILDING TEACHING WRITING

RAFAEL MONEO
BUILDING TEACHING WRITING

FRANCISCO GONZÁLEZ DE CANALES AND NICHOLAS RAY

YALE UNIVERSITY PRESS • NEW HAVEN AND LONDON

For Nuria and Beatrice

Designed by +SUBTRACT

Printed in China

ISBN: 978-0-300-13912-9
Library of Congress Control Number: 2015945632

A full catalogue record for this book is available from
The library of Congress and The British Library

Frontispiece   Rafael Moneo: Logroño town hall, 1973–81. View from the eastern colonnade
towards the western range. Detail from a photograph by Michael Moran.

CONTENTS

Rafael Moneo is one of the most thoughtful architects born in the twentieth century. His work has received numerous awards and has been a major inspiration for a younger generation of architects, particularly Spanish and American, and of course his projects have been published internationally. Yet his name is not as well known to the public as that of some of his contemporaries, such as Norman Foster or Frank Gehry. His work resists easy categorization and is particularly self-reflective. He has taught for many years, in Barcelona, Madrid and Harvard, where he was Chairman of the Department from 1985 to 1990, and has published essays and books on historical subjects, and (unusually for an architect currently engaged in practice) on the work of his contemporaries, as well as on his own buildings. These writings collectively begin to describe a personal position with important implications for the discipline. Moneo's attitude challenges contemporary assumptions, which suggest that the architect's role has somehow been superseded, and questions the position of those who (in his words) 'wish to think of architecture only in relation to instantaneity and action'. It is probable that his stance will be seen in years to come as a valuable counter to what has almost become a prevailing orthodoxy.

Despite this, there is currently no critical monograph on Moneo's life and work.[1] The most extensive publication is the reproduction of three editions of the Spanish architectural journal *El Croquis* (2004). The present book seeks to remedy that omission and bring to the attention of architects, architectural students and a wider public the work of an important contributor to the culture of architecture.

The book is arranged in three complementary sections and an appendix. The first covers Moneo's biography, and describes a number of his buildings, a few of which are discussed in some detail. The second section analyses seven key buildings, chosen to best illustrate the range and importance of his contribution to architecture. These case studies, selected from his work from

---

1   A 120-page introductory book by Marco Casamonti has a brief essay on the work and illustrates eleven constructed projects and three at design stage; there are also reprints of three essays by Quelga, Vitale and Leone; Marco Casamonti, *Rafael Moneo*, Milan: Motta architettura, 2008. In 2013, CSAE (the National Association of Spanish Architects) published a book under Moneo's supervision to celebrate his Spanish gold medal; Juan Antonio Cortés and Duccio Malagamba, *Rafael Moneo International Portfolio 1985–2012*, Fellbach: Edition Axel Menges, 2013.

1 Rafael Moneo, photographed at home in
Madrid in 1995, on the day on which
he heard he would be awarded
the 1996 Pritzker Prize

the 1970s to the early years of this century, explore the moments at which particular aspects of his approach became first evident, and hence were most important as a contribution to architectural debate at the time; this is not to say
that later buildings do not demonstrate equal quality and intelligence. There
follow, in the third section, essays that seek to explain Moneo's theoretical
stance. The ideas discussed refer back to experiences and personal encounters already described in the biographical section, and their implications for
his own work are illustrated by employing that thinking in re-readings of the
seven case studies. His thought is contextualized in relation to the theoretical
debates on architectural issues in Spain, in Italy and other European coun-
tries and the East Coast of the United States, and the ways in which his own
approach relates to broader philosophical positions are explored. We have
also taken the opportunity to examine in some detail the pedagogical texts
that Moneo published in connection with his teaching appointments; since
these have not been translated into English before, this provides an opportunity for the principles he outlined to be seriously examined and discussed for
the first time.

In bringing together the strands of biography, significant buildings and the ideas evident in his teaching and writing, we seek to argue the relevance of Moneo's work for the twenty-first century. Included as an appendix is a translation of a crucial essay by Rafael Moneo entitled *The Life of Buildings*, published here in English for the first time – a study of the Mosque at Córdoba. It is an inspiring essay to read in itself, but one of the aims of this book will have been achieved if its profound implications can be more fully understood in the light of the teaching, theoretical thinking, and practice of the architect and author himself.

A fuller note of acknowledgement is appended on page 299, but we would like to record here our gratitude to Professor Fernando Pérez Oyarzun, who first introduced Nicholas Ray to Moneo's work and was instrumental in initiating the present book and contributing some preliminary drafts.

Francisco González de Canales
Nicholas Ray
London, March 2013

For many Spaniards, the place where they were born and grew up remains 'el pueblo' ('the village'), no matter how infrequently they may return, or how far abroad their career may take them. Sooner or later they will come home to re-encounter their ancestors, to celebrate a significant birthday, or to bury their relatives. José Rafael Moneo Vallés was born in the city of Tudela, Navarra, on 9 May 1937, and is no exception to that rule. Despite his international career, he has never forgotten the place of his formative emotional experiences and intellectual awakening. It was there that he received his first architectural impressions and, later, his first commissions.

Located some 90 kilometres south of Pamplona, and with a current population of almost 30,000, Navarra's capital city Tudela is strategically sited where the Queiles River meets the Ebro. The region of Tudela was inhabited by humans from the earliest times. The history of the city itself dates back to a Roman settlement, and there is evidence that its current location was certainly a Celtic-Iberian settlement, and possibly an even older one. The present autonomous community of Navarra comes from one of the most ancient kingdoms of the Iberian Peninsula, halfway between Castilla and the Basque country. Navarra borders France at its northern edge, Aragón and the Basque country to the east and south-east, and Rioja to the south. In the fifteenth century, Tudela remained loyal to the king of Navarra when Fernando, 'The Catholic', incorporated the kingdom into Castilla. During the Middle Ages, the city was exemplary for the coexistence of three monotheistic religions: Catholicism, Islam and Judaism. The city has an interesting historic district, which includes a beautiful late Romanesque–early Gothic cathedral attached to an older cloister. The rich agricultural land surrounding Tudela supports vines and vegetables that are exported all over Spain, and agriculture remained the principal economic activity until industry and tourism grew in the middle of the twentieth century. Since the nineteenth century, Navarra has been generally regarded as a broadly conservative region, particularly influenced by traditional, and Catholic, ideas characteristic of movements such as Carlism, which still affected its character during the first half of the twentieth century.[1]

---

1 Carlism is a traditionalist movement that emerged in Spain at the beginning of the nineteenth century. It sought to restore an alternative lineage of the Bourbon family in the succession of the

At the time of Moneo's birth, Tudela was still comparatively small, with around 10,000 inhabitants, and was in the throes of the Spanish Civil War. Its recent history, during the Second Spanish Republic (1931–9) had been turbulent: strikes and civil disobedience were common. Franco's supporters swiftly put down any resistance in the early weeks of the war, assisted by Carlists and other traditional groups with the connivance of the Catholic Church.[2] On 13 August 1937, just a couple of months before Moneo was born, Tudela was bombed by the Republican air force, but compared to the significant resistance mounted by leftist and Republican supporters at the beginning of the war, there was little obvious opposition to the new regime, neither during wartime nor in the post-war period.[3] According to Moneo himself, 'Life in Tudela during the 1940s was popular and traditional, with the typical forms of life of the Spain of those times.'[4]

Spanish monarchy. Their political views were anti-liberal, counter-revolutionary and profoundly Catholic, proposing a return to the Ancien Regime. Although it had a certain impact in Valencia, Aragón and more particularly Catalonia, the centre of Carlism was predominantly in Navarra and the Basque country; indeed the city of Estella in Navarra was the Carlist capital during the third and last Carlist war (1872–6). Carlism became influential again after the Spanish defeat during the 1898 USA–Spanish war, which entailed the loss of the last three Spanish overseas colonies (Cuba, Puerto Rico and The Philippines), and then had an important role during the Spanish Civil War supporting Franco's uprising in Navarra. The Carlist movement waned during Franco's regime, lost its influence after the restoration of democracy in Spain, and is now insignificant and politically marginal.

2   The Spanish elections of 16 February 1936 were won by the leftist party, the Frente Popular, which formed a government consisting exclusively of left-leaning ministers, presided over by Manuel Azaña. After years of violence and confrontation, this final triumph of the left was seen by traditionalist and fascist sectors as a major threat. On 18 July, generals Francisco Franco, Emilio Mola and Gonzalo Queipo de Llano, among others, led a revolt against the legitimate democratic government of the Second Spanish Republic, which took over much of the west of the peninsula, including Navarra under Mola. Tudela was one of the most brutally repressed cities in the region as it was the only one in Navarra where the feared Frente Popular had won the elections, since other Navarran cities generally supported conservative parties. Navarra was already pacified by 1937, and the battlefront moved to the East of the peninsula. The war officially ended on 1 April 1939 when Franco declared his complete victory and started a dictatorship that would last until his death on 20 November 1975.

3   There were multiple imprisonments and at least 65 executions in the Tudela region at the beginning of the war, continuing the pre-war campaign in the Ribera area to suppress the predominantly leftist movement, and to control active workers' unions such as the Federación de Trabajadores de la Tierra and de la Unión General de Trabajadores, which mainly represented peasants without land.

4   Translated from an interview with Rafael Moneo conducted by Francisco González de Canales, 5 December 2012.

Rafael Moneo was raised in an upper middle-class family; his father, Rafael, was an engineer who worked in an electric company. His mother's family was from Aragón, and she had been born in Huesca. His siblings included a younger brother, by one year, Mariano, who also became an engineer like his father, and a sister, Teresa. The house of his grandparents on his father's side was above a fabric store on the beautiful Plaza de los Fueros, or Plaza Nueva, the city's central public space, which had served as a bullring during the eighteenth century. Rafael Moneo has often recalled that living in a relatively small community allowed him to have a more complete vision of the social reality of his times:

> A boy who is raised in a big city only sees the world of his parents; the reality of the social environment of his own family. In a smaller community, such as Tudela, the familiar environment is not the only one from which reality is apprehended. Reality is more widely understood, the relationship of city/countryside, the professions, the social groups . . . you have a more comprehensive anticipation of what the world is going to be about, and are not confined by your own social group.[5]

Tudela in the 1940s reflected the dreary tone of Spanish fascism, without any political or public life. In the hard early post-war years, when food scarcity and rationing were common, Spanish culture was completely isolated from the rest of Europe and people with intellectual curiosity mostly had to seek refuge in their own professional or private activities. In these years of his childhood, always with his brother Mariano, Rafael Moneo attended the Jesuit school in Tudela, housed in a severe nineteenth-century building. He pursued his primary studies there from 1947 to 1954. Jesuit education was regarded as the finest in Spain at the time, but not without its difficulties. We can compare his experiences with those so memorably depicted by James Joyce in his *Portrait of the Artist as a Young Man*, with its famous chapter describing a Jesuit sermon – indeed reading Joyce's novel seemed to leave a strong impression on Moneo. In this period he became interested in philosophy, literature and plastic arts, and inspired by the work of Spanish intellectuals such as Miguel de Unamuno and, most fundamentally, Ortega y Gasset,

---

5   Ibid.

whose books were mandatory reading for all those of his generation with any cultural ambition. His early digestion of their writings helped him to fashion an image of the role in society of the Spanish intellectual that would remain with him all his life. Moneo recalls his years in the school as follows:

> I see myself as an anxious and inquisitive child and teenager, attracted by the intellectual life that the Jesuit School in Tudela offered to me. The school also allowed me a deeper understanding of what life in a community was like. I remember the years at school as an intense period when peer relationships were particularly important. On the other hand, a conventional Catholicism was practiced in the Jesuit college, not particularly enthusiastic or devout, and generally considerably liberal, even though the system of Catholicism had to be seen as unavoidable and impossible to break with. This limitation would be resolved later in Madrid. I see myself in those years influenced by literature, philosophy and painting. In fact, my first approach to culture was going to be through painting, a hobby that I practiced almost since my childhood as an amateur artist, and later enthusiastically developed during my adolescence and early adulthood.[6]

Moneo left Tudela in 1954 to pursue his professional studies after a test (*reválida*) held at the Instituto Plaza de la Cruz, in Pamplona, under the aegis of the University of Zaragoza. He was in general an outstanding student, able in most of the school subjects but inclined towards philosophy and art. The idea of breaking with conventional thinking and developing his own intellectual and artistic personality became an obsession, and was accompanied by an increasingly polemical and controversial personal position. He was yet to recognize his future vocation as an architect; in fact it seems to have been difficult for him to choose his career.

---

6   Ibid.

Moneo arrived in Madrid to begin his university education in September 1954. Madrid was a city still recovering from the privations of the war, with its concomitant political repression reflected in the architecture of the period. In the first fifteen years of his dictatorship, Franco had sought to create monuments to celebrate his regime and the result was a series of megalomaniacal historicist buildings such as El Valle de los Caídos (1940–58). But by 1955, Spain was beginning to recover from an enfeebled economy and from its cultural isolation from the rest of Europe, and indeed the world. Agreements were struck with the United States, Spain joined the United Nations, and gradually fascist ideologists in important government positions were succeeded by efficient technocrats, some of whom were associated with Opus Dei, a conservative Catholic group that became increasingly important in the country.[7] In the second half of the 1950s, Spaniards experienced a transition from stifling autarchy to a livelier period of development known as the *desarrollismo* ('developmentalism'), during which foreign investment was encouraged in support of the economic and technological modernization of the country. Unsurprisingly, this shift was also reflected in the world of design, and a new architecture, faithful to the principles of the Modern Movement, began to be promoted. The first interesting contributions to this paradigm include Alejandro de la Sota's Civil Government building in Tarragona (1956–61, fig. 2), and José Antonio Corrales's and Ramón Vázquez Molezún's Spanish Pavilion for the Brussels World exhibition of 1958.

---

7   Founded in 1928 by the Spanish priest Josemaría Escrivá de Balaguer, Opus Dei is a Personal Prelature of the Catholic church, which promotes an orthodox catholicism based on the principle of 'sanctification through work', as its Latin name suggests. During the Civil War, Opus Dei members at first supported Franco's uprising, which became something of a crusade against the anticlericalism of Republican Spain. Some important architects of the 1950s, such as Miguel Fisac, were closely related to the group, which is still influential in Spain today. In the late 1950s (1957–9), the fact that, almost overnight, three prominent members of Franco's government – Ullastres, Navarro Rubio and López Rodó – were members of this Catholic group, must be understood more as a reflection of the position of an intellectual elite at that time than as some special relationship that Franco had with the organization. John F. Coverdale makes a clear distinction: 'In recent years, "technocrats" grouped around Laureano López Rodó also figured prominently in Franco's cabinets. This group was sometimes identified with Opus Dei, the Catholic lay association to which López Rodó belonged. Opus Dei, however, always protested against the use of its name in this context, pointing out that its members held diverse political views quite independent of their membership in the organization.' John F. Coverdale, *The Political Transformation of Spain after Franco*, New York: Praeger Publishers, 1977, p. 15.

2 Alejandro de la Sota: Gobierno Civil,
Tarragona, 1956–61. An important contribution
to the regeneration of modernism to Spain

Moneo arrived in Madrid still uncertain as to what he should study. His first encounter with the city was through painters, such as Cristino de Vera and Rafael Canogar, whom he met in the studio of Daniel Vázquez Díaz, one of the most remarkable painters of the time. They introduced him to a sophisticated cultural environment of art galleries and ateliers: to Luis Feito and the painters around the Fernando Fe Gallery at the Puerta del Sol. For the young Moneo, Vázquez Díaz epitomized everything that modern painting had to offer: in international terms, he practised a moderate and somewhat tepid modernity, indebted in some sense to Cézanne, but his was nevertheless the most advanced painting to be found in contemporary Madrid. With a group of friends from Tudela, including Rafael del Real and Ramón López de Goicoechea, Moneo founded the literary magazine *Cierzo*, a provincial publication typical of a group of young men with shared intellectual preoccupations. In Madrid he lived in a Jesuit dormitory, sharing a room with his inseparable brother Mariano and with the future architect Rafael Manzano, who was a precocious disciple of the historicist architect Fernando Chueca Goitia and went on to become professor in the history of architecture at the newly founded School of Architecture in Seville. Although Moneo was still linked to a Jesuit institution, he found in these years a freedom of thinking and action that was impossible in the school of Tudela. Manzano remembers the young Moneo as impetuous and adventurous, always boasting that he had just returned from running the bulls in Pamplona, or had met this or that girl, or making similar claims that his young friends realized had been creatively embroidered.[8] Moneo's youthful impulsiveness would be tempered over time to develop into the serene and reflective personality for which he was known in his maturity. As Juan Daniel Fullaondo pointed out in 1975, in comparison to his earlier years, 'we could say he has already lost his polemical angularities'.[9]

Moneo's uncertainty about which studies to pursue persisted, but he was attracted to the idea of studying philosophy and the arts because of his broad interest in philosophical thinking, literature and painting. With this intention he showed his parents the seductive world of art galleries and ateliers each

8   From a conversation between Francisco González de Canales and Rafael Manzano in Seville, 6 March 2012.
9   Juan Daniel Fullaondo, 'Notas de Sociedad', *Nueva Forma* 108, 1975, p. 6.

time they came to visit him and his brother in Madrid, and confessed that he intended to devote himself to the life of an artist. But Moneo's parents, like many before and since, advocated a professional career, with all the benefits of security that that would bring. He was persuaded to enrol in the common science course, which was the gateway to both engineering and architectural schools.[10]

To be admitted to the architectural school was no easy task. For most students, it took more than four years of preparation in order to succeed. In general, the two Spanish schools of architecture at the time – one in Madrid and the other, a younger foundation in Barcelona – reflected the confusion of the period. The Madrid school was part of the Polytechnic University but was organized in a traditional manner, following the structure of the Beaux-Arts School in Paris. This meant that students were required to pass two very stringent exams, one science-based and the other of drawing, before entering the school. Students were prepared for the sciences exam, which was common to all science-based degrees, at a foundation-year course at the School of Basic Sciences, directed by the notable professor José Barinaga; whilst training in drawing, in preparation for the particularly demanding test for architecture applicants, was normally undertaken in private academies. Moneo enrolled on the science classes, where he would study during the morning, and work on perfecting his painting and drawing skills in the evenings. There, those aspiring to enter the architectural school first met, and exchanged their impressions of its academic ambience and the leading teachers of the moment. Moneo became close friends with Emilio Mendívil, a young man from Bilbao who went on to study architecture in Barcelona.

During the period when Moneo was preparing his application to the school of architecture, the drawing examinations were changed, so that evaluation was based on a series of eight or nine exercises integrated into the so-called *cursillos* ('small courses') that were taught at the school. The final examination exercises consisted of charcoal drawings of classical figures, typically

---

10   'It might have been my father, who had a great penchant for architecture, who helped to set me on the path and leave the study of philosophy or painting to one side, both of which attracted me powerfully.' Fernando Márquez and Richard Levene (eds), 'Three Step Interview: Spring 1985', in *Rafael Moneo 1967–2004: Imperative Anthology*, Madrid: El Croquis Editorial, 2005, p. 16.

using chalk and ink wash techniques. Traditional though these may seem, the *cursillos* were intended to contribute to the modernization of the teaching in architecture, since they allowed examiners to compare the skills of different applicants who previously only had the opportunity to show their talent in one examination with a single drawing. Moneo passed the sciences examination exceptionally quickly, enjoying the teaching of Barinaga, and also performed remarkably well in the *cursillos*, obtaining admission to the school in the unusually short time of two years.

When Moneo started his studies at the school of architecture in 1956, the first student revolt occurred in Madrid. It began as a homage, ultimately frustrated, to the memory of the influential philosopher Ortega y Gasset, who had died the year before, but ended with the arrests of a group of young intellectuals who were critical of Franco's regime and would later become important pro-democratic political leaders.[11] During the revolts, when young Falangists confronted young liberal students, the university remained closed, which led to a scandal that was rumoured to be the cause of the resignation of both the Dean of Universidad Complutense, Pedro Laín Entralgo, who had supported the homage to Ortega, and the Minister of Education, Joaquín Ruiz-Giménez. The events of 1956 instigated a series of protests against Franco's regime that would continue to be a feature of university life in Madrid during the 1960s and 1970s.

In the summer of 1957, Moneo took his first extended trip abroad, living for about six weeks in Paris. Rather than concentrating on architecture, he was attracted to the cultural life of the city, the bookshops of the Rive Gauche, the new abstract painters such as Fautrier and Soulages, and the writings of Camus and Sartre.[12] He had not yet found an all-consuming passion for architecture.

---

11 These included Miguel Sánchez Mazas, Dionisio Ridruejo, Ramón Tamames, Enrique Múgica, Javier Pradera, José María Ruiz Gallardón and Gabriel Elorriaga.

12 'I see myself visiting all the art galleries at "La Rive Gauche", all museums, the book stores at the "Boulevard Saint Germain", the French abstract painters such as Fautrier, Soulages … also the discovery of a painter, Grommaire, today almost unknown, but at that time enjoying a great recognition. I remember sharing some of those Parisians moments with a good friend from Tudela, the journalist Montxo (Ramón) López de Goicoechea, but overall it was a quite lonely experience . . . France for us was mostly Camus and Sartre, not so much the philosopher, but the public man, playwright, essayist . . . I remember having seen Sartre in a cafe. Those were the interests of that first trip, which has little

During his studies at the Madrid School of Architecture, Moneo gained a reputation as something of a rebel. In one of the exercises during the *cursillos*, students were asked to produce a model of a simplified Corinthian capital, to be executed in paper, cardboard or clay. Moneo's solution resulted in an unexpected sculptural shape, which he controversially named 'asterisk in space', and which resembled some works of rope and stones that the Spanish sculptor Angel Ferrant was creating at the time. But Moneo was skilful in the medium of ink and charcoal, and soon earned the respect of his peers. His classmate Juan Daniel Fullaondo remembers him during his time at the school as perpetually embroiled in controversies: 'His beginnings at the school of architecture were memorable, confronting some of the professors, as a kind of Buffalo Bill in the Bronze Age of "contestation".' He was a maverick at the very start of what was to be a period of academic turmoil.[13] In his first year at the school, his design professor was Luis Moya, an academic architect of the old school, but a cultivated and talented individual who in the 1940s had designed a suggestive structure inspired by Surrealism – *Sueño Arquitectónico para una exaltación Nacional* ('Architectural Dream for a National Exaltation'). At the time he was teaching Moneo, Moya had just completed his most important work, the eclectic and historicist Laboral University of Gijon (1946–56). In his second year the design professor was Luis de Villanueva, but his assistant was Alejandro de la Sota, one of the most brilliant architects of his generation. When Moneo had completed his second year, De la Sota was asked by architects who needed help in their offices to suggest two students, and he recommended José Ramón Marticorena and Rafael Moneo, who subsequently worked for Fernando Cavestany for some months. It was not until his third year that he encountered a young emerging architect, Francisco Javier Sáenz de Oíza, who was shortly to become his employer and in many ways his mentor: at this stage he started to lose interest in the university and focused on collaborating with Oíza. This was not a decision he took lightly.

---

architecture . . . I don't remember going to see buildings with other classmates, but with this whole group of friends linked to painting and literature rather than to architecture.' Interview with Rafael Moneo by Ana Esteban Maluenda, 'Sustrato y sedimento. Los viajes en la formación y evolución del arquitecto: el caso de Rafael Moneo', in *Viajes en la transición de la arquitectura española hacia la modernidad*, Pamplona: Universidad de Navarra, 2010, p. 154.

13 Fullaondo, 'Notas de Sociedad', p. 6.

During his student years, Spanish schools of architecture were in the midst of a process of modernization, trying to re-fashion the chaotic curriculum that students were forced to endure. While the structure of the schools continued to be based on a Beaux-Arts paradigm, the new ambition of its tutors was to teach from a strictly scientific and technical position. Students of the time tended to be confused, uncertain of their ultimate goals and not surprisingly unhappy with the education they received. While Moneo recalled with pleasure the courses on architectural history by Leopoldo Torres-Balbás, whom he venerated, and appreciated the rigour of the stricter scientific courses of professors such as Barinaga, ultimately he found the last years in the school of architecture uneventful and uninspiring since he did not respect the approach to design teaching in general.[14]

14 'I don't believe that the education of the school in the years I studied had laid a particular stress on the technical aspects. Nor that what was taught there had permeated my work. I remember with pleasure those subjects which had to be pursued at the School of Basic Sciences. We also enjoyed an exceptional teacher of History of Architecture: Leopoldo Torres-Balbás.' Rafael Moneo in Conversation with Félix Arranz in 'Rafael Moneo: Autor de Arquitectura', *Scalae: documentos periódicos de arquitectura* 1, 2003, p. 1.

3 Sáenz de Oíza: plans of the Torres Blancas,
Madrid, 1961–9. An example of flamboyant
organicist modernism

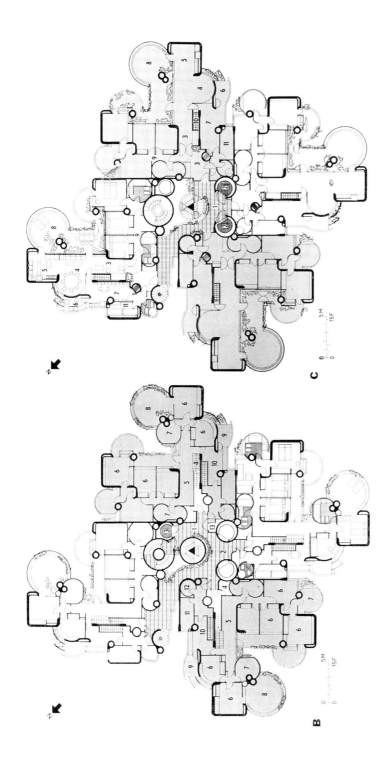

Sáenz de Oíza, whom Moneo consistently acknowledges as his master,[15] first became aware of the young Moneo when he was part of the panel evaluating the *cursillos*. He had seen some of Moneo's works such as the 'asterisk in space'. Oíza asked José Erbina, an older and more experienced student that he knew, to recommend a talented student to help him on a new commission he had recently received – Torres Blancas (fig. 3).

Francisco Javier Sáenz de Oíza had been born in Caseda in 1918, and was therefore also from Navarra; he had completed his education at the school at Madrid in 1946 and then had travelled in the United States, where he was able to study the buildings of Mies van der Rohe and his disciples. Oíza's generation, that of the 1950s, was the first to escape the monumental historicism of Franco's regime and to openly – even fervently – embrace modern architecture. Oíza himself was widely regarded as the brightest of his generation, and was highly respected as a professor of architectural design.[16] He exuded an aura of a modern young professor with advanced ideas, arriving at the school daily in his DKV car. Beyond his professional and academic achievements, Oíza was a charming, unpredictable and charismatic character – probably the most exciting person to work with in Spain.[17]

When Moneo first met him, Oíza had already completed a well-known sanctuary, Nuestra Señora de Aránzazu (1950–55), with the architect Luis Laorga in collaboration with the prominent Basque sculptor Jorge Oteiza. The Aránzazu project, with its abrupt relationship to the landscape in which it was situated, represented a first transition towards modernism, but it still maintained an echo of traditional architecture. Oteiza's contribution was critical to the final project, not only in fulfilling an ideal of integrating the arts, but also by helping to embody in the building something of that primitive Basque

---

15 'What did my work with Oíza mean to me? I have often said the same thing: with Oíza, I learned what it could mean to be an architect, and his attitude to the profession undoubtedly had a profound effect on my future. It was quite clear to me: I wanted to be an architect like Oíza; putting the same tremendous self-demand and overwhelming enthusiasm into my profession as he did.' Márquez and Levene, 'Three Step Interview: Spring 1985', p. 17.

16 In this his career anticipates the path that Moneo's own was to take, with its mixture of practice and theoretical reflection and teaching.

17 Moneo had a high opinion of Oíza as an exceptionally gifted architect. In the text on the young days of Oíza that Rafael Moneo wrote in 1988 he described him as a 'modern Vitruvius'. Rafael Moneo, 'Perfil de Oíza Joven', *El Croquis* 32–33, 1988, p. 176.

character that infused his own art. Oíza and Oteiza collaborated on another significant, but unbuilt, project, the chapel in the Camino de Santiago (1954), which received the National prize of Architecture.[18] But from the mid-1950s Oíza abandoned this more nuanced position and participated in the rush to compensate for the missing chapter of Spanish modernism. His masterpieces in Madrid were the luxury apartment block Torres Blancas (1961–9), a heroic expressionist concrete tower somewhat in the manner of Paul Rudolph or Eero Saarinan, and Banco Bilbao (1971–81), a meticulous and elegant glass and steel tower with slightly rounded corners. This tower was located on the Paseo de la Castellana, the central artery of Madrid's business district, and had an ingenious concrete structure. Both buildings are representative of the ambition of architects of Oíza's generation to produce buildings in Spain of an authentic modernist character.

When Moneo started working for Oíza there were only the two of them in the office, and no architectural technicians or draughtsmen. Later, others joined them, such as Juan Manuel Alonso Velasco and Juan Daniel Fullaondo. During his time in Oíza's office, Moneo contributed to the early stages of Torres Blancas, where he was mainly involved in the study of different solutions for the towers by analyzing the work of modernist masters such as Louis Kahn, Le Corbusier and, most relevantly, a project by Frank Lloyd Wright, the Price Tower in Bartlesville, Oklahoma (1952–6).[19] His work at Torres Blancas remained at the level of the sketch. According to Moneo, the resulting ideas were a mix between Le Corbusier and Wright with a bit of Paul Rudolph, and were very typical of the sensibility of the most avant-garde architecture in Madrid at that time.[20] He also worked on other smaller projects, such as houses, and design competitions, but, most importantly, on the design of an exhibition space for Juan Huarte in the basement of his headquarters at Castellana Avenue in Madrid. This particular project was in fact the one on which Moneo carried out his most concentrated work during his time collaborating with

---

18 For further information on this work and the collaboration between Oíza and Oteiza, see Francisco Javier Sáenz Guerra, *Francisco Javier Sáenz de Oíza, José Luis Romany, Jorge Oteiza: A Chapel on St. James Way*, 1954, Madrid: Rueda, 2004.

19 See Valeria Koukoutsi-Mazarakis, 'José Rafael Moneo Vallés, 1965–1985', PhD dissertation, MIT, 2001, pp. 29–32 and 197.

20   From an interview with Rafael Moneo conducted by Francisco González de Canales, 5 December 2012.

Oíza, and it was fundamental for his education as an architect. The rhetorical and eclectic approach to design and the free use of quotations from De Stilj, the Bauhaus and Aalto, alongside other examples of the modernist architectural legacy, could even be seen as anticipating the work that would emerge out of the 'New York Five'; it indicates a certain sensibility absorbed by the young Moneo, whose ideas were influenced at the time by his admiration for the refined and eclectic personality of the architectural historian and architect Leopoldo Torres-Balbás, and by his readings of Heinrich Wölfflin.[21]

From Sáenz de Oíza, Moneo not only learnt the fundamental technical elements of the profession (drawing and construction), but also seems to have acquired his passion – not to say obsession – with the act of design. The fact that Oíza was interested in designing everything, from the structural frame to the handrails or light fittings, using his rigorous technical skills to hone the aesthetic effect of his architecture, could not fail to impress the young student.[22] It was also in this period during the late 1950s, as he sought to emulate the outstanding architectural erudition of Oíza and the teachings of Torres-Balbás, that Moneo discovered and began to exercise a passion for architectural knowledge, its history and theory – a characteristic that marks the remainder of his career.

---

21 'But above all we spent most time on a new commission from Juan Huarte and Co., the Head office at the Castellana Ave, which is now unfortunately demolished.' Márquez and Levene, 'Three Step Interview: Spring 1985', p. 17. Juan Daniel Fullaondo also remarks on the importance of this project to Moneo's development: 'Oíza was a man always alert to the trends of our time . . . Oíza was a man who oscillated, was sensitive to alternative evocations of rationalism and their expression. Oíza, an up-to-date man, a man of many keys, a mirror of many things, who needed the endorsement of ideas that were generally foreign to him to further his own thinking . . . Moneo witnessed this from his initial experiences in the office of the great Navarra architect, just at the time he was developing the project for an exhibition space. Rationalism? Certainly, an eclectic and inventive overview of quotations from neoplastic, Bauhaus . . .' Fullaondo, 'Notas de Sociedad', p. 7.

22 'It was probably the contact with Francisco Javier Sáenz de Oíza which taught me how to be an architect. Many things attached to the professional work in its more direct condition as well: how to evaluate scale and measurements, how to draw, how to put one material beside the other when one is thinking on a detail or a color. In one word, never seeing architecture as something located far from reality. But upon every other thing, what I value the most in my learning with Oíza is that he transmitted to me his intellectual curiosity and to see the architect as someone that contributes to the cultural discourse to explain the world around us.' Rafael Moneo in Conversation with Félix Arranz in 'Rafael Moneo: Autor de Arquitectura', p. 2.

But even though Moneo always credited Oíza as his true master, he was also critical of his work from the start. His first published article, in 1961, was devoted to Oíza's low-income housing project Poblado Dirigido de Entrevías, and essentially took him to task for pursuing the aesthetic ideals of modernism without taking the real needs of the inhabitants sufficiently into account.[23] Later, he continued to criticize Oíza's generation for pursuing the principles of early modernism in a dogmatic way, just at the time when those principles were being called into question everywhere else.[24]

It was also during his years as an architectural student in Madrid that Rafael met Belén Feduchi, who would later become his wife. Belén was the daughter of Luis Martínez Feduchi, a well-known Spanish architect of the first half of the twentieth century. He was not only the architect, with Vicente Eced, of the Capitol Building (1931–3), one of the modernist icons of Avenue Gran Vía in Madrid, but was also the author of several books on the history of Spanish furniture and, most famously, a compendium of five volumes on Spanish vernacular architecture.[25] The fact that she had grown up among architects (indeed one of her brothers was also himself a well-known architect), and that she had been able to enjoy frequent visits abroad, had given her a sophisticated education. Belén remained a crucial figure in Moneo's career, not only as wife and mother, but also as a source of invaluable, ongoing advice.

It is not clear how much his father-in-law, Luis Martínez Feduchi, helped launch the young Moneo's career. Feduchi was a reasonably well-known architect in Madrid in the 1950s when he changed the direction of his career by concentrating on furniture design. Though interest in modern furniture in Spain was mainly concentrated around Barcelona-based architects during the 1950s, Feduchi was certainly the most influential figure in that field in Madrid. Nevertheless, it is probable that Moneo's relationship with the Huarte family had a greater importance.

---

23   Rafael Moneo, 'El poblado dirigido de Entrevías', *Hogar y Arquitectura* 34, May–June 1961, pp. 3–28.

24   Rafael Moneo, 'Madrid 78: 28 arquitectos no numerarios', *Arquitecturas Bis* 23–4, 1978, pp. 22–54.

25   Amongst his works on furniture design are: Luis M. Feduchi, *La casa por dentro*, Madrid: Afrodisio Aguado, 1948; *Interiores de hoy*, Madrid: Afrodisio Aguado, 1955; *Historia del mueble*, Madrid: Abantos, 1966; and *Estilos del mueble español*, Madrid: Abantos, 1969. His extensive research into popular architecture was published in Luis M. Feduchi, *Itinerarios de arquitectura popular española*, Barcelona: Blume, 1974–84 (5 volumes).

Moneo met Félix Huarte, the founder of the Huarte and Cia construction company, when working for Francisco Javier Sáenz de Oíza in the late 1950s. Huarte had started a construction company back in 1927, but was able to adapt himself sufficiently to the post-civil war context to obtain important commissions from Franco's government, including the construction of El Valle de los Caidos. He was politically and culturally engaged, financed the editorial group Alfaguara and promoted some of the most important artistic personalities of his time. These mostly came from the Basque and Navarra region and included the sculptors Jorge Oteiza and Eduardo Chillida, the musician Luis de Pablo and Sáenz de Oíza himself, from whom he commissioned Torres Blancas as a showcase for his concrete. It helped that, like Huarte, Oíza's young assistant Rafael Moneo also came from Navarra. During his period with Oíza, Moneo worked not only on Torres Blancas, but also – in fact mostly – on the Huarte Gallery, an important project during which he got to know the Huarte family very well. Juan, one of Félix Huarte's sons, continued his father's philanthropic mission, financing Los Encuentros de Pamplona and also the magazine *Nueva Forma*, which was crucial in promoting modernist architecture in Madrid. Moneo was the first architect of his generation to receive a full monograph in its January 1975 issue. Not only did Juan Huarte found the furniture company H Muebles, in order to promote the production of modern furniture design in Spain (and their first competition was won by Moneo), but it was through Huarte's relations that Moneo received his first architectural commission in Madrid: the Gómez-Acebo House (fig 11) , built by Juan Huarte's aristocratic brother-in-law Alfonso Gómez-Acebo. Throughout his career, Moneo has maintained his relationship with the Huarte family. His most recent commission from the family is the Contemporary Art Museum of the University of Navarra (2011–14), to hold the collection of Juan's sister María Josefa Huarte.

Feduchi's furniture designs certainly influenced Moneo's attitude to the details of his own furniture, which are often reminiscent of the suave lines of the 1930s. In fact, Moneo's first two successes in design competitions were related to furniture design. In 1960, whilst still a student, he won the competition run by H Muebles, who wanted to advertise the quality of Spanish design and offered, in addition to reasonably generous prize money, to manufacture and market the winning entry. Moneo's successful design was made of folded

4 Rafael Moneo: prize-winning
design for H Meubles of a chair
made from folded plywood, 1960

plywood, which proved difficult to manufacture in Spain and resulted in a long
journey by Moneo himself through England, Denmark and Sweden, using the
prize money to find furniture producers to help him with its production (fig.
4).[26] One year later, he won one of the prizes in a competition organized by
the Minister of Housing for furniture designed for low-income housing. In
this competition he was able to put to good use the furniture manufacturing
techniques he had observed on his trip to Northern Europe.[27]

26   'As nobody in Spain knew how produce this industrially I thought of using part of the prize to make
      a journey to find who could do it. I called on many offices to see if they could advise me on the mat-
      ter. I had seen some school furniture and desks by Ernö Goldfinger, the Hungarian architect of some
      importance in the fifties who had emigrated to England. Goldfinger told me that the machines that
      did this kind of work were all in Sweden and that I had to go there . . . In Denmark I was not so lucky,
      though I visited all furniture stores . . . So then I went to Sweden, where I did obtain the address of
      small factories who could do what I was looking for. And there also I began to think about visiting
      some architecture. I was tantalized by Asplund, from the first sight . . . his Woodland Cemetery . . .
      And then I met Ralph Erskine. I knew where the boat in which he lived and worked was moored and
      I went to greet him.' Esteban Maluenda, interview with Moneo from 'Sustrato y sedimento', pp. 154–5.
27   After the disappointment of his prototype for H Muebles, this second chair was finally manufactured
      commercially and properly marketed. According to Moneo: 'It can be said that this chair was the
      result of the 1960 trip'. Ibid., p. 156.

In 1961 Moneo qualified as an architect, just as Oíza won a competition to build the Inland Revenue Headquarters in San Sebastián and started to produce the construction documents for Torres Blancas. According to the professional conventions of the time, once Moneo had qualified, if he were to remain in Oíza's office, he would be entitled to an equal share in the commissions. So, after staying three years in Oíza´s office, Moneo felt it was time to expose himself to international influences.[28] That year he obtained a scholarship from the Spanish Ministry of Exteriors to work abroad. The sum involved was modest and it was necessary to earn an additional small salary to survive, but the award allowed him to travel and offered him a better chance of being accepted into a good international office.[29]

As a young architect from Madrid, Moneo had championed a late-modern organic style, which represented what from the late 1950s came to be called the 'School of Madrid': expressive plastic forms within the constraints of the modernist ethic of truth to materials, inspired by Bruno Zevi's *Verso una architettura organica*, the architecture of Aalto and Wright, and the recent works of Le Corbusier, Paul Rudolph and Eero Saarinen. The results of the 'School' were best seen in some of Antonio Fernández Alba's work (the first architect to set this trend), especially in Alba and Feduchi's Feria de Muestras en Gijón (1966), in Sáenz de Oíza's Torres Blancas, and in the emerging contributions of a new generation of architects including Juan Daniel Fullaondo, Fernando Higueras and Rafael Moneo himself, who were probably the architects who promoted this change of sensibility with the best results.[30] Moneo

28 'In those years architectural corporativism was very strong. According to the ideas of the time, the fact that I was already a qualified architect would force Oíza to share his commissions with me. I didn't want this situation to arise so I decided to leave Oíza before it happened.' Translated from an interview with Rafael Moneo conducted by Francisco González de Canales, 5 December 2012.

29 According to Moneo this scholarship was really modest as the cost of living in Spain was very low in comparison to that in Denmark where he hoped to work. Moneo remembers it as around 2,000 pesetas a month during 1961, which is equivalent to $10 US in 1961, or about $100 US today. Ibid.

30 The term 'School of Madrid' (Escuela de Madrid) was first used by Juan Daniel Fullaondo in 1968 to define a generation of Madrid-based architects practicing a modern organic style (1958–68). Juan Daniel Fullaondo, 'La escuela de Madrid', Arqu*itectura* 118, 1968, pp. 11–21. For the School of Madrid, see also the special issue of the magazine *Arquitectura Bis* 23–4, July–September 1978, with articles by Rafael Moneo and Antón Capitel. Also Juan Miguel Hernández de Leon, 'The Impossibility of the School of Madrid', in *UIA International Architect* 2, 1983, p. 10. The notion of the School of Madrid emerged as a counterpoint to the so-called School of Barcelona, a term coined by Oriol Bohigas. The work and

5 Fernando Higueras in collaboration
with Rafael Moneo: entry for the
Restoration Centre at the University
of Madrid, awarded the National
Architecture Prize in 1961

and Higueras had collaborated on an entry for a restoration centre for the
University of Madrid that was awarded the National Architecture Prize in
1961, a design that was seminal to what was later constructed by Higueras
and Miró (1962–76), and also paradigmatic of the intentions of the School of
Madrid. It was because he wanted to pursue his own ideas that Moneo did not
continue to collaborate with Higueras, who was older than him, and whose
exuberant Expressionist Constructivism was soon to earn him recognition as
the newest representative of the School of Madrid.[31]

ideology of the School of Madrid was promoted by the magazine *Nueva Forma* (1967–75), most editions being supervised by Oíza's disciple Juan Daniel Fullaondo. Apart from Fullaondo himself, Corrales, Molezún, Vázquez de Castro, Oíza and Fernández Alba were all closely involved in *Nueva Forma*.

31 Higueras was a charismatic personality, seven years older than Moneo, who graduated from the Madrid School of Architecture in 1959. Following early success in competitions in the 1950s, Higueras'
work was representative of the fresher and more interesting aspects of the School of Madrid. He
gained international recognition in the 1960s with his winning entry for a multi-purpose building
for Monte Carlo (1969). Other relevant works are La Macarrona Residence in Somosaguas, Madrid

It was not surprising therefore that Moneo's chosen mentor, when he sought work abroad, was Jørn Utzon, one of the most significant representatives of Scandinavian architecture, and for many, a worthy successor to Aalto in representing Nordic sensibilities. In the early 1960s, Utzon was working on the Sydney Opera House, a competition he had won in 1956 (Eero Saarinen, by no coincidence, being the most influential member of the jury).[32] Antón Capitel has described Moneo's failure at his first attempt, by correspondence, to be employed in Utzon's studio. Since Utzon had failed to reply to Moneo's letters, he decided to knock on the office door in Hellebaek in order to convince Utzon to hire him.[33] Fullaondo also describes this frequently recounted episode of Moneo's biography, which for him epitomizes the tenacity and perseverance of the architect. According to Fullaondo:

> He seems absolutely inexhaustible, immune to discouragement, with a great ability to react to the unexpected. Actually, architects tend, with the passing of time, to adopt the character of a person who has lost faith in almost everything. After a period without seeing them, you realize how bad they look, how disappointed, with lowered expectations, their professional respect diminished . . . Nothing of this applies to Moneo, completely absorbed in a natural, unfettered and obsessive optimism.[34]

Moneo was employed, and lived for a year in the Solbakken hostel in Hellebaek, close to Utzon's house and office and enjoying fantastic views over the sea. In the end, it seems Utzon was well pleased with his young assistant, because his rigorous training in structural design, and especially in geometry, was to prove extremely useful.

When Moneo arrived at the office, the podium of the building was already under construction and the architects were working on a new solution for the auditorium's shells. These had been revised a number of times over

(1971–6), the Fierro House in Marbella (1971), and the office building at 266 Castellana Avenue, Madrid (1974–8).

32 For Utzon generally, and the role of Saarinen in the competition judging, see Richard Weston, *Utzon: Inspiration, Vision, Architecture*, Hellerup: Blodal, 2002.

33 Antón G. Capitel, 'Apuntes sobre la Obra de Rafael Moneo', *Arquitectura* 236, 1982, p. 16.

34 Fullaondo, 'Notas de Sociedad', p. 5.

several years, in collaboration with the Anglo-Danish engineer Ove Arup, who was working on the project on the recommendation of Leslie Martin in part because of his ability to speak Danish. The architects were determined to be true to the design concept as presented in the competition stage, and that accounted for their rejection of alternative solutions (multiple ribs, a steel substructure, or double shells) before they reached the final one. While Arup was able to see how the shells could provide mutual support, it was Utzon's team that resolved the geometry of the shells by assimilating them to the section of a sphere. This also allowed the possibility of prefabricating the shells and their cladding.[35] All this was already decided when Moneo started to work for Utzon, but it was the precise location of the triangular spherical sections within the shells that required geometrical description, and this was Moneo's task. As the work was all done by hand, this was an arduous process of trial and error, and required someone with a proficient education in geometry, which only Moneo possessed in the office.[36] This was also the first time Moneo had the opportunity to work with an international group of young architects, as the seven or eight employees included Danes, Norwegians, Australians and Japanese.

Since he was well equipped to deal with the complexity of the Sydney Opera House geometry and to understand the difficulties of its structure, Moneo was also appointed as the intermediary between Utzon's studio and the London office of Ove Arup at 13 Fitzroy Street. He needed to travel frequently to London, where he could meet Belén Feduchi, who was living there

35   Rafael Moneo offered an extended description of his work at Utzon's office in a lecture given at the Colegio Oficial de Arquitectos de Madrid in 2003. The lecture was transcribed in 2007 in Rafael Moneo, 'La geometría de la Ópera de Sydney', in Paloma Alarcó Canosa, Xavier Antich, Javier Arnaldo, *Estudios de Historia del Arte en honor de Tomas Llorens*, Madrid: Machado libros, 2007, pp. 435–51.

36   'My task was to locate the triangles on the sphere . . . Of course everything was necessarily done by hand at that time, and although there was a protocol which meant that you could approach the problem with a certain confidence by the use of descriptive geometry, you never knew whether the initial points you chose from which to draw the larger circles would effectively result in what Utzon was looking for. In other words, to get each of the shells right you probably needed to go through five or six attempts . . . The truth is that the knowledge of descriptive geometry that we got from the school of architecture in Madrid allowed us to do all that, and it was clear that I was the only one in Utzon's office capable of undertaking that kind of work.' Esteban Maluenda, interview with Moneo from 'Sustrato y sedimento', p. 158.

to improve her English language. It was a happy chance, allowing him to be paid to fly to London and stay in first-class hotels whilst visiting his girlfriend.

Thus it was that Moneo, as a young architect, had the privilege of being involved for one year in the development of one of the most significant works of the twentieth century, as well as of enjoying a close relationship with one of the most respected masters of Nordic architecture. During his stay in Northern Europe he also had the opportunity to travel to Sweden and look at the work of Gunnar Asplund, which would become fundamental to his career – the Woodland Cemetery in Stockholm, designed with Sigurd Lewerentz (1915–40), and especially his extension to the Gothenburg Law Courts (1913–37; p. 246, fig. 85). He was also able to visit the Finnish master Alvar Aalto in his own office in Munkkiniemi, near Helsinki, and study some of his projects at first hand. Moneo's meeting with Aalto was remarkably extended: it seems that the personal recommendation of Utzon, and two bottles of Rioja that Moneo brought from Spain, facilitated it.[37] Particularly influential for Moneo's subsequent work were Aalto's use of brickwork in buildings such as Säynätsalo town hall (1949–52) and the University of Jyväskylä (1951–8), and his mastery of light, seen for example in the church at Imatra (1957–9).

In 1961–2, Moneo, whilst still a student, started work on a modest housing design for a local developer in Tudela. This was his first commission. He also entered several competitions: for a school centre in Soria, with some school friends (1961); later, by now qualified, for a planning commission in the Asúa Valley in Bilbao with Carlos Ferrán (1962); and for a market in Caceres (also 1962), which had an interesting large roof structure and was awarded second prize.

Moneo's involvement in the Sydney Opera House project might have taken him to Australia to be part of the construction process if other circumstances had not arisen to prevent it. In 1962 he returned to Madrid to participate in the competition for a Cultural Centre in El Obradorio Square at Santiago de Compostela (figs 6, 7). The site was extraordinarily difficult, as El Obradorio Square is one of the most historically and culturally charged spaces in Spain, presided over by the legendary Romanesque Cathedral of Santiago and

---

37 Fullaondo, 'Notas de Sociedad', p. 9.

6 (top) Rafael Moneo: model of competition
entry for the cultural centre in El Obradorio
Square, Santiago de Compostela, 1962, prepared
to gain Moneo's place at the Royal Spanish
Academy in Rome

7 (bottom) Rafael Moneo: elevation of
competition entry for the cultural centre in El
Obradorio Square, Santiago de Compostela, 1962

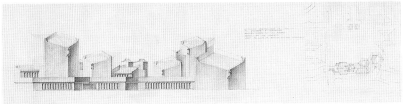

flanked by the Spanish renaissance master work Hostal de los Reyes Católicos
– the climax and culmination of Europe's foremost pilgrimage route. Moneo's
project employed hexagonal geometry, which had emerged in some of his
studies of Wright's work for Torres Blancas, and was also typical of the design
patterns of the period, lying somewhere between Doxiadis' grids and Dutch
Structuralism. It was also already apparent in the influential Spanish Pavilion
at Brussels of 1958 by Corrales and Molezún, even if filtered through an expressionist and strangely gothic sensibility. However, the delicate articulation
and fragmentation of the pieces in relation to the site, its modest scale, and
the careful choice of materials and construction systems, seem more closely
matched to the humanistic approach, with a respect for context, that was
starting to be promulgated by some Italian architects of that time. As a result
of his scheme, he was awarded a scholarship, along with another young architect, Dionisio Hernández Gil, to stay in the Spanish Academy in Rome for
two years. He chose Rome instead of Australia, but before departing married
Belén Feduchi in Madrid.

The wedding took place in El Escorial and the young couple travelled to Ibiza, Palma and Sicily for their honeymoon. Moneo particularly remembers the journey from Palma to Palermo on board the Saturnia, a boat built during the Mussolini era, and the spectacle upon the arrival at the port of Palermo, where families welcomed their relatives coming from the United States with a wild choreography of agitated hats and kerchiefs.[38] The young couple travelled slowly across Sicily, visiting Agrigento, Segesta, Catania and other sights *en route*.

In Rome, Moneo joined some talented young Spanish contemporaries – not only his fellow architect Dionisio Hernández Gil, but also the sculptors Francisco López and Francisco Toledo, the painters Isabel Quintanilla, Manuel Alcorlo, Antonio Zarco and Agustín de Celis, and the musician Amando Blanquer, all of whom held two-year scholarships at the Spanish Royal Academy. They lived together in a Roman palace, with concierges, waiters and secretaries, but their stipend was very low and their life-style correspondingly modest. During the first year of the scholarship, those specializing in architecture were required to work on a Roman building constructed before the year 1000. Moneo chose Santa Costanza, but this was more of a formality and he never produced anything very substantial on it, spending the first year visiting every church and palace that he could.[39] The second year of the scholarship was usually devoted to traveling. In fact, Moneo used his period in the Royal Academy of Spain in Rome to establish a certain distance from the immediacy of office work, as he had experienced it with Oíza and Utzon, and to reflect on architectural history and theory, and his personal position. For this reason he spent much of his time on the detailed study of Western architecture, and not only by visiting buildings. On Monday evenings he regularly attended Bruno Zevi's lectures at the Palazzo Taverna, where he met Paolo Portoghesi and Manfredo Tafuri for the first time. It might be expected that Zevi would be the principal influence on a young Madrid architect, in view of the widespread influence of his organic theories, but the Bruno Zevi that

---

38 Esteban Maluenda, interview with Moneo from 'Sustrato y sedimento', p. 159.

39 'To tell you the truth I did not do any specific research in Rome, absolutely nothing; however, I got to know Rome perfectly well, church by church, house by house, shop by shop . . .' Rafael Moneo, on being questioned about what he did in Rome, as described in Anton Capitel, 'Mis Memorias en la Escuela', 2009. http://acapitel.blogspot.com.es/2009/05/mis-memorias-de-la-escuela-de.html.

Moneo encountered was rather different to the figure who was held in such high esteem in Madrid. Paradoxically, it seemed that meeting Zevi face-to-face encouraged Moneo to reflect on the importance that an understanding of the history of architecture as a discipline had for contemporary practice.[40] Moneo was also able to attend some of Rudolf Wittkower's lectures on the Italian renaissance and baroque; while he appreciated his own thorough grounding in the technical aspects of architecture that he had learned in Madrid, which had indeed proved essential during his time in Utzon's office, he realized that the depth of historical knowledge and level of architectural discourse that he experienced in Rome was of a different order, and he sought to obtain as much as he could in compensation. In the process he was able to distance himself from the conception of the architect as a 'technocrat', promoted in Spain at the time, and embrace a wider humanist vision of the architect as a cultured intellectual.

Whilst in Rome he also took the opportunity to study at first hand the work of architects such as Franco Albini, Ignazio Gardella, Luigi Moretti, Ludovico Quaroni and Giuseppe Samonà – architects who had challenged the orthodoxy of the Modern movement from the early 1950s by acknowledging the force of issues such as tradition, material realism, the human dimension, history and context. Gardella's work in particular left a deep impression in the way that it dealt with the specifics of the site, the detailed needs of the occupants and the realities of constructional disciplines. Further afield, in Italy, he visited the work of Carlo Scarpa in the Veneto and BBPR in Milan, although it was not until later that he was to have strong links with Milanese architects and their theories of the city.

Moneo's interests were not confined to recent architecture; he took a trip to southern Italy, Greece and Turkey to see ancient buildings, especially Greek architecture, a crucial educative experience for him at the time.[41] He also visited Vienna, Amsterdam and Paris on shorter trips. He was determined to learn

---

40   Moneo discussed this question and also recorded his new-found appreciation of his history professor in Madrid, Leopoldo Torres-Balbás, in the first article he sent from Rome to the architectural magazine *Arquitectura*: Rafael Moneo, 'Sobre un intento de reforma didáctica (En la facultad de Arquitectura en Roma)', Arq*uitectura* 61, January 1964, pp. 43–6.

41   What he learnt during this trip was recorded in 'Notas sobre la arquitectura griega', *Hogar y Arquitectura* 59, July–August 1965, pp. 67–82.

as much as he could from the direct encounter with all canonical examples of Western architecture, from Greek Temples to the Venetian Palaces, from Hagia Sophia to Ville Savoye, from Borromini's Chiesa Nuova to Hoffman's Stoclet Palace. Oscar Tusquets, a Catalan architect who accompanied him on a trip through central Greece, Attica and the Peloponnese with some of the scholars of the Royal Spanish Academy, remembers Moneo's absolute passion for examining architecture on the spot, and how he insisted on checking the dimensions of all the stones of the most important buildings in order to record their geometry and proportions.[42]

While Rome in itself was a vivid lesson in art and architecture, his period in the city also allowed him to participate in current architectural debates, which affected his thinking. His fluency in Italian had improved as he devoured all the articles he could find in journals and periodicals. With a newfound confidence in the language, he embarked upon the translation of Bruno Zevi's *Architettura in Nuce*, a crucial book for the development of Moneo's architectural thinking, which was published in 1969.[43] He also began writing critical reviews for journals, initiating another strand of architectural activity that would continue all his life. Between 1964 and 1969 he was a regular contributor to the Spanish magazine *Arquitectura*, published by the Colegio de Arquitectos de Madrid and widely regarded as the most authoritative architectural journal in Spain, but he also wrote for other publications, such as *Hogar y Arquitectura* and *Nueva Forma*. As someone who was still fashioning a personal polemical position, he was famous for his continuing confrontations with the editor of *Arquitectura*, Carlos de Miguel.[44] The subject matter of his articles ranged from theoretical reflections, arising out of his studies during his time in Rome, to reports on his reaction to particular paradigmatic works of modern architecture, to criticism of contemporary works by his

42   'Rafa brought with him a metallic measuring tape and we spent the days measuring the height of the Pentelikon, the perimeter of the columns, the distance between columns (truly, how totally fascinated with architecture was this man!).' Oscar Tusquest Blanca, *Todo es comparable*, Barcelona: Anagrama, 1998, pp. 60–61.

43   Bruno Zevi, *Arquitectura in Nuce, Una definición de arquitectura*, Madrid: Aguilar, 1969 (translated from the Italian by Rafael Moneo).

44   Fullaondo, 'Notas de Sociedad', p. 6.

8 Rafael Moneo, with Fernández
Casado (engineer): bullring extension,
Pamplona, 1966–7

colleagues. Writing became an essential part of his reflective practice from
then on.

During his Roman sojourn Moneo found time for some architectural commissions, such as the extension of the Pamplona Bullring (1966–7; fig. 8), and
the Diestre Transformer Factory (1965–7; figs 9, 10), which would be completed
in Madrid, as well as a number of competition entries; amongst these were the
New York International Exhibition Pavilion and the 1964 Madrid Opera House
competition. Both projects were formally bold and expressive, and continued
to reflect the influence of the exuberant and organic school of Madrid. Moneo
was particularly pleased to be appointed for the Pamplona Bullring extension:

9 Rafael Moneo: Diestre Transformer
Factory, Zaragoza, 1965–7. The top-lit
interior

10 Rafael Moneo: Diestre Transformer
Factory, Zaragoza, 1965–7. Exterior
showing the free Aaltoesque
composition

not only was it the first important competition that he had won, but he had always been an enthusiastic supporter and admirer of bullfighting.[45]

Personally, Rome was like a second honeymoon for Rafael and Belén, who enjoyed the company of a group of artistic friends and acquaintances, both in the city and on trips together; their first daughter, named Belén after her mother, was born there.

45 In 2011, Moneo was chosen to give the opening speech at the Seville bullfighting festival. This is one of the most important events for bullfighting lovers around the world. Before him, other personalities such Mario Vargas Llosa (2000) and Carlos Fuentes (2003) had given the address which precedes the Resurrection Sunday bullfight in Seville. In his speech, Moneo recounted how his father had brought him to the bullfights in Tudela since he was a child. He also remembered himself playing with two horns with his brother, Mariano, simulating the fight between bull and bullfighter, and how in his youth he liked to run the bulls or fight small bulls in festivities (*vaquillas*) as typical proofs of bravery for his age. Rafael Moneo, *XXXI Pregón Taurino. Sevilla 2011*, Sevilla: Real Maestranza de Caballería, 2011, pp. 38–40.

After the Roman years, Rafael and Belén returned to Madrid where he established his practice as a young architect, and where their second daughter, Teresa, was born.

Moneo's first achievements as an architect were connected to his home region, Navarra. Among them, the Bullring enlargement in Pamplona, completed in 1967, was immediately recognized as a serious work. The project speaks not just about the personal passion of Rafael Moneo for bullfighting but also of his early interest in structure and technique, which had been honed during the time he worked with Utzon. Carlos Fernández Casado, one of the most talented engineers of his generation, was the structural consultant and made a major contribution. The extension is conceived of as a straightforward concrete skeleton that crowns the old building, slightly expanding its diameter whilst keeping its character and giving it new and more graceful proportions.

During the same years Moneo completed the Diestre factory near Zaragoza, again a commission in which functional and constructional issues apparently dominate. The factory makes electrical transformers and the spatial design of the building reflects the production sequence: the space is open throughout, except in the area where flammable materials are handled. As the components reach their final form the roofs become higher, so that the ultimate bay contains gantries for lifting the completed transformers onto the inspection bays, from which they are eventually dispatched. The volumes are elided slightly and clad uniformly in brick with asymmetrical pitched roofs, recalling the freedom and sensitivity with which Alvar Aalto treated industrial buildings. The Casa Gómez-Acebo (1966–8; fig. 11), on the other hand, reflects a predominantly Wrightian inspiration, with its hipped roofs and slight internal changes of level, though its repetitive piers give it a less cozy and more monumental character than the typical Prairie House.

Less well documented are some of the early projects that Moneo worked on for his hometown, Tudela. Among the most important are a housing block (1965–7) and a school (1966–71; fig. 12), the latter arising out of a competition for which he had been awarded second prize in 1966, and which he was later to adapt in the Elvira España School (1969–71). Both the housing and the school have a very urban, solid and robust character, and reflect on the role of architecture in a traditional city, whilst still indicating the continuing influence of the School of Madrid. Rational and systematic in plan, both buildings

11 (facing) Rafael Moneo: Casa Gómez-Acebo,
La Moraleja, 1966–9, showing Wrightian influence

12 Rafael Moneo: Tudela school, 1966–71,
showing semi-circular rooflights

employ sensual curvilinear corners, large cantilevered tiled roofs and a rich use of brick to create different textures in the façade, achieving a subtle organic expression within a forceful whole. In these two buildings Moneo also began to investigate how the internal logic of the building might help to structure its spaces. The circulation areas of the schools, for example, are beautifully articulated by means of a series of semicircular skylights, which wash selected wall areas with an atmospheric light.

Other buildings in Navarra include the remarkable Irati housing block in Pamplona (1967–70; fig. 13), and an interesting small housing development for Químicas Ebro in Cortes (1967–8). In these two other projects the organicist sensibility is reduced to the minimum, since both buildings are compact orthogonal pieces and are more concerned with the particular structural organization of the housing units than with the eloquence of its resulting shape.

13 Rafael Moneo: Irati housing,
Pamplona, 1967–70

A certain play of setbacks in the turning of the façade at the corner and at
the encounter with the adjacent block is the only expressive moment that
the architect allows himself in the development of the design of the Irati
building. The houses in Cortes are even more elementary and work as four
clusters of houses around two crossing walls, a plan which may remind us
of Hejduk's later North-East-South-West House, but according to Moneo was
influenced by Frank Lloyd Wright's Suntop houses.[46] Each of these reveals a
clear intention to treat the new architecture as a modest intervention in the
urban grid that contributes to its continuity. The Real Casa de la Misericordia,
an old people's home for a religious community, was commissioned and
built not much later (1972–83). It is a massive building, occupying a complete
urban block, and summarizes some of Moneo's views on urban typology,
which was already an emerging concern. In all of these projects, the imprints
of his Italian experience are visible: a certain abstraction of classical elements

46   Francisco González de Canales (ed.), *Rafael Moneo: Una Reflexión Teórica desde la Profesión. Materiales de Archivo* (1961–2013), La Coruña: Fundación Barrié de la Maza, 2013, p. 144.

and the strong presence of the urban fabric as a determining factor in the resulting architectural project.

Moneo also participated in some urban projects in the north of Spain. In 1968, with Carlos Ferrán and Eduardo Mangada, he prepared an Urban Plan for Sector 8 in Vitoria. Here Moneo proposed a series of organic oval blocks around a park, which were nevertheless strictly modern in their housing typology – an approach that combined the interest of the School of Madrid with a preoccupation with urban form learnt from Italy. The same year that he completed the Irati building he submitted a scheme for the refurbishment of the Plaza de lo Fueros at Pamplona (1970) with Estanislao de la Quadra-Salcedo. This design, which dealt with a complex road gyratory and how to connect and make sense of its interior, would not be realized until 1974–5.

A first monograph on the work of Moneo was published in the most important Spanish architectural magazine of the time, *Hogar y Architectura,* in 1968.[47] The issue also celebrated what was considered his greatest success to date: being shortlisted for the Amsterdam Town Hall Competition (figs 14, 15).[48] His design was a moderated organic exercise, skilful in the organization of the programme, and able to integrate the building within the existing urban landscape through a volumetric play of different heights and setbacks. A systematic repetition of prismatic skylight structures gave coherence to the whole. The design acknowledges Dutch structuralism and also traditional Dutch architecture, as well as being sensible to the scale of Amsterdam, a city

---

47 'Obras de Rafael Moneo', Special issue, *Hogar y Arquitectura* 76, May–June, 1968. The issue featured the Diestre Transformers Factory (1964–7), Pamplona Bullring (1963–7), the Housing Block in Tudela (1965–7), Gomez Acebo House (1966–9) and the boutiques for Confecciones Gallego in Tudela and Calatayud (1966).

48 The Amsterdam Town Hall Competition became one of the most significant international architectural events of the period. Competitors were required to decide on the appropriate expression for a political building in a liberal country such as the Netherlands just at the time when traditional political institutions were coming under increasing criticism from the citizens. The competition received 803 entries from all over the world and only seven were shortlisted to be further developed in a second stage to be submitted in 1969. The range of proposals received could be considered representative of the diverse spectrum of the architecture of the time, from venerable modern masters such as Arne Jacobsen, to the Team X members De Carlo, Bakema and Van der Broek, to the Dutch structuralism of Herman Hertzberger and the 'high-tech' Richard Rogers. The final winning entry was a formidably monumental composition by the Austrian architect Wilhelm Holzbauer. For more on this competition, see the informative webpage *Amsterdam Town Hall Competition* published by the Netherlands Architecture Institute in the summer of 2005: http://static.nai.nl/stopera/.

14 Rafael Moneo: elevation, section
and plan for the Amsterdam Town Hall
Competition, 1967–8. A fluent exercise
in 'structuralism'

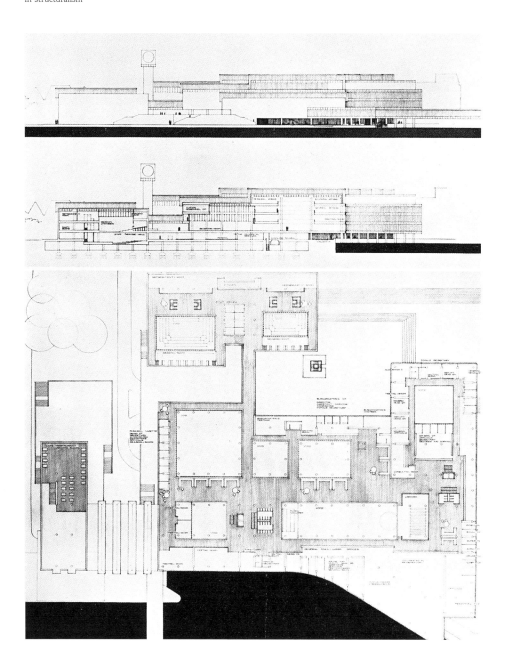

15 Rafael Moneo: model for the
Amsterdam Town Hall Competition

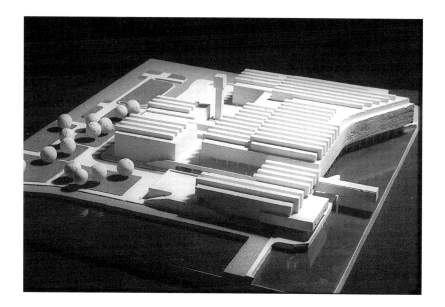

that Moneo knew from an earlier visit. According to the jury it was the only
entry that truly succeeded in relating the building to the Amstel River. In a
remark that tells us about the ambiguous impression the project made, the
jury member and modernist architect Huig Maaskant said that 'the design is
a cross between a parliament building and a station'.[49]

Moneo continued both to participate fully in the Spanish architectural
debate and to look beyond its boundaries and make important international acquaintances. In the mid-1960s he regularly attended the 'Pequeños
Congresos' (Small Congresses), organized by the editor of *Arquitectura* magazine Carlos de Miguel and the Catalan architect Oriol Bohigas, to discuss
projects by Spanish and foreign architects in a group drawn from members of both the School of Madrid (represented by Oíza, Corrales, Molezún,
Fernández Alba and others) and the School of Barcelona (Bohigas, Correa
and Domenech) along with other Spanish architects. Moneo was very active in the second period of the 'Congresos' from 1966. It was at one of these

49   Ibid.

congresses, in Tarragona in 1967, organized by the Catalan group, that he met Aldo Rossi for the first time – a figure who proved to be a fundamental reference for his career throughout the 1970s. As Moneo recalls, during the late 1960s, Rossi's book *The Architecture of the City* 'truly impressed me'.[50] In 1968, the group was asked to represent Spain and Portugal in an international architectural conference in Aspen, chaired by the American architect Elliot Noyes. The Spanish representation was composed by Fernández Alba and Moneo from Madrid, Correa, Bohigas, Domenech and the designer Antoni Blanc from Barcelona, and Nuno Portas from Portugal. Moneo's English was rudimentary at the time, but the group was able to establish a strong relationship with Peter Eisenman through the medium of Federico Correa, who was the only one amongst the Spaniards able to speak the language. This first acquaintance with Eisenman was also to prove fundamental for his career from the late 1970s, when by re-establishing his contact with the New York architect he was able to visit architectural institutions in the United States. Meanwhile, the Aspen conference offered Moneo his first opportunity to see Chicago, San Francisco and New York.

Given his career and his education, as well as his intellectual concerns, it was natural for Moneo to gravitate towards teaching and it is not surprising that he began to teach at the School of Architecture in Madrid, if only as a part-time assistant at first. In 1966, Moneo and his fellow architect in Rome, Dionisio Hernández Gil, were recruited to teach on the course entitled Análisis de Formas (Analysis of Forms), then under Professor Adolfo López Duran. The experiment was unsuccessful and the following year Moneo moved across to the Elementos de Composición course (Elements of Composition, usually conceived of as the first year of architectural design studio) and then, in 1968, to the Proyectos (architectural design studio) of the fourth year. Moneo remembers these as difficult years at the university: the Architectural School in Madrid had been slow to adapt, and various half-hearted attempts at modernization were now largely superseded by the ideas and ambitions of the student generation of the end of the 1960s. As happened in many other parts of

---

50   Luis Fernández-Galiano, 'Entrevista con Rafael Moneo', *El País*, Babelia, 4 August 2001, pp. 22. Republished in 'Se construye con ideas: Rafael Moneo, una conversación', *Arquitectura Viva* 77, March–April 2001, pp. 71–3.

Europe, students tried to meet their social and political ideals with a vision of an architecture that would embrace new-found technological freedom with a total disregard for history, urban tradition and the disciplines of tectonics. The chasm between 'the myth of Archigram', which students pursued, and the teaching on offer by the old professors of Madrid was too large to be bridged; students had no respect for the teaching on offer and classes frequently went unattended.[51] Moneo remembers the efforts he made to gain the attention of the students each day, directing them to topics he thought would stimulate their interest. Seduced as they were by the dream of a techno-scientific world, they demanded a design methodology that would ensure a systematic and reliable outcome. His experience would prove crucial for the pedagogical approach that he would go on to develop in future years.[52] Students remember him as a gentle and approachable man, his shoulders slightly bent, who erratically fingered his hair when talking. His wife Belén recalls that even though Moneo was not much older than his students, he always used the respectful address 'usted'. Anton Capitel, his student at that time, also noted that he used 'usted' just with the student's Christian name, which was quite an unusual combination.[53] Such a construction exhibits the mix of respectful distance and familiar closeness that Moneo liked to establish with students and collaborators. In order to reinforce familiarity, he very quickly learnt his students' full names, and he also liked to know about their family, city of origin and hobbies; he would remember these details, and ask after them when they subsequently met.

51   In Madrid, the fashion for 'Archigramesque' architecture was led by another young tutor, José Miguel de Prada Poole. A year younger than Moneo, he had graduated in 1965 and began teaching in the school straight away. He enjoyed incredible success among the younger generations of architects, and produced two pneumatic structures emblematic of the time. The Instant City (1968–70), an open inflatable structure, was built in 1971, at the request of two students from the School of Architecture of Barcelona, Fernando Bendito and Carlos Ferrater, to host participants at the International Congress of Design ADI–FAD held in Ibiza. The second inflatable structure was produced for the Pamplona Meetings of 1972, one of the most important and heated cultural occasions in Spain before the end of Franco's dictatorship. Three years later, his 'Heliotron', an inflatable ice rink built in Seville, was awarded the National Prize of Architecture, which is indicative of Spanish architectural fashion at the time.
52   See Márquez and Levene, 'Three Step Interview: Spring 1985', p. 15.
53   Capitel, 'Mis Memorias de la Escuela de Arquitectura'.

The following academic year, 1969–70, Moneo did not teach at the school. He was preparing himself for the forthcoming professorship competition. As some of the students of that time recall, the presence of Moneo in the School of Architecture library, day after day, contributed to his reputation as an erudite architect with an insatiable cultural appetite.[54]

54   Conversation between Francisco González de Canales and Antón Capitel, Rafael Moneo's former student at ETSAM, Madrid, in the late 1960s, London, June 2011.

In December 1970, interviews were held in Madrid for the professorship of Elements of Composition, by the usual process in Spain of 'oposiciones', or public examination for the purpose of obtaining a professorship. It became something of a national architectural event. Three positions were on offer, one in each of the three main Spanish schools of architecture: Madrid, Barcelona and Seville. But there were five candidates, three of whom had already acquired a considerable reputation: Antonio Fernández Alba, Alejandro de la Sota and Federico Correa. Candidates for the professorship were required to be interviewed by a specially convened committee, to describe their *curriculum vitae* to date, explain their approach to teaching in principle and submit details of their proposed courses. Naturally the occasion was not without a certain tension. A serious amount of time and effort was required in preparation, and Moneo used the occasion to work out a synthesis of ideas that he drew from his own education and his subsequent experience. As a result of an outstanding submission and performance at interview, Moneo was selected, with Antonio Fernández Alba and Alberto Donaire, in preference to the charismatic masters of an older generation, Alejandro de la Sota and Federico Correa. Fernández Alba and Donaire chose Madrid and Seville, leaving Moneo to take the Barcelona chair. Moneo himself was only 33.

The course that Moneo prepared for the Elements of Composition professorship, following his stay in Rome, was a comprehensive attempt to summarize his personal approach to design. He had clearly profited from the experience of teaching in Madrid and his first contacts with architects whose ideas were to have a major influence on his thinking – Manuel de Solà-Morales and newly emerging international figures such as Peter Eisenman and Aldo Rossi.[55] Moneo's teaching programme was required to follow on from a course entitled 'Form Analysis', and itself inherited the traditional designation of the French Academy (Éléments de Composition). But the method Moneo proposed was far from traditional: his educational intention was to reconcile theoretical and practical education, combining analytical reading and discussion with the students' own creative proposals. Each lesson set a particular design problem (which informs us just what architectural issues most preoccupied

---

55   Rafael Moneo, *Programa de la cátedra de Elementos de Composición*, Cátedra de Elementos de Composición, Monografía 1, Barcelona: Ediciones de la ETSAB, 1972.

Moneo at the time), and suggested a set of references; these in turn were backed up by an extensive bibliography. Moneo was acutely conscious of the irrelevance of traditional syllabus divisions and tried to fashion a course that avoided both the inherited academic tradition and the alternative modern orthodoxy of the Bauhaus *Vorkurs*. An unusually inclusive bibliography was one result, ranging from the classic treatises of Vitruvius and Palladio up to contemporary theoretical texts by Rossi and Christopher Alexander.

One thing that becomes clear in studying these courses is Moneo's unusual capacity to connect philosophical and historical concerns with quite concrete issues in design. His general conviction of the importance of university education in raising social, cultural and economic standards, and his view that the teaching of architecture constituted a contribution to the discipline of the humanities, led him to publish the content of his courses and workshops.[56] He was assisted in his disciplined and thoroughly grounded course in Barcelona by the most brilliant young Catalan architects of their generation – José Llinás, Francisco Pernas, Helio Piñón, Teresa Rovira, Elias Torres and Albert Viaplana. He also supervised Piñón's doctoral thesis, and those of other architects who were to become important scholars of the Barcelona School of Architecture, such as Ignasi de Solà-Morales and Josep Quetglas.

The first academic year at Barcelona that Moneo taught was 1971–2, and he was soon recognized as one of the most gifted, as well as demanding and critical, teachers, quickly assuming a leading position within the institution.[57] He taught there for ten years, staying in Barcelona for two or three days each week, whilst he continued to live and practice in Madrid. In 1974, he was one of the founders of *Arquitecturas Bis*, which swiftly gained international respect and served to promulgate the thinking of the avant-garde to Spanish readers. By 1975, the journal would appear to have superseded *Nueva Forma*, which had served a similar purpose at the Madrid school. Moneo has described the

---

56 The Barcelona course between 1971 and 1977 is described in the following project publications: Rafael Moneo, *Ejercicios del curso de Elementos de Composición 1972–1973*, Barcelona: Cátedra de Elementos de Composición, ediciones de la ETSAB, 1973; *1973–1974*, 1974; *1971–1972*, 1975; *1974–1975*, 1975; *1975–1976*, 1976; *1976–1977*, 1977. Later, Moneo published his courses in Madrid from 1980–85, and his teaching in Harvard in his book *Theoretical Anxiety and Design Strategies in the Work of Eight Contemporary Architects*, Cambridge, Mass.: MIT Press, 2004

57 Tusquets Blanca, *Todo es Comparable*, p. 61.

many extended meetings at the house of Rosa Regàs, the editor, with the rest of editorial board, which included Oriol Bohigas, Federico Correa, Manuel de Solà-Morales and, from a younger generation, Lluís Doménech and Helio Piñón, as amongst the most intense and fruitful intellectual experiences of his career.[58] The intellectual distance between his new interests and the organic tradition of the Madrid school appeared to increase. In January 1975, in an issue of *Nueva Forma*, Juan Daniel Fullaondo observed that Moneo had become a member of Barcelona's contemporary 'radical chic'.[59]

Throughout the 1970s, in addition to his teaching and practice, and complementing it, Moneo maintained a formidable pace of publication. He made full use of the traditionally close relationship between Barcelona and Milan to study in more depth the work of La Tendenza and Aldo Rossi, whom he visited in Italy, establishing connections that would prove crucial for the younger generation of Spanish architects.[60] His writings ranged from commentaries on the work of his contemporaries to essays on historical figures such as Durand, and several pieces that were to become highly regarded internationally, such as 'On Typology' and 'The Life of Buildings' (see pp. 267–83). His 'Comentarios sobre el dibujo de 20 arquitectos actuales' ('Commentaries on the Drawings of 20 Contemporary Architects') anticipates his concern for the means of representation that architects employ.[61] In addition to his contributions to the Spanish publications *Arquitectura*, *Nueva Forma* and the recently founded *Arquitecturas Bis,* Moneo's writings now appeared in international journals such as *Oppositions*, *Lotus* and *Contraspazio*.

---

58   At a public conversation between Rafael Moneo, Shumon Basar and Beatriz Colomina at the Architectural Association, to discuss *Arquitecturas Bis* on the occasion of the exhibition 'Clip, Stamp and Fold', Saturday 10 November, 2007.

59   Fullaondo, 'Notas de Sociedad', p. 7.

60   La Tendenza (literally, 'the tendency') was the name adopted by a group of Italian neo-rationalist architects, of whom the most important figure was Rossi himself.

61   See Rafael Moneo and Juan Antonio Cortés, *Comentarios sobre dibujos de 20 arquitectos actuales*, Barcelona, Cátedra de Elementos de Composición, Ediciones de la ETSAB, October 1976. See also Rafael Moneo, 'La Propuesta Pedagógica de Jean-Nicolas-Louis Durand', in *J.N.L.Durand, Compendio de Lecciones de Arquitectura (1802–1805)*, Madrid: Pronaos, 1981; 'On Typology', *Oppositions* 13, 1978; 'La Vie de bâtiments. extensions de la Mosquée de Cordoue', in *DA Informations* 62, 1979, pp. 23–45.

In a brief article of the late 1970s entitled 'Designing and Teaching – The Re-organization of a School of Architecture',[62] Moneo wrote about the 'transformation of the institutional and political framework within which Spanish society moves today' as an influence on the position of the school in Barcelona. He regrets the survival of 'the old nineteenth century rules of administration that give the school the right to bestow a degree', claiming that they are 'a serious obstacle to any academic change'. He also regrets the large numbers of students that the school is required to cater for. He describes the school as 'pluralistic', as it has to be in responding to the problems of the day, and he then devotes a paragraph or two to the departments of Structures (Buxadé, Margarit), Town Planning (Ribas, Manuel de Solà-Morales), Theory and History (Sostres, Ignasi de Solà-Morales, Quetglas), and the Department of 'Architectural Projects' (Bohigas, Correa, Moneo, Muntañola, Piñón, Viaplana, Torres). The range exhibits the plurality he speaks about and that he accepts: some who 'still feel themselves called by the preaching of the architects of the Tendenza', others who are attracted by American neo-rationalists, and those who attempt 'a timid synthesis in which the abstract concepts of "realism" and "formalism" would be integrated'. The 'mass-production of professors and students seems to justify this "new eclecticism"' he concludes, and this is the cause of some anxiety. It is possible to detect a problem that was to preoccupy Moneo here: eclecticism, he believes, is the only way forward, in view of the situation, but some method is required to prevent it from being merely 'timid'. Moneo's own theoretical position can be seen as the result of trying to come to terms with this issue.

The built work that Moneo achieved in parallel during the Barcelona years is what transformed his role from that of a talented and promising young architect to being considered as one of the leading architectural talents of the time. The Urumea Building in San Sebastián (1968–72; figs 16–18) was his most significant building in progress. Occupying half of a block in the nineteenth-century expansion area of the city, it apparently conforms to the expected typology of adjacent apartment blocks, with light wells overlooked by the service rooms of the flats whose principal rooms would look out onto the

16 (top) Rafael Moneo, in collaboration with Marquet,
Unzurrunzaga and Zulaica: Urumea building, San
Sebastián, 1968–73. Plan of the apartments

17 (bottom) Rafael Moneo, in collaboration with Marquet,
Unzurrunzaga and Zulaica: Urumea building, 1968–73.
Viewed from across the Urumea river
in San Sebastián

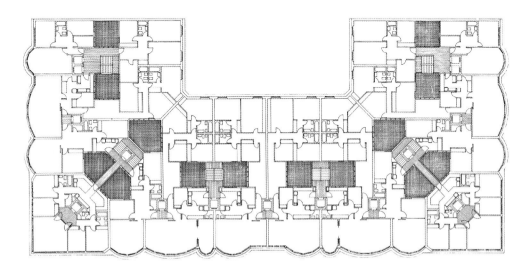

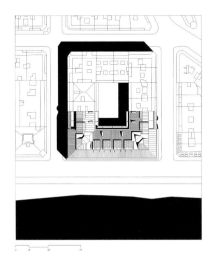
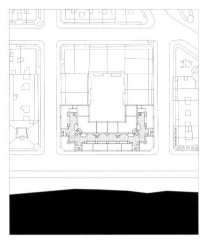

river or into the central courtyard. But Moneo manipulated the plan so that
the central light well, divided by a common staircase, is overlooked by only
one flat, though the arrangement is more complicated at the corners. Central
bays have wide curving forms that allow windows to look up and down the
Urumea river, while rectangular metal balconies on all levels at the corners establish a visual connection with the neighbouring blocks. The design of this
urban intervention initiates a continuing dialogue in Moneo's mind between
the demands of pre-existing typologies and the authority of the architect to
make inventions within those constraints.

During the years he taught at Barcelona, Moneo developed two of the most
significant works within his oeuvre: the Bankinter building in Madrid (1972–6;
see pp. 111–17), and Logroño town hall (1973–81; see pp. 118–26). In Paseo de La
Habana (1973–8), in Madrid, he designed a stone-clad group of apartments that
are linked to address a common entrance area; they have an intricate plan
combining diagonal geometries with a radiused layout and exhibit the kind
of formal fluency he had inherited from his more organic period. Around the
same time he also submitted entries to several competitions, including the
Colegio de agentes de cambio y bolsa at Madrid (1973), and the refurbishment
of the city centre of Éibar (1972–3), which was awarded first prize. Neither
project was realized, but both indicate clearly Moneo's new interests, with a

significant nod to Rossi. His only architectural interventions in Barcelona at the time were two small galleries, which tends to suggest that his intellectual work mainly developed in Barcelona, while his professional activity was mostly confined, for the present, to the Madrid environment, or to his own home region.

In the early 1970s, there were usually around five people in the office, which was run as a studio. In addition to the two major commissions of Bankinter and Logroño, there were numerous smaller jobs. Moneo usually spent two days at the office, two in Barcelona and one visiting work on-site, although this could vary according to specific commitments. He tended to produce fully developed sketches of his solution before presenting a project to his collaborators – his practice was not even to tell his employees about a new project until he had already determined the approach that would be adopted. Thereafter everyone was free to discuss and contribute to the project, but Moneo retained absolute control. Sometimes, when the project was fairly well developed, he would explain it to new members of the office by means of a cardboard model, which was also his usual method when teaching or describing his schemes to clients.[63] The model was coloured to represent materials; thus it avoided the conventional abstraction of most architects' models. In the early 1970s, his studio was therefore still a small one, and the relatively few substantial commissions allowed him to dedicate himself fully to a reflective and thoughtful architectural practice. Meanwhile, on a family note, in 1975, Moneo's youngest daughter, Clara, was born in Madrid.

63   From an interview between Nicholas Ray and Enrique de Teresa at the Círculo de Bellas Artes, Madrid, 4 April 2012.

19 Rafael Moneo: Cannaregio project,
Venice, 1978–9. Low-rise housing on an
unmodified grid pattern

Cannaregio Venezia
Rafael Moneo

In 1975, when Moneo was less than 40, the influential *Nueva Forma*,
edited by Juan Daniel Fullaondo, had already devoted a complete issue to his
work; Fullaondo describes Moneo both as the youngest representative of the
Madrid School, and as the architect probably responsible for putting an end to
it. Previously, only the work of significant figures such as de la Sota had been
treated in special issues. Fullaondo knew Moneo well and his article consisted
of a mixture of personal biography and architectural critique. His intelligence,
culture and architectural knowledge are highlighted. Behind the apparently
naïve passion for architecture, exhibited in his public persona, lay a tenacious,
coolly analytical mind and a strategic sensitivity. Fullaondo, whose portrait
did much to reinforce Moneo's reputation – already a quasi-mythical figure
to his younger contemporaries – underlined the seminal importance of Frank
Lloyd Wright and the personal impact of Sáenz de Oíza. For him, Moneo's position, which he considers at once eclectic and original, was a response to those
historical circumstances that he had been compelled to confront. In addition
to the long article by Fullaondo, *Nueva Forma's* issue presented one of the
most complete illustrations of Moneo's work to date.[64]

In the late 1970s, the political situation in Spain was still confusing, and the
economy in recession. Moneo used the opportunity to travel and cement the
wider international connections that he had begun to forge during his years

---

64 *Nueva Forma* 108, January 1975. This is an exhaustive compilation of works, including in the following order: Urumea Building in San Sebastián (1969–73), Extension of Pamplona Bullring (1963–7), Obradoiro Square Proposal for the Prix de Rome (1962, first prize), Diestre Transformer Factory (1964–7),
Opera de Madrid Competition entry (1964), Madrid Stock Exchange Building Competition entry
(1973), National Prize of Architecture with Fernando Higueras (1961), Proposal for a Housing Block in
Paseo de La Habana, Madrid, with Ramón Bescós (1966–8), Gómez-Acebo House in La Moraleja, Madrid (1966–8), Schools in Tudela (1966–71, following a winning competition entry), Housing in Cortes
(1967–8), Asua Valley Competition entry with Carlos Ferrán (1962), Urban Plan for Sector 8 in Vitoria
with Carlos Ferrán and Eduardo Mangada (1968), Cofecciones Gallego in Tudela (1966), H Muebles Furniture Competition entry (1960, first prize), Ministry of Housing Furniture Competition entry (1961,
first prize in the armchair category), Amsterdam Town Hall Competition entry (1968, shortlisted),
Zaragoza Historical Centre Refurbishment Competition entry with Manuel de Solà-Morales (1969,
second prize), Hostel in San Miguel de Aralar Competition entry (1965), House in Santo Domingo, Madrid, 1970–72, Huesca Provincial Government Headquarters Competition entry (1974), Altos Hornos de
Vizcaya Madrid Headquarters Competition entry (1974), Market in Caceres Competition entry (second prize, 1962), Irati Housing Block in Pamplona, 1967–70, Square in Éibar Competition entry (1972–3,
first prize), Los Fueros Square in Pamplona with Estanislao de la Quadra Salcedo (1970–75, following
a winning competition entry), and Bankinter Headquarters in Madrid (with Ramón Bescós, 1973–6).

20 Rafael Moneo, in collaboration with
Manuel de Solà-Morales: first prize-
winning entry to the competition for the
residential district of Aktur de Lakua,
Vitoria, 1976–80. This was an important
project for Moneo at the time, dependent
on a strong typological approach

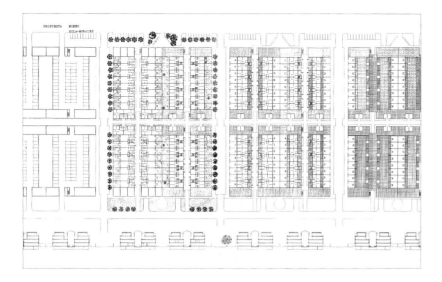

at Barcelona. In 1976–7, he took sabbatical leave and was a visiting fellow at
the Institute of Architectural and Urban Studies (IAUS), in New York, at the
invitation of Peter Eisenman.[65] Here he encountered, and formed friendships
with, Diana Agrest, Kenneth Frampton, Mario Gandelsonas, Rem Koolhaas,
Jorge Silvetti and Anthony Vidler, and met for the first time Frank Gehry and
James Stirling, who were also visitors to the institute. His initial teaching engagement in the United States was at the Cooper Union, directed by the charismatic John Hejduk. He decided to extend his stay for a further semester and
taught at Syracuse University in the fall of 1977. In that year he gave his paper
'The Life of Buildings' at the Graduate School of Design in Harvard. Thereafter
he was invited to teach at the École Politechnique Fédérale of Lausanne, in
Switzerland, in 1980, and at Princeton in 1982.

In tandem Moneo continued developing his professional work. During the
second half of the 1970s he began one his most fruitful collaborations, with
Manuel de Solà-Morales; they were brought together by a shared interest

65   Moneo had met Eisenman in Aspen and visited him again in 1974 with a group of young tutors from
Barcelona. Peter Eisenman in turn had connections with the Barcelona group and participated in
some architectural discussions organized by Oriol Bohigas.

in the theoretical ideas of La Tendenza. Amongst their joint projects was a typological study of Aranjuez (1974–5), which was later incorporated into the Aranjuez Special Plan of 1982, and an important project for the residential district in Lakua, Vitoria (1977; fig. 20), which also used typological investigation to reformulate the idea of a residential neighbourhood; unfortunately it was never realized. Another key project of the period, also unbuilt but very important symbolically for Moneo's career, was for *10 Immagini per Venezia*, an event held in Venice in 1978, during which a group of architects prepared schemes for housing in the Cannaregio neighbourhood of the city (fig. 19).[66] Moneo was invited to participate in this ideas session together with some of the most well-known architects of his generation, including Peter Eisenman, Aldo Rossi, John Hejduk and Raymund Abraham. This conjunction of talents working on the same project represented one of the most interesting intellectual encounters of recent architectural history. Cannaregio lies to the east of the railway station, and the site was just to the south of the area where Le Corbusier's unbuilt late project for a hospital had been planned. Moneo's strategy maintained the predominantly horizontal character of the Venetian townscape by using cross-walled houses as the building type rather than flats, and by interlacing the housing with a network of canals. But he quite deliberately did not modify his proposed layout in the light of the accidents of the local context, with its arbitrary geometry of boundaries, and thereby he maintained a strong figurative character to his scheme just as Le Corbusier's hospital project had. Meanwhile in Spain, one prize-winning project, in 1979–80, was for the extension to the Bank of Spain in Madrid, where Moneo's attitude to context resulted in the controversial decision to use the classical language for its façade (see pp. 254–6).

In 1980, the School of Architecture at Madrid was suffering a period of revolts and strikes, and threatened to descend into chaos. Moneo was invited by a provisional council of the school to take up a vacant post, previously occupied by Victor D'Ors. Moneo accepted, and thus was able to practice and teach

---

66 The results of the 'seminar' (often wrongly described as a competition) are published in Francesco Dal Co (ed.), *10 immagini per Venezia: Raimund Abraham – Carlo Aymonino – Peter Eisenman – John Hejduk – Bernhard Hoesli – Rafael Moneo – Valeriano Pastor – Gianugo Polesello – Aldo Rossi – Luciano Semerani: mostra dei progetti per Cannaregio ovest; Venezia, 1 aprile–30 aprile 1980*, Venice: Officina Edizioni, 1980.

in the same city after his ten-year spell at Barcelona. He was 43 years old and already involved in what would be one of his best-known works of the period: the National Museum of Roman Art at Mérida, an ancient Roman site in Extremadura, south-western Spain (see pp. 127–38 for a detailed description of this important project).

The 1980s, in retrospect, were a golden era for Spanish architecture. The political transition, from a dictatorship to a democracy with a titular king, unfolded successfully, the economy grew impressively, and architectural commissions came easily. Successive governments saw the benefits of major investment in public work, from infrastructure to public spaces, new museums and the preservation of historic monuments, providing unparalleled opportunities for architects to display their talents. Moneo's reputation had been enhanced by the international recognition of buildings such as Logroño town hall and Bankinter, and he attracted several new commissions. He maintained his contacts with Venice and New York, and his collaboration with *Arquitecturas Bis*, while his international prestige continued to grow.

Moneo's primary focus in the office in the early 1980s was on the substantial new commissions for the Mérida National Museum of Roman Art (1980–86), the Bank of Spain in Jaén (1980–88), the insurance company headquarters Previsión Española in Seville (1982–6), the Colegio de Arquitectos de Tarragona (1983–92), and the transformation of Atocha railway station (1984–9). According to members of the studio at that time, Moneo worked consistently long hours. He regularly appeared at the office in the early morning and was highly disciplined in allocating his time between teaching, writing, site visits and office design reviews. Even though he tried not to stay late at the office, it was mainly in the evenings that he looked over the boards and made revisions to the drawings that his assistants had worked on during the day. Always self-critical and equally demanding of his staff, he maintained control of all the important design decisions.[67]

In the 1980s, work in the office dealt with two principal issues: how public buildings in the newly democratic Spain should be fashioned, and how particularly awkward sites should be treated, building in historic contexts being one of the questions that was hotly debated at the time (as Moneo explained in 2010[68]). So, for instance, Moneo treated the problem of the offices for Previsión Española, Seville, as primarily a question of how to reinforce the edge of the city, since the site ran along the line of the old city walls

---

67 Conversation between Francisco González de Canales and Luis Moreno Mansilla, Cambridge, Mass., February 2006.

68 Rafael Moneo, *Remarks on 21 Works*, New York: The Monacelli Press, 2010, pp. 137–41.

21 Rafael Moneo: Previsión Española,
Seville, 1982–8. The wall-like character
of the office building reflects the old
Almohade wall on the right

(fig. 21). Thus the expression is wall-like and strongly horizontal, with a continuous band of windows, an intermediate stone strip and a strong cornice;
every fourth course of the brickwork is deeply recessed. But, where the building cranks, the corner is emphasized by a strong parapeted prow. The whole
acts as a backdrop to the Torre del Oro, a survival from the time of the old
city wall structure, which stands between the Previsión Española and the
river. Along the river frontage the name of the office is inscribed in large letters on the stonework, and again as a gilded inscription on the parapet above,
rather as the popes in Rome would announce their patronage on a square in
Trastevere. But the owners have changed, and the new occupants have removed the name of Moneo's patrons and substituted their own – a graphic
demonstration of the relative impermanence of contemporary institutions
compared to those that architects could expect to celebrate in the past.[69]

Another building of this period makes use of large-scale graphics to announce its presence in the city: the Banco de España in Jaén. This is a modest
four-storey building, but expressed as a cubic volume from which much of
the material has been removed, that forms a giant canopy sheltering single
and two-storey structures in the front portions. The removal of material from
a cube, as a design strategy, seems to refer back to Jorge Oteiza's sculptures,
in particular his *cajas metafísicas* (metaphysical boxes) of the 1950s, which
Moneo, in common with many Spanish architects, much admired. The building, its screen walls and adjoining ancillary structures, are uniformly faced
in red Alicante stone and ordered on a strict 2.4 metre square module; by this
means the composition achieves a presence on the street that is quite dispro-
portionate to its actual size.

Atocha railway station, on which Moneo began work in 1984, was not only
a much more significant building in terms of size, but, because its brief encompassed a series of urban and architectural problems, was also a project
that demanded a particularly coherent and strategic architectural control
(figs 22–4). The primary task facing Moneo's office in their proposals was organizational, on plan and section. The plan brings together an international
rail terminal, a suburban station, a bus station and the underground, with

---

69   Moneo notes this with regret on p. 150 of *Remarks*; indeed it is something he is prone to say whenever
he passes the building when visiting Seville.

22 (top) Rafael Moneo: plan of Atocha Railway
Station, Madrid, 1984–92. The original building
designed by Alberto del Palacio is on the left, the
national tracks at the bottom of the plan, with the
suburban station above. The piers of the cylindrical
lantern register in the concourse behind

23 (bottom) Rafael Moneo: Atocha Railway Station,
Madrid, 1984–92. Aerial view, with the original
building on the right

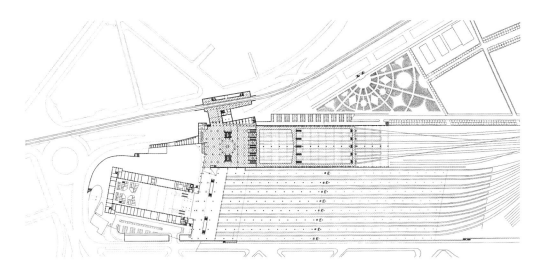

24 Rafael Moneo: Atocha
Railway Station, Madrid, 1984–92.
Aluminium car park domes

24 Rafael Moneo: Atocha
Railway Station, Madrid, 1984–92.
Aluminium car park domes

all the necessary apparatus of a transport interchange including taxi ranks, private parking and car hire arrangements, and Moneo needed to reconcile complex levels, where the roads were some six metres above the level of the national train tracks, which were themselves at a higher level than the suburban tracks. The whole had to respect the context and setting of the existing nineteenth-century shed designed by Alberto de Palacio, with its glazed and vaulted roof, which had been dwarfed by the recent road construction at a higher level still. Moneo decided that it was simplest to accept the elevated road position rather than to try and bring vehicles down to the lower level, and to carve out a predominantly pedestrian space around the Alberto de Palacio building, which is retained as a generous planted garden onto which shops and ticket offices open; it acts as a kind of foyer to the stations beyond, and sports a prominent new brick clock tower. Moneo had proposed something similar in an entry for the Amsterdam Town Hall Competition in 1968, and also installed a clock at Logroño, its purpose being as much to symbolize civic virtues as to record the time. The ensemble of buildings at Atocha thus creates a low-level court adjacent to the old train shed as a kind of oasis in all the bustle of the station. A second major formal gesture is the introduction of a 'lantern' – a cylinder of brick piers – which marks the principal place of arrival and vertical circulation, skewered through the multiple levels of the

complex. The suburban station, despite its subterranean location, is naturally lit through skylights that emerge on the roof above as the supports for a
gridded field of aluminium domes, which in turn act as sunshades for the car
park (fig. 24). Next to the suburban station, and at a slightly higher level, is the
international station, and here Moneo's new enclosure does not attempt to
emulate the form or character of the nineteenth-century building, but instead
behaves as a vast but somewhat neutral canopy held on multiple concrete
columns – these are the equivalent of four stories high and create a kind of
hypostyle hall. Each column carries a square steel tray with expressed ribs,
both orthogonally and diagonally, and there are rooflights on all four sides
between the trays. But the trays are not quite square, because the international tracks (which are parallel with the suburban tracks) do not come into the
concourse at right angles. Rather than exploit the tension that this misalign-
ment might provoke, Moneo defuses it by slipping the whole column grid and
making each apparently square metal tray into a rhomboid. This neutral (yet
subtly composed) four-storey high train shed roof stops well away from the
roof of the Alberto de Palacio building, the junction being effected by a single-
storey saw-toothed glazed canopy. By disengaging the different structures of
the stations from each other and from the nineteenth-century shed and keeping them horizontal rather than vaulted, Moneo enhances the dignity of the
old vault and prevents an embarrassing collision.

Nearly twenty years after the completion in 1988 of Moneo's Atocha station, London's St Pancras was extended, to general acclaim, to cater for the
Eurostar; the design also turned much of the old station over to retail uses,
and employed a flat roof for the extended platforms. But the flat roof simply
abuts Barlow's magnificent shed without any articulation at all.

William Curtis sensed in the Atocha station (and the airport at Seville) 'an
aesthetic fatigue' in comparison to the museums at Mérida and for the Miró
foundation.[70] But it is surely to be expected that the repetitive structures nec-

70   William Curtis, 'The Structure of Intentions', in Márquee and Levene (eds), *Rafael Moneo 1967–2004:
     Imperative Anthology*, p. 569. Seville Airport was one of the projects awarded by the national govern-
     ment to prestigious Spanish architects to cater for the festivities of 1992; Ricardo Bofill, for example,
     designed the airport at Barcelona. The project had to be completed to a very tight timetable, at a time
     when Moneo was the chair of the Department of Architecture Harvard Graduate School of Design
     and was simultaneously working on the Illa Diagonal, Pilar and Joan Miró Foundation, Barcelona
     Auditorium, Thyssen-Bornemisza Museum, and other commissions. The standard of detail and con-

essary for larger transportation buildings will yield less in the way of aesthetic interest than an art gallery or museum. Seen from afar, the clock tower, brick and glass lantern, and the glistening aluminium car park domes, combine to create a memorable image of a complex that is important as a transport hub but is intended neither to carry the aesthetic impact of an institution nor to challenge the presence of the earlier Alberto de Palacio building.

The commission for Atocha certainly lies in a difficult area of work, partly concerning the provision of infrastructure but essentially to do with the representation of public space. Moneo grasped it as an opportunity to demonstrate how architecture could contribute to the solution of an urban problem, rather than merely be an excuse for formal or aesthetic experiments, though it involves the inventive manipulation of many formal languages. But the quality of execution is not as high as it is in most of Moneo's buildings: the contract with RENFE (the Spanish railway company) required that the architect be employed up to scheme design stage and retained only in a consultative capacity during detailed design and construction, which may go some way to explain this.

Moneo's teaching syllabus in Madrid was substantially different to that in Barcelona. In Barcelona he had taught the first year of Architectural Design (Elementos de Composición) in the students' second year of studies, while in Madrid the similarly named Composición was a history- and theory-based course taught in the fourth year, with special emphasis on the understanding of relevant concepts and case studies useful for the design composition challenges that a young contemporary architect could be expected to face. His main assistant in Madrid was Juan Antonio Cortés, who had collaborated in his office for several years in the 1970s, and was later to become an important Spanish architectural critic. Moneo developed this course as a masterclass in

struction is low, and the result is one of Moneo's least successful projects. Moneo has acknowledged this, although he has continued to defend the ideas behind the design. For his acknowledgment of the problems, see for example the interview in 2002: Francisco González de Canales and Ignacio Fernández Torres, 'Del Kursaal al Prado', in *Diario de Sevilla*, 31 January 2002, p. 67. Moneo discusses the notion of a 'mat building', the importance of the roof plan as a generator of the design, and the reference to local architectural traditions at the Seville airport in *Remarks*, pp. 200–210. It was probably because of the impossibility of maintaining architectural control in Spain that Moneo decided to return to Madrid in 1990.

which to discuss the ways in which architectural ideas and theoretical principles were embodied in particular architectural works; he would structure
the debate around concepts such as 'free plan' or 'typology', and how these
were reflected in a detailed study of historical works across a wide range
of periods, while concentrating on works by well-known modern masters
such as Le Corbusier, Mies van der Rohe, Aalto and Kahn, but also those by
Asplund, Hoffmann and Loos. In his university lectures he began to analyse
the work of his contemporaries, and the design strategies in the architecture
of Hejduk, Eisenman, Stirling, Venturi, Graves, Meier and Moore, anticipating what would later be the procedures in his masterclass at Harvard GSD.[71]
These were intense and concentrated sessions, and he preferred to lock the
classroom door at the beginning of his lectures so that students could not
come in and out and disrupt the flow of his ideas. Emilio Tuñón, his student
and later one of his closest collaborators over a ten-year period, recalls that
Moneo was once telephoned at ETSAM by his family to inform him of the
death of a relative. The ETSAM concierge asked the young student Tuñón to
interrupt Professor Moneo, but he was forced to wait until the lecture had
finished, and the door was unlocked.[72]

In the spring of 1982, Moneo returned to the United States to teach at
Princeton, and that November participated with some of the most influen-
tial American architects at an invited conference in the University of Virginia.
At its core was the network of architects that Peter Eisenman had gathered
together at IAUS. Moneo met Harry Cobb, I. M. Pei's partner and at that time
Chair of the Department of Architecture at the Graduate School of Design at
Harvard. Some 18 months later, in the summer of 1984, Moneo was proposed
as Cobb's successor at Harvard, and a committee headed by Dean Gerald
McCue visited Madrid to inspect Moneo's built work. Moneo was offered the

71   As we can see from this list of names, Moneo was becoming increasingly interested in East-Coast
     American architects, with whom he was establishing strong contacts, and set aside the Italian ar-
     chitects (Rossi, Gregotti, etc.), on whom he had concentrated when teaching in Barcelona. For more
     on the Madrid syllabus, see the five-year summary published by the ETSAM, *Programas de Curso
     y Ejercicios de Examen. 1980–1981, 1981–1982, 1982–1983, 1983–1984*, Madrid: Cátedra de Composición II,
     Ediciones de la ETSAM, 1985.

72   From a conversation between Emilio Tuñón and Francisco González de Canales, March 2014. Accord-
     ing to Tuñón, this was before Rafael Moneo became his tutor.

chairmanship for a period of five years, beginning in the winter term of 1985, and was invited to teach a course in the spring of that year.

Before leaving, and in a sense in anticipation of the imminent internationalization of his practice, which up until then had consisted almost entirely of work in Spain, Moneo entered several competitions, for Prinz-Albrecht-Palais, Berlin (1983), Progetto-Bicocca for Pirelli, Milan (1985), and the IACP competition for Campo di Marte (1985), where he was awarded first prize *ex aequo*. In projects such as Bicocca, his work began to distance itself somewhat from his earlier enthusiasm for the typological studies of the Italian school; the project is defined by infrastructural decisions and the form that emerges establishes its own character more naturally.

25 (top) Rafael Moneo and Manuel de Solà-Morales:
L'Illa Diagonal, Barcelona, 1987–94. Plan

26 (bottom) Rafael Moneo and Manuel de Solà-
Morales: L'Illa Diagonal, Barcelona, 1987–94. Section

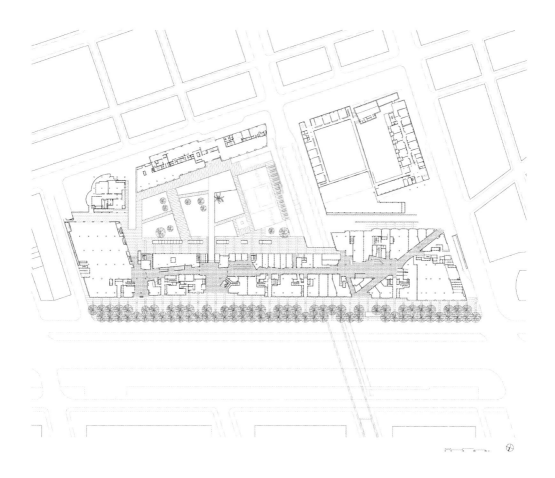

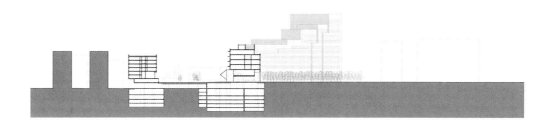

When Moneo was appointed at Harvard in 1985, he moved with his wife, Belén, and their three daughters, Belén, Teresa and Clara, to live in Cambridge, Massachusetts. At the time, their two elder daughters were already living and studying in New York. They rented a small house on a privileged site facing the Charles River. Moneo apparently revelled in the opportunity that the new position gave him; he has frequently recalled how well he was treated by American universities in the 1980s. Despite being rooted in his native Spain and attached to Madrid, and even to his home town of Tudela, he appreciated the opportunity offered by this more isolated way of life, enjoying the best aspects of the American campus. During this period, and no doubt partly owing to his international exposure at Harvard, his reputation grew exponentially. Even in Spain, it was the prestige attached to his new academic position that probably accounted for the substantial new commissions he attracted, which compelled him to work out the difficult balance between his academic obligations in the United States and the supervision of projects in Spain.

Just before his appointment at Harvard, in April 1985, *El Croquis*, an architectural journal that had been founded by two young architects Fernando Márquez and Richard Levene in the early 1980s and had developed extraordinarily in the years since its inception, dedicated a special issue to his work. To be published in a journal that had become so influential internationally, and was now bilingual, represented a very significant public recognition. Later on, *El Croquis* would publish two other issues on Moneo, one dealing with his work between 1990 and 1994, and another for the period from 1995 to 2000.[73] The 1985 publication highlighted buildings such as Bankinter, Mérida and Logroño, each illustrated by specially commissioned photographs by Lluis Casals. In addition to an introduction by Márquez and Levene themselves, critical articles about the buildings were written by Josep Quetglas, Ignasi de Solà-Morales, Juan Antonio Cortés, José Luis González Cobelo, Enrique Sobejano and Fuensanta Nieto. The seriousness with which his built work was treated served to reinforce his growing international status.

The position at Harvard meant a new concentration on academic affairs; Moneo had long been connected with universities but had never undertaken

---

73 The compendium volume *Rafael Moneo, 1967–2004* encompassed and completed the three previous publications.

administrative responsibilities, let alone experienced the reality of a full-time position in a North American university. At the time of his arrival in Harvard, American architectural education was under attack for its exclusive interest in theoretical debate and speculative paper-based architecture, and apparent lack of concern for the actualities of practice. Moneo, who was both a considerable figure in the theoretical debates of the time and a respected active practitioner, was expected to help to bridge the gap. His Kenzo Tange Lecture at Harvard in March 1985 specifically addressed the question, highlighting the importance of construction in giving consistency and authenticity to the work of architectural practice, and illustrating how, in his own work, theoretical ideas could be understood as developing out of practical solutions.[74]

Among his obligations as Chair of the school, was that of organizing the curriculum, hiring new faculty staff and inviting visiting lecturers, but in addition to his administrative duties, Moneo regularly taught in the studio and gave seminars on contemporary architecture. Thus the quality of the academic life of the school rested to a large extent in his hands. For his course entitled 'Introduction to Design and Visual Studies in Architecture', aimed at the first year M.Arch students, Moneo delivered a series of lectures based on those he had already taught at Barcelona and Madrid. But for the American lectures he started using a case study system – already made famous by the Harvard Business School – discussing a chosen subject by means of paradigmatic case studies. These lectures discussed buildings such as H. H. Richardson's Sever Hall at Harvard, Carrère and Hastings' New York Public Library, twentieth-century buildings by Kahn and Le Corbusier, and more recent work by BBPR and Stirling. In the succeeding years he found it more appropriate to try to contrast different ways of conceiving architectural design by using a single architect's body of work, rather than taking a particular theoretical concept as the thematic organization. So it was that he began to fashion what were to become famous lectures concerning selected architects of his own generation,

74   Rafael Moneo, 'The Solitude of Buildings', Kenzo Tange Lecture, Harvard University Graduate School of Design, 9 March 1985, *A+U 227*, August 1989, pp. 32–40. The interesting question of how theory may develop out of practice, rather than the other way around, which is the normal assumption, is discussed in more detail in the essays on his thinking, below.

such as Stirling, Rossi, Venturi, Eisenman, Siza and Gehry, a group that he subsequently expanded over the years as architectural culture progressed.

Moneo's presence at Harvard was a good advertisement for Spanish architecture, which by then had gained a considerable international reputation. He
was able to incorporate younger staff into the faculty, who in turn brought
fresh ideas to bear on the curriculum; these included Prescott Scott Cohen,
Mohsen Mostafavi, Homa Farjadi, Michael Hays, Wilfred Wang and others.
Lectures and exhibitions played a central role in the students' education, and
here too Moneo's opinions had a major bearing on the school's direction; he
quite deliberately promoted his personal views and values. One example was
the exhibition 'Emerging European Architects', which included some relatively unknown names at the time, amongst them Herzog and de Meuron,
Diener and Diener, and David Chipperfield. Exhibitions featuring the work
of Ignazio Gardella, Steven Holl and other significant figures were also organized. Lectures were the occasion to learn about any important architect
at the period. Students of that time remember Moneo's chairmanship at the
GSD as a period of particular architectural intensity.[75]

As already noted, despite his distance from Spain, Moneo began to receive
further commissions there during his chairmanship at Harvard. He established a small office in Cambridge, Massachusetts, close to Harvard Square,
and some of his assistants from Spain came over for periods to work there.
But the main office remained in Madrid, and he trusted Emilio Tuñón with
the difficult task of managing it alongside a number of trusted collaborators.
Tuñón himself was architect in charge of the Atocha Station, Luis Moreno
Mansilla of the Seville Airport and the Thyssen Museum, Luis Rojo of the
Miró Foundation and the Kursaal, and Maria Fraile and Lucho Marcial of the
Barcelona Auditorium. Nevertheless, Moneo maintained a close control on
administrative issues, trivial as they may seem compared to the central task
of design. Because he was seldom in Madrid, when he did appear he could be
extremely demanding. Some of his collaborators recall that though Moneo
generally tended to be in a good mood and made jokes about everything

---

75   From a conversation between Francisco González de Canales and Luis Eduardo Carranza, a Harvard
      GSD PhD student at that time, who was present at the school throughout most of the period during
      which Moneo was chair, Cambridge, Mass., April 2006.

27 Rafael Moneo and Manuel de Solà-Morales:
L'Illa Diagonal, Barcelona, 1987–93. A consistent
façade with numerous articulations

imaginable, if he saw something he disliked in the office, such as a design
drawing or a decision about the purchase of office supplies, he could became
quite tough on his young collaborators.

Two of the most significant projects that Moneo developed in this period were in Barcelona: the Illa Diagonal Building (1987–93; figs 25–7), and
the Auditorium (1987–99). The first of these was a huge and complex project
that he won in limited competition jointly with Manuel de Solà-Morales in
1986. The site had a 300-metre frontage on to Avinguda Diagonal, which was
a major route into the city, and was at the edge of a relatively homogenous
nineteenth-century development and looser twentieth-century clusters of
higher buildings. The brief for the multi-purpose building called for shops,
offices, a hotel and even a school. In the past, the largest buildings, such as
cathedrals or palaces, tended to be the most important, and an established
architectural language could be called upon to express their significance, but
that is not necessarily the case more recently. L'Illa is large because the commercial realities of contemporary development mean large developments are
more profitable than small ones. Their construction requires myriad other

professionals, and the buildings have to be flexible enough to adapt over time
to different programmatic needs. Consequently the symbolization of uses
can no longer be a reliable prop to architectural invention.[76] The project tried
to reflect the complexities of the programme and resolve those of the urban
location. Moneo and Solà-Morales chose to concentrate on maintaining the
consistency of the fabric, meeting the brief in a continuous travertine-faced
superblock along the Diagonal, with a more varied grouping of other buildings behind. Numerous entrances puncture the main block, and every excuse
is found to vary the frontage by slight set-backs, which register strongly on
oblique views, while the expression of the façade is kept absolutely regular.
This procedure is the very reverse of that which is often applied: monumental
blocks with minimal articulation, decorated in multiple ways.

The site for the Auditorio de Musica de Barcelona was in an unpromising
urban location, close to Plaza Las Glorias, which was a major traffic intersection, where the context offered little to which the new building could respond.
Moneo placed the two required auditoria back-to-back, with separate foyers,
but sharing a central covered plaza, rather along the lines of a Beaux-Arts
'vestibule'. This is treated as a 'lantern' and decorated with an abstract graphic
design by Pablo Palazuelo. The separate foyers lie as destinations beyond the
auditoria, that for the larger symphony hall being around a courtyard, and
this arrangement allows for multiple entrances along the flanks of each hall.
Below the level of the auditoria is a continuous basement, so that services can
be shared. The auditoria themselves are quite autonomous; the symphony hall
seats 2,340 and is broken up into sections in much the same way as at Hans
Scharoun's Berlin Philharmonie. In contrast to such particularity, the external and internal expression of the skin of the building is deliberately mute
– a framework of concrete with in-fill panels of steel externally and timber
paneling internally brought flush with the frame, in the manner that Louis
Kahn explored at his Mellon Gallery in New Haven. The project was initially
conceived as part of the urban transformations for the Olympic Games but it
was delayed and the building eventually took more than 20 years to complete.

---

76 Rem Koolhaas has eloquently explained this. Moneo refers to Koolhaas's categorization of buildings
    by size in his discussion of L'Illa. Moneo, *Remarks on 21 Works*, p. 225.

28 Rafael Moneo: upward isometric projection
of the Thyssen-Bornemisza Museum, Madrid,
1989–92

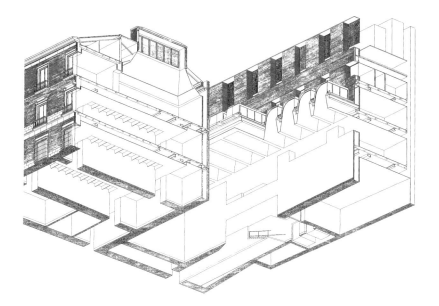

28 Rafael Moneo: upward isometric projection of the Thyssen-Bornemisza Museum, Madrid, 1989–92

In 1987 Moneo was commissioned to design a new airport for Seville, a building that has provoked some critics because of its literal reference to the local
architecture. The simple linear arrangement of this small airport (with only
five stands for aircraft) allows for straightforward expansion. But in terms of
expression, Moneo refused to indulge in the romance of flight as an inspiration, as, for example, Santiago Calatrava does at his Bilbao airport. Moneo's
building is eminently ground-based, with a parking structure built around
gardens, and a terminal vaulted with blue, top-lit domes – the 'unabashed use
of an element . . . well known throughout the history of architecture'.[77]

Other significant commissions in Spain during this period include two of
his best known museums: Pilar and Joan Miró in Palma de Mallorca (discussed
in detail on pp. 139–45), and the Thyssen-Bornemisza Museum in Madrid,
which involved the transformation of an old building located in Paseo de la
Castellana, in front of the Prado Museum (fig. 28). The building had already

77   Ibid., p. 207.

29 Rafael Moneo: the Davis Museum, Wellesley
College, Massachusetts, 1990–93, set beyond Paul
Rudolph's 1950s Jewett Art Centre

suffered multiple alterations and all that remained was the basic volume and
the façades. Within these constraints, Moneo organized the interior in two
main stories and a double-height naturally lit entrance hall. Moneo avoids the
use of corridors by making each of the regular new rooms behind the retained
façade lead into each other. The top floors, where rooflights are possible, are
given special profiled ceilings and lanterns of different sizes, and there is a
lot of attention given to the building's finishes, such as the coloured marble
floorings. This *parti* on the upper floors, densely packing rooms of differing
sizes, is recognizable in Moneo's later museums such as those in Houston and
Stockholm, and Moneo refers to the precedent of projects by Scamozzi.

Moneo's first commission in the United States arrived during his tenure at Harvard: the Davis Museum at Wellesley College, Massachusetts (fig. 29). Buildings on the idyllic 500-acre, undulating and well-wooded campus at Wellesley, just outside Boston, date from 1914, following the destruction by fire of the nineteenth-century college hall, and have been added to in each decade. The immediate context was the Jewett Arts Center, an auditorium linked at first-floor level with a library, which was the first major building by Paul Rudolph, of 1955–8. It is predominantly horizontal and brick-faced, but has enameled sun-screens, prominent rooflights and a spiky profile that associates it with its neo-gothic neighbours on the campus. Moneo's adjacent art gallery is more solid and vertical, a stubby tower in fact, linked to a lower screen room and temporary gallery whose geometry relates it to Rudolph's building. The main cubic gallery space is bisected by a double staircase system, allowing mezzanines within the two-storey spaces and a choice of routes up and down. Moneo intended the ascent to the top to relate to the development of art, but in reverse chronology, with the earliest pre-Columbian art as the climax; subsequent curators' installations have not always followed this narrative.[78] Urbanistically, the plain brick volume becomes a destination for Rudolph's somewhat over-elaborated steps beneath his library–auditorium link, and thus recasts our understanding of the whole complex.

In May 1990, Moneo delivered the Walter Gropius lecture upon the completion of his term as Chairman of the Department of Architecture.[79] A few days before, he had finished and sent to Spain his entry for the Kursaal Auditorium competition at San Sebastián. He went on to win that competition (the project is discussed on pp. 146–53), which marked a new stage in his career. After his period as chairman, Moneo continued to be attached to the Graduate School of Design as the Kenzo Tange Professor, which meant that, while living in Madrid, he would return for one semester a year to teach at the school. In 1991, he was appointed as the first Josep Lluis Sert Professor at the GSD, a position that he still holds today.

---

78   Ibid., p. 357.
79   Rafael Moneo, 'Reflecting on Two Concert Halls: Gehry versus Venturi', Walter Gropius Lecture, Harvard University Graduate School of Design, 25 April 1990, *El Croquis* 64, 'Rafael Moneo 1990/1994', February 1994, pp. 156–75.

On his return to Madrid, Moneo was 53. His permanent home ever since has been in the so-called 'colonia' of El Viso, where he lived intermittently since the 1970s.

El Viso was designed by Rafael Bergamín in 1933–6, in collaboration with Luis Blanco-Soler and Luis Felipe Vivanco. The scheme remains one of the first examples of international modernism by Spanish architects, members of the so-called 'Generation of 1925'.[80] Located at what was then the outskirts of Madrid, the 'colonia' was conceived of as a cooperative of affordable housing for workers and public employees under the Ley de Casas Baratas (Economic Housing Act) of 1925, but was soon occupied by upper-middle class professionals and intellectuals.[81] The design of the small villas drew upon modernist housing precedents, in particular the dryness of the work of Adolf Loos.[82] Many Spanish intellectual personalities, such as José Ortega y Gasset, Rafael Sánchez Mazas and Salvador de Madariaga, lived there. The area was soon connected to the rest of the city through the *ensanche*, and is today an exclusive residential central area popular with celebrities. Though Moneo always believed that it was important for a man to live in a good neighborhood, his style of living has never been sumptuous. The house in Miño Street, El Viso, is comfortable, with some fine materials such as the wooden flooring

---

80 The architectural historian Carlos Flores introduced the term 'Generación del 25' to define the first group of Spanish architects to attempt to absorb the architecture of modernism, formally if not theoretically. The group (Fernando García Mercadal, Rafael Bergamín, Casto Fernández Shaw) took its name from the 1925 International Exposition of Modern Industrial and Decorative Arts in Paris, where they had been impressed by the radical work of Le Corbusier and Melnikov. Other important architects of this generation were Carlos Arniches, Agustín Aguirre, Luis Blanco Soler, Martín Domínguez, Luis Lacasa, Manuel Sánchez Arcas and Miguel de los Santos. A complete study can be found in Sofia Diéguez Patao, *La generación del 25: Primera arquitectura moderna en Madrid*, Madrid: Cátedra, 1997.

81 The Ley de Casas Baratas was influenced by movements in Britain and France, such as the Labouring Houses Act or the Societé française des habitations à bon marchè. The first Ley de Casas Baratas was passed in 1911, and extended in 1921. In 1925, under the dictatorship of Miguel Primo de Rivera, the Ley de Casas Baratas was extended again to include the middle classes.

82 The small villas were sensible, somewhat condensed versions of the typically bourgeois residence, without any superfluous ornamental features. For affordable housing, the villas were extraordinarily well equipped, enjoying the latest technologies in heating, electricity and water supply. They were also spatially generous: the average villa had four or five bedrooms and a small office space, hall, living and dining room, kitchen and service spaces, two toilets, storage areas, a car parking area and a private terrace.

and staircase, but unpretentious in expression, to match Moneo's preference for material asceticism. The general atmosphere is warm and modest, ceilings are low and furniture pieces are few but carefully selected. The low-ceilinged living room, with plain wooden bookshelves lining its longer sides, is a cave-like space. The small art pieces that are displayed are almost lost within the books, drawing little attention to themselves, even though amongst them could be original Miró or Le Corbusier drawings. More books are in the semi-basement, where his personal library is located, opening on to a small backyard. The house as a whole has a sense of austerity, with its few pieces of furniture (usually of a modern ancestry), no decorative features and an absence of household clutter.

Moneo's office has also always been in El Viso. From 1965–80, his house and office shared the same villa, at Oria 17. For a short period (1979–80), the office moved to an independent building at Urola 8, just opposite. But from 1980 to the early 1990s, the two were again reunited when he moved to his present house in Miño Street, the office occupying the basement. On his return from the United States in 1991–2, Moneo refurbished another of the El Viso villas, in Cinca 5, still within walking distance of his house.[83] By then he needed space for more than twenty employees. The office is consequently not unlike his own house; it respects the villa structure in being fragmented into a number of rooms, the smallest of which allows groups of two or three to work together. But on the right of the ground floor there is a generous room, open to the entrance, which can take five or six assistants, and to the left a pair of rooms, interconnected with a sliding door, the smaller of which is occupied by Moneo and his personal assistant, Cristina Carriedo. Moneo, who refuses to have a mobile telephone, uses the landline there. The other room has a large table for meetings and a smaller table for the numerous books that Moneo has recently bought or been given. The only decorations, throughout the office, are selected drawings of projects – not necessarily presentation drawings but those that capture their conceptual essence and illustrate their construction – Bankinter, for example, and two favourite sectional axonometric views

---

83 Moving from the house basement to the new office space was difficult, and it was not until 1995 that the new office space was fully in use.

of the Mérida Museum (see fig. 50, p. 129). The semi-basement is used as the office archive, storing rolled drawings, boxes of models and further books.

By 2013, most of his collaborators were young architects; of the older generation there remained only Fernando Iznaola, who began his collaboration with Moneo in 1989, and Hayden Salter, who joined in 1994 to take charge of the Los Angeles cathedral. For 20 years Sandra Domínguez looked after the office archive, until 2013 when she returned to Philadelphia with her husband Martín, son of the exiled Spanish architect of the 'Generation of 25', Martín Domínguez. Francisco González Peiró, the office quantity surveyor ('aparejador') since the mid-1960s, remains in this position today.

Some architects, such as Louis Kahn, do not begin to attract substantial commissions until they are in their 50s. This was not the case with Moneo; nevertheless the 1990s can be seen as representative of the maturity of an international architect. The Pilar and Joan Miró Foundation (pp. 139–45), the Davis and Thyssen-Bornemisza museums, the Illa Diagonal building in Barcelona, and the San Pablo Airport in Seville, which was required for the 1992 International Exhibition, were all completed, and the Auditorium in Barcelona substantially finished during this decade. New commissions included the Los Angeles cathedral (pp. 163–9), the Beirut Souks, the Royal and General Archive of Navarra (1995), the Contemporary Museum of Art and José Beulas Foundation (1999), and most complex of all, the Prado Museum in Madrid, described in more detail below. He participated unsuccessfully in a number of major competitions, such as for a concert hall in Lucerne, and the Potsdamer Platz in Berlin. But in two other competitions he was successful: the Palazzo del Cinema on the Lido at Venice (1990), and the Museum of Modern Art and Architecture in Stockholm (1991–8; fig. 30).

The Venice Palazzo del Cinema, a simple volume with a monumental canopy suspended over the canal, was designed to cater for the Film Festival, with two large screens and a cluster of smaller screening rooms. But it joined the list of projects for that city by Wright, Le Corbusier, Kahn and indeed Moneo's own 1978 Cannaregio project, that have never been constructed. Fortunately, however, the Museum of Modern Art and Architecture in Stockholm, located on the beautiful Skeppsholmen island looking towards the Stockholm Bay, was built during the 1990s. It was probably the modesty of Moneo's approach that won him the commission. His building plays on the linear character of

30 (facing) Rafael Moneo: the Museum of
Modern Art and Architecture, Stockholm, 1991–8,
on Skeppsholmen island

31 (below) Rafael Moneo: Don Benito Cultural
Centre, Badajoz, 1991–7. Storks can be seen
nesting on the rooflights

the island's ridge, using the change in level across the narrow section, and,
with its multiple repetitive roofs, it sits happily in the context of the adjacent
earlier buildings. Only its colour seems to have provoked a reaction.[84] Most of
the surrounding buildings are yellow or cream, and Moneo proposed either
red walls with copper roofs, or grey walls with zinc roofs. In the event, the
roofs were constructed in zinc, but the wall colour was red. The roofs define
clusters of top-lit gallery spaces of differing scales, an elaboration of the ideas
first investigated at the Thyssen-Bornemisza Museum.

Moneo also received direct commissions for a hotel in Potsdamer Platz,
Berlin, the Murcia town hall (pp. 155–61), and the delightful cultural centre in
Don Benito in Extremadura, in southern Spain (fig. 31). The latter was a modest and appropriate addition to a small town, and a fascinating demonstration of architectural ingenuity – a *tour de force* of the motifs that Moneo had

84 See Andreas Gedin, 'Moneo on Moderna Museet in Stockholm: To Locate a Large Building on
    Skeppsholmen', 1998. www.artnode.se/artorbit/issue1/i_moneo/i_moneo.html.

been exploring in the last few years. It has prominent roof lights, on which storks make their nests, and through which the light penetrates a top floor gallery, and illuminates a reading room on the floor beneath through shallow domes. Externally, a simple rendered façade receives horizontal incisions of differing scales depending on conditions of adjacency, or the desirability of emphasizing certain moments, such as the corner entrance.

The full brief for a small site had encouraged Moneo to use a 'compact' form, as he explained in his valedictory 1998 lecture at Harvard, 'End of the Century Paradigms', where Don Benito is one of the five examples (and by far the smallest) of his work that he refers to.[85] He tried, in that lecture, to illustrate the continuing validity of certain architectural principles, in the face of the pressure to indulge in fragmentation, the use of unprecedented sculptural form, the indulgence in wilful 'stylelessness', or the concentration on surface and skin at the expense of volume and mass. So this modest little building bears a potentially heavy theoretical load.

These years of the return to Spain therefore were dense both in projects and in building completions. A general overview of his production during the period reveals a tension between two poles: on the one hand, Moneo continued to exercise some of his concerns of the 1970s and 1980s, among them a careful insertion of new work into the pre-existing urban fabric and a sophisticated reference to history and to traditional composition. The brick mass perforated by regular windows of the Berlin hotel and the elaborate interpretation of Andalusian historical architecture in the San Pablo airport would illustrate that. Even the complex morphology of the Illa building in Barcelona can be interpreted in that way, addressing the problem of how to subdivide and articulate in different architectural segments a 400-metre long building that had to meet a very complex programme and yet perform as an urban piece that reads at the scale of the city. On the other hand, the late 1980s had been the time when Moneo began to explore a freer and more complex approach to composition. The Museo Miró in Palma de Mallorca and the Kursaal Auditorium in San Sebastián (pp. 146–53) are probably the clearest expressions of that tendency. In both cases, the reference to landscape and to the

85   Rafael Moneo, 'Recent Architectural Paradigms and a Personal Alternative', *Harvard Design Magazine*, Summer 1998, pp. 71–4, reprinted in Márques and Levene (eds), *Rafael Moneo 1967–2004: Imperative Anthology*, pp. 651–9.

geographic conditions of the respective sites justifies the approach. That this exploration, in an urban context rather than using a landscape analogy, would lead towards very new results at Murcia town hall should not surprise us, when we take into account his initial contacts with organic architecture and his admiration for Wright, first observed by Fullaondo. A more organic or informal approach to composition does not mean that Moneo abandoned his usual precision in managing the design geometry, however. Form was never dissolved, but was handled differently as he explored more complex issues. His exploratory position not only allowed him to confront new situations and architectural challenges but also reinvigorated the relationship between his own work and that of his contemporaries, which had followed a number of divergent paths following the relative consensus of the 1970s and early 1980s.

One of the explorations undertaken in those years, and perhaps one of the most original of them, which we have already touched on, originates in the design for museums: the idea of the container combined with a non-hierarchical division of the plan. Beginning with Thyssen-Bornemisza and continuing with the Davis Museum and Stockholm Museum, Moneo's approach to the project can be seen as producing carefully modulated architectural boxes – a species of magical containers – and the treatment of the auditoria within the Kursaal is similar. They seek to respond both to the urban context (though from a more abstract position than that of exploring traditional typologies), and to accommodate the specific requirements of exhibitions or other aspects of the brief. In many respects Moneo's architectural production can be seen as a personal reflection on contemporary architecture, just as his research and teaching, during the various versions of his seminar at Harvard, reflects on the buildings of his contemporaries, and would culminate in his book *Theoretical Anxiety and Design Strategies* (2004). His explorations of multiple possibilities for the Murcia façade, for example, echo Gehry's approach to architectural form in using a considerable quantity and variety of models. In a similar way, one can sense some of Venturi's ideas about architecture as an ordinary container, especially behind the series of museum plans and sections. However, Moneo never gets tempted into using those containers merely decoratively, nor into making iconographic references to pop culture. In his museums, Moneo has consistently developed the idea of a non-hierarchical plan that he has related back to Scamozzi. The idea is to divide

32 (facing) Rafael Moneo: Prado Museum
extension, Madrid, 1998–2007. Roof plan

33 (following spread) Rafael Moneo: Prado
Museum extension, Madrid, 1998–2007.
View towards the south east, showing the
new entrance suppressed beneath a parterre,
and the terracotta pavilion which encloses the
re-built cloister of Los Jerónimos

the plan in an uneven grid, which offers a series of different room sizes, usually naturally lit through roof lanterns. Avoiding corridors, rooms are directly
connected to each other. Their different proportions accommodate different
types and sizes of art works. The pattern is not unlike that used by Venturi
in the National Gallery in London. Nevertheless the specific treatment given
by Moneo to this idea produces characteristically varied volumes, usually
crowned by lanterns of different sizes. The same *parti* is used at the Thyssen,
Houston and Stockholm museums, though the rooflight pattern is more successful in southern latitudes than in Sweden, with its low sun angles.

The high-profile competition for the Prado extension (figs 32–6) proved
to be a major point of friction between Rafael Moneo and other Spanish
architects. As work had been scarce since 1992, the first Prado competition of
1996 attracted no fewer than 766 entries, and the result was eagerly awaited.
The jury panel, which consisted of architects and politicians, failed to agree
on a winner.[86] Moneo's 1996 project was heavily criticized by most of the
architects on the panel, but widely defended by the politicians.[87] The compromise, which caused enormous frustration to all participating architects,
was to select ten practices to compete again. At this stage Dürig and Rämi,
and Matos and Martínez Castillo, were considered front runners.[88] The
second-stage competition, held in 1998, had a new brief, new site conditions
and a new jury, which was eminently political. The only architect in the jury
panel of eight was Antonio Fernández Alba.[89] When Moneo was announced
as the winner of the second round of the competition, other architects,
especially Matos and Castillo, saw this as a personal betrayal and the result of

86   The architects on the panel included Mario Botta, Pedro Ramírez, Dan Eytan, Rogelio Salmona, Herman Hertzberger, Francesco Venezia, Krysztof Chwalibog and Antonio Fernández Alba. The politicians were recently elected right wingers including Esperanza Aguirre (Minister of Culture) and
Miguel Ángel Cortés (State Secretary of Culture), and the Director of the Prado, Fernando Checa.

87   Fernando Samaniego, 'Un jurado de arquitectos y políticos declara desierto el concurso para ampliar
el Prado', in *El País*, 7 September 1996.

88   The eight others were Arana, Aroca and Población, Barrionuevo, Molino and Daroca, Govela, Hernández Gil and Olalquiaga, Marco, Moneo, Pardo and Zoido. The results of the competition were published in 'The Competition', *AV Monografías* 62, November–December 1996.

89   Other jurors for the second competition were Benigno Pendás representing the Ministry of Culture,
Fernando Checa and José Antonio Fernández Ordóñez, representing the Prado Museum; César Franco and Francisco Jurado, for the archbishopric of Madrid; Luis Armada, representing the municipality of Madrid; and José Manuel Rueda, for the regional government of Madrid.

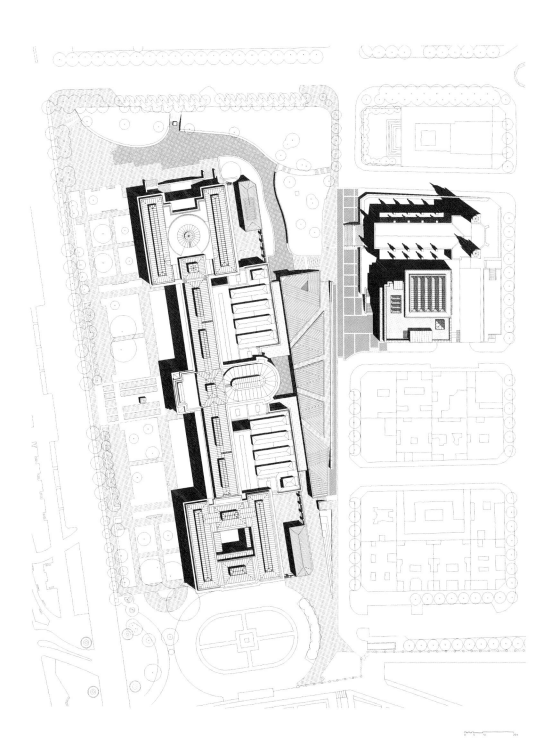

34 Rafael Moneo: Prado Museum extension,
Madrid, 1998–2007. Lower-floor plan

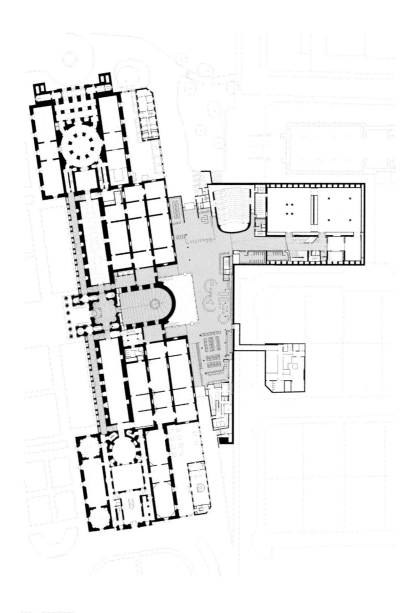

PRADO JERÓNIMOS: PLANTA ACCESO +635.30

35 Rafael Moneo: Prado Museum extension,
Madrid. Main gallery-level floor plan

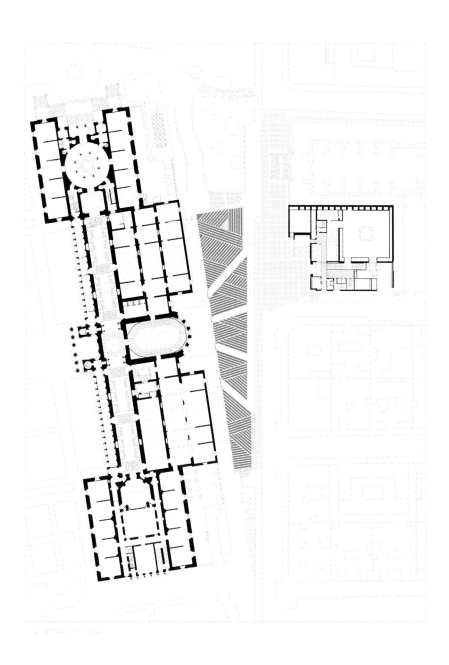

36 Rafael Moneo: Prado Museum extension,
Madrid, 1998–2007. Section looking north. The
existing museum is to the left and the new
extension, incorporating the cloister of Los
Jerónimos to the right

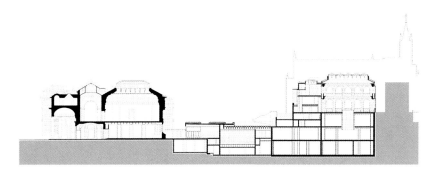

political manipulation. There was also the precedent of the Murcia Town Hall Competition, where Moneo had succeeded Alberto Noguerol and Pilar Díez: his completed building, admired though it was by architects, was at least as unpopular with local inhabitants as the earlier project had been.

The Prado Museum extension proved to be one of Moneo's most complex and difficult projects. By the time of the 1999 competition, the museum's requirements and the available site were precisely determined, a constraint that Moneo welcomed in his competition report, quoting Paul Valéry: 'the greatest freedom arises from the greatest rigour'.[90] The project was subject to a number of delays, but on completion, though probably too compromised to rank among his greatest works, it has an air of inevitability that is the hallmark of skilful architecture. The Prado is one of the richest and most substantial collections of European art, displaying fine examples of Italian, German, Dutch and of course Spanish art, the work of Goya and Velázquez being especially well represented. The collection had been housed since 1819 in a building started in 1785 and intended as a natural history museum, but substantially constructed from 1809 by Juan Villanueva, an architect Moneo deeply admires. This was originally a dumbbell on plan: two square pavilions linked by a long central north–south block. Opposite the central western entrance was a galleried oval room. Early in the twentieth century, new galleries were built to the east of the central linking range, and further construction in the 1950s

90   Márquez ad Levene (eds), *Rafael Moneo 1967–2004: Imperative Anthology*, pp. 520–25.

and 1960s eventually swamped the oval room. Only a small proportion of the museum's extensive collection can be shown at any one time, and there are two additional separate buildings, the Casón del Buen Retiro and the Palacio de Villahermosa (the Thyssen-Bornemisza Museum, converted by Moneo himself as we have described, and subsequently extended further), which house portions of the work. There are multiple entrances to the substantial main building: in addition to the central entrance from the west (Puerta de Velázquez), there are also entrances on two levels from the north and from the south. Across to the east, on Ruiz de Alarcón street, stands a nineteenth-century neoclassical institute, in red brick with a prominent portico and flight of steps, and the sixteenth-century church of Los Jerónimos, similarly raised above street level, with the remains of a two-storey seventeenth-century cloister, designed by Alonso Carbonel.

The programme required the incorporation of the Los Jerónimos cloister into the Prado Museum complex, and Moneo achieved this by the expensive and controversial expedient of demolishing it stone by stone and re-erecting it in precisely the same place, above a new building that partially encloses it at upper levels as well as containing space for temporary exhibitions, conservation offices and a capacious storeroom and loading bay. The new building and cloister are connected to the Prado underground, as it were, since Moneo excavated a space for a generous linking area and covered it with a raised garden of box hedges. The long triangular linking block, whose floor slopes gradually southwards, contains the museum shop, in a group of low semicircular metal-cased bays, and is cut into by a small courtyard embracing the radiused end of the Villanueva oval gallery. Beyond the shop is a café, and a window towards the trees of the Botanical Gardens to the south, which the Prado's deputy director Gabriele Finaldi described as Moneo's 'nod to the right-hand door at the back of the room in Las Meninas'.[91]

The sophistication of Moneo's proposal is evident when one considers the temptations that he resisted. There were three other galleries, or gallery extensions, constructed in the early years of the twenty-first century in Madrid: the Reina Sophia by Jean Nouvel, the Caixa Forum by Herzog de Meuron,

91 Xavier Bray, 'Giving the Prado Space to Breathe' in *Apollo*, 7 January 2008 (www.apollo-magazine. com/features/434546/giving-the-prado-space-to-breathe.html).

and the extension to the Thyssen-Bornemisza Museum by BOPBAA.[92] Each of them is a remarkable building: Nouvel made a dramatic blood-red canopy over an internal courtyard, which is expressed on the Ronda de Atocha; Herzog de Meuron performed a piece of structural gymnastics by removing the ground floor of the existing building to leave it apparently suspended in mid air, and created a sculptural rusting steel attic; BOPBAA made a powerfully contrasting new white extension to the pre-existing red brick of the Palacio de Villahermosa. Moneo's intervention at the Prado is altogether lower-key and its ambition is primarily organizational. By removing the lecture hall and temporary gallery functions, he made it possible again for visitors to use the central 'Velázquez' entrance and reach a reception point in the very centre of the Villanueva building, from which access to all parts of the gallery is possible. His linking building also provides a generous new entrance (Puerta de Los Jerónimos), but this is subsidiary and not signalled as a major event. Moneo avoids the addition of a new architectural element of any kind in the narrowing space between the rear of the Prado and the church and other buildings lining the street behind – there is no pyramidal glass light as I. M. Pei had made in the Louvre for example.

In suppressing the entrance link, Moneo leaves the expression of the substantial expansion of the Prado almost entirely to the new building, Edificio Jerónimos, which he makes sure to compose as a well-behaved addition to Ruiz de Alarcón Street. It is treated as a red-brick pavilion, backed by a rectangular stone-clad residential building designed by the Diocesan architects, entirely filling the block, and has the complicated formal task both of taking its place as one of a series of pavilions on the street, and of acting as a wrapping to the Los Jerónimos cloister. Unlike the other buildings that address the street, it has no need for a central entrance, yet it is required to signify its importance as something more than a block of flats. Moneo's solution is to give it a projecting portico composed of twelve square-brick piers which rest on a rusticated brick base; the rustications are achieved by setting in every sixth course of bricks, but it is only the portion beneath the piers that is so treated. The projecting section, and the building as a whole, sits on a

92   The founder members of BOPBAA, in 1990, were Josep Bohigas Arnau, Francesc Pla Ferrer and Iñaki Baquero Riazuelo.

granite-clad plinth, the height of which varies according to circumstance, moving up and down to accommodate the slope of the site, and the relationship to the pavements and terraces that surround it. The flight of steps to the terrace between the extension and the church of Los Jerónimos, instead of running down to the calle, is set at right angles and consequently is masked by a plinth and balustrade composed of the same brick and stone cladding. It rises to a mezzanine entrance, and continues up to join the terrace in front of the church. The asymmetry this creates to the lower part of the façade is further emphasized by the placing of a single window at first floor and a monumental set of gates (which are more like window shutters) to the ground floor. The bronze doors were designed by Cristina Iglesias, an artist born in San Sebastián but based in Madrid. They are treated as a representation of trees, or luxuriant vines, a reflection of nature that is appropriate in this location, opposite the new roof landscape of the Prado link, running down to the Botanical Gardens to the south. When the doors are open, a view is revealed from the Edificio de los Jerónimos of the whole rear elevation of the Villanueva Prado building.

Internally, public circulation in the Edificio de los Jerónimos is arranged around a flight of escalators running from the ground floor (the apparently below-ground) level up to the rebuilt cloisters. There are two large spaces for temporary exhibitions at the lowest level, where there is also an auditorium in the link, and at the intermediate or mezzanine level a small exhibition space and a second large exhibition area; this contains a central light well, bringing natural light down from the cloisters above and also acting as a rooflight to the large gallery beneath. The two-storey cloisters themselves are roofed by five skylights running north–south above metre-deep coffers. The central well has a timber-clad edge to balustrade height. There are five bays to each side; to the north there is the nearby flank of the church of Los Jerónimos, and to the east the apartment block. The other two sides are clasped by the new building, but this stops one bay short of the end of the west-facing elevation. Thus a single bay has an unobstructed view back towards the Prado. By not quite enclosing the whole courtyard, Moneo both permits this release at the corner and ensures that the new building with its prominent portico is shifted southwards, allowing the façade of Los Jerónimos to breathe. The displacement is not abrupt, however; rather, it is managed in three steps, the first being the line of the portico proper, the second marking the area of internal circulation, and the third the edge of the corner staircase connecting the conservation offices and their library. These staff and study areas are intricately planned, with carefully positioned roof lighting on the upper floor.

The second half of the 1990s confirmed Moneo's international reputation, especially enhanced by a number of prestigious awards: the Arnold W. Brunner Memorial Prize from the American Academy of Arts and Letters, the Prince of Viana Prize, the Swedish Schock Price for the Visual Arts, the Pritzker Prize for architecture, and the gold medals of the Spanish Government for the Merit in Arts, the French Academy of Architecture, the International Union of Architects and the Royal Institute of British Architects. In 2012, he was awarded the prestigious Prince of Asturias Prize in Arts, and became the most honoured Spanish architect in history.

Having settled permanently in Madrid, he continued to teach at Harvard during the spring term and travel extensively to supervise work on site. He interrupted his frantic professional activity, which involved frequent flights around the world for lecturing, as well as visiting sites and meeting clients, with peaceful holidays in Mallorca. There, he purchased a rural property close to the sea and planted its grounds with olives and different fruit trees. A preexisting traditional Mallorcan house was enlarged, shielded by old trees and canvas awnings on hot summer days, and this remained a retreat for him and his family.

Amongst his competition entries, those for the expansion of Helsinki railway station and a theatre in Basel were the most important. The Arenberg campus library in Leuven and the Cranbrook Academy of Arts extension in Michigan were both commissions in which Moneo exercised his skill in setting up a dialogue with pre-existing buildings. At Cranbrook, Moneo's addition to the existing building by Eliel Saarinen is particularly careful in its insertion of volumes and the manipulation of their height, whilst at the same time the new building complements, and distinguishes itself from, that of Saarinen. It accepts, and denies, its symmetry and introduces a new material sensitivity.

Another commission, in 1997, for the Gregorio Marañón Maternity and Pediatric Hospital in Madrid, was also a building type that was new to him (fig. 37). The challenge here was to reconcile a brief that stressed technical questions at the expense of other issues, such as the experience of those who use it, and its material expression as a compact and dense building on an already crowded site. It was conceived as part of a comprehensive scheme for the hospital area, replacing outdated buildings and setting the pattern for future development, which would involve the demolition of buildings that have been erected pragmatically to deal with short-term problems in the past, and that currently spoil the relationship between pre-existing buildings and their open spaces. Inevitably, some of that re-configuration is yet to come, since the temptation is always to invest in what will yield the immediate return of new floorspace to meet a pressing need. This building is one of Moneo's most systematic and rationally organized, with a rigorous separation of internal routes and a consistent external expression. There are eight internal deep courts or light wells, and all the perimeter corridors are single-sided, ensuring that the interiors are unusually well lit. Patients' rooms, usually in groups of no more than five, look into the courts, with staff offices on the perimeter. The whole building is glazed, but mostly the glass is etched on the outside and mirrored internally. The horizontal glazing bars project so that the external appearance reads as an abstract, pearly glass composition. This is relieved by a number of projections and recessions, and a ramp to the adjacent below-ground car park that is strongly textured in concrete. Internally, the intention was to create a bright and sanitized environment, which would symbolize the clinical standards of the institution while still being sufficiently articulated to make the patients feel at home. The skin is clearly in the line of development from the internal courtyard of the Barcelona Music Centre, and the cladding, curved externally but flat internally, was also used at the Kursaal in San Sebastián, the designs for which were finalised as those for the Gregorio Marañón hospital were being conceived.

The Chivite winery was the first of a number of projects related to wine, which had been a passion of Moneo's for a long time. In fact, in 2007 he began producing his own wine at La Mejorada, Olmedo (Valladolid), where he had the opportunity of reusing an old eighteenth-century monastery as the main building, which sits beside a delicate Mudéjar chapel from the early fifteenth century.

After the year 2000, Moneo could enjoy both his architectural maturity and international prestige. Amongst the fruit of those years was the completion of the Museum of Fine Arts in Houston (fig. 38), and Our Lady of the Angels

37 (facing) Rafael Moneo with José María de
la Mata: Gregorio Marañón hospital, Madrid,
1997–2003

38 (below) Rafael Moneo: Museum of Fine Arts,
Houston, Texas, 1992–2000

Cathedral (pp. 163–9). The contrasting approach to each project is evidence
of Moneo's versatility, and his conviction about the connection between the
specific architectural *parti* of a project, the conditions of the brief and the
character of the site. While the museum is compressed into a single and
relatively simple volume that contains the kind of exhibition rooms he had
previously developed for Thyssen-Bornemisza or Stockholm, the cathedral
generates its own urban precinct, and exhibits a great richness of volumes, sur-
faces and material textures. In the Chivite winery, as at Cranbrook Academy
and the Arenberg library, Moneo demonstrated a continuing elaboration of
complex themes relating projects and place, never reducing the forms to a
simple mimesis of the existing architectural elements. The contrast is even
greater in the Leuven library, where the remains of the old cloisters were reused or extended, while the white volume of the reading room is inserted as a
complete contrast within the brick fabric of the cloister.

A list of new commissions received since the beginning of the twenty-first
century reveals an impressive catalogue of work for any architect who has

39 Rafael Moneo: Northwestern building,
Columbia University, New York City, 2005–10.
The bridging function of the building, over an
existing gymnasium, accounts for the emphatic
diagonals on the façade.

practised for more than half a century.[93] Rafael Moneo has maintained a consistently hectic pace of practice from his office in Cinca 5, Madrid, on national
and international projects and competitions, assisted by a small and dedicated team of young architects. He continues to gather prizes, and his work is
regularly reviewed and exhibited. But, as seen with the Prado, Moneo's continued ability to gather patronage for significant projects has provoked a certain
amount of resentment amongst younger colleagues. In the 1990s, a younger
generation of Spanish architects, now in their 50s, was highly critical of the
status quo of Spanish architecture, which they considered conservative, outdated and exhausted. The omnipresent figure of Rafael Moneo, ex-Harvard
GSD chair and the only Spanish Pritzker Prize recipient, was the paradigmatic representative, with some of his most prominent (and slightly younger)
followers in Seville and Barcelona, such as Antonio Cruz, Antonio Ortiz, Elias
Torres and Helio Piñón. The younger critical generation of architects included Iñaki Ábalos, Manuel Gausa, José Morales, Juan Herreros, Federico
Soriano, Vicente Guallart, and Alejandro Zaera Polo, and even some of Rafael
Moneo's disciples such as Emilio Tuñón and Luis Moreno Mansilla, who occupied an intermediate position.[94] Though there were differences in the way
each of these architects expressed themselves, they all sought to break with
the previous generation of Spanish architects, who had finally gained international recognition through commissions related to the events of 1992 – the
Barcelona Olympics and Seville Universal Exposition, and, less importantly,
Madrid's year as European Capital of Culture. As a consequence of his international reputation, Moneo in particular had received prestigious public
commissions directly from government institutions, such as those for Seville

93 Housing at Tres Creus in Sabadell (2000–5, with Elias Torres); LISE for Harvard University at Cambridge, Mass. (2000–7; fig. 81); the Roman Theatre Museum in Cartagena (2000–8); Chase Centre for
the RISD (2000–8); Aragonia building complex in Zaragoza (2000–2010); 'El Miradero' Convention
Centre in Toledo (2000–12) Housing in the area of Rabbijn Maasenplein, The Hague (2001–6); the
Bank of Spain extension in Madrid (2001–6); the University of Deusto Library in Bilbao (2001–9); the
Iesu Church in San Sebastián (2001–11); L'lla Diagonal Bahosa Hotel in Barcelona (2002–7); a laboratory for Novartis in Basel (2005–8); the Northwest Science Building at the University of Columbia
(2005–10; fig. 39); Atocha Station extension in Madrid (2007–12); the Contemporary Art Museum of
the University of Navarra (2011–13).

94 Others of this generation include José Alfonso Ballesteros, Xavier Costa, Eduardo Arroyo, Willy
Müller, Enric Ruiz-Geli and Fernando Porras.

Airport and the Barcelona Auditorium. In their eagerness to showcase the best of Spanish architecture, government organizations neglected to hold public competitions, and a younger generation felt marginalized.[95] The economic crisis that followed the events of 1992 compounded the problem, and younger architects were increasingly frustrated. Around 1996–7, when the economic recovery began, this generation, by then in their 40s, started to campaign for their right to take over commissions on public works that the previous generation had already enjoyed. To distance themselves from Moneo and his followers ideologically, they rejected the long association between Spanish and Italian architecture, which had been especially intense from the 1970s and had been promoted by Moneo and Solà-Morales, in favour of other European and American models.[96]

In the midst of running a busy office, Moneo still found time to write and reflect on his own work and that of his contemporaries. His 2010 *Remarks on 21 Works* is of course a fundamental text for the understanding of his own *oeuvre*. But, in 2013, at the age of 76, he was preparing a new seminar series

---

95 Seville Airport was a direct commission to Moneo from the Spanish Ministry of Public Works, while the client for the Barcelona Auditorium (part of the National Plan of Theatres and Auditoriums of the Spanish Ministry of Culture) was the Auditorium Consortium, which had national, regional and local representation: the Spanish Ministry of Culture, the Regional Government of Catalunya (Generalitat), and the Barcelona municipality.

96 There were a number of strands to this new ideological position: it resisted the attempt to construct the discipline from within the culture of architecture itself in favour of seeking inspiration in other related disciplines and practices such as landscape, ecology, urban studies, information theory, and performance and land art; it was sceptical of architectural theories based on identity, place and memory; it was less interested in discursive and linguistic practices than a more material approach to the profession, which also involved a revaluation of minimal art; but at the same time it vindicated architectural plurality and diversity, especially in housing typologies, as a response to the plurality and diversity manifested in society. In the late 1990s, the work of these architects began to exert its influence through two *El Croquis* issues entitled In Progress (issues 96/97 and 106/107, published in 1999 and 2002), the Metapolis festival in Barcelona (1999 and 2000), the teachings at the UIC School of Architecture (especially in the period 1997–2005), and architectural magazines under the direction of the same young architects, such as *Fisuras*, *Bau*, *Exit* and especially *Quaderns*, edited by Manuel Gausa (1991–2000), and the emergent printing press Actar (1994–) under Ramon Prat. Some of the thinking of the group is compiled in: Willy Müller, Manuel Gausa, Vicente Guallart, Federico Soriano, José Morales, José and Fernando Porras (eds), *The Metapolis Dictionary of Advanced Architecture: City, Technology and Society in the Information Age*, Barcelona: Actar, 2006. Another compilation of paradigmatic texts of these architects can be found in Ricardo Devesa and Manuel Gausa (eds), *Otra mirada: Posiciones contra crónicas, La acción crítica como reactivo en la arquitectura española reciente*, Barcelona: Gustavo Gili, 2010.

at Harvard, entitled *Masters at the Beginning of the Twenty-First century*, to discuss the most interesting work of his peers. There he analyzes not only the work of Rem Koolhaas and Herzog & De Meuron (who were already present in *Theoretical Anxiety*) but also considers architects such as Sejima & Nishizawa, Steven Holl, Zaha Hadid and David Chipperfield. Rafael Moneo's career, therefore, is still driven by a characteristic self-reflectiveness and by his enthusiasm for contributing to current debates in order to generate a living architectural culture.

40 Rafael Moneo with Ramón Bescós:
Bankinter Headquarters, Madrid, 1972–6.
View from Marqués de Riscal with the Mudela
villa on the right

The Bankinter building marked an important milestone in Moneo's career –
his first major building in the capital city of Spain, an early exploration of
that contextualization of modern architecture which was to become one of
his most recognisable skills, and the beginning of a creative period from 1972
to 1977 that was to see the completion of the apartment blocks on Paseo de la
Habana (also in Madrid) and the design work on the Logroño town hall. The
project was undertaken with Ramón Bescós (1936–1993), who had studied with
Moneo and subsequently, like him, had gained both educational and practical experience abroad. He had taken his Masters in Architecture and Urban
design at Cornell, and then returned to Madrid where he worked for the municipality, though he had left by the time Bankinter began. A second important contributor was Carlos Fernández Casado (1905–1988), one of the most
well-known structural engineers in Spain at that time. According to Moneo,
the engineer Javier Martínez de la Hidalga chose Moneo and Bescós as architects on the advice of an architectural student, Francisco G. Quitana.[1] Moneo
also established a good relationship with Jaime Botín, the younger brother of
Emilio Botín, who was the founder of Bankinter, a Spanish bank supported
in equal shares by Santander and Bank of America. Jaime Botín was close to
the Huarte family, and Moneo would work for him not only on this and other
buildings for Bankinter, such as the headquarters in Valencia (1979–80) and
Seville (1984–6), but also on the refurbishment of his family's large country
house in Almuradiel, Ciudad Real (1978–9).

  If the Urumea building in San Sebastián had received significant attention
within Spain, it was probably Bankinter, a building that many still consider
one of the major landmarks of Moneo's career, that initiated his international reputation. The building is sited on the Paseo de la Castellana, a road described by Moneo as the backbone of the city of Madrid, along which many
of the city's most important institutions have been located over the years.[2]
Moneo's building sits behind an existing nineteenth-century villa that fronts
the Paseo, designed by Álvarez Capra for the Marqués of Mudela (figs 40, 41).
Moneo retained and restored the villa as part of the bank's premises, but his

---

1   Rafael Moneo, 'Sede de Bankinter', in Francisco González de Canales (ed.): *Rafael Moneo: Una Reflex-
     ión teórica desde la Profesión*, La Coruña: Fundación Barrié de la Maza, 2013, p. 247
2   Rafael Moneo, *Remarks on 21 Works*, New York: The Monacelli Press, 2010, p. 45.

41 Rafael Moneo with Ramón Bescós: Bankinter
Headquarters, Madrid, 1972–6, showing the
forceful modelling of the façade and the bronze
reliefs on the top storey

new building does not join it physically; only a curved driveway from the subsidiary street, Marqués de Riscal, links the two structures organizationally. Sitting behind the existing building, and rising well above it, the task of the new structure is both to act as a backdrop, and to engage in a dialogue with the older building. Organizationally, the dignified pre-existing building would accommodate the executive offices, whilst the new building would create spaces with a closer connection to their everyday use by the public.

In determining the retention of the earlier building, the architects would create problems for themselves if they were to exploit the maximum amount of development permitted. The new building to the rear would need to rise well above the three-storey villa, but it was also necessary to accommodate the rights of light of the apartment buildings immediately behind. These constraints account for the formal complexity of the project, though they do not explain the manifest skill with which the forms were ultimately handled, which reveal a compelling combination of eclectic references and geometrical control. At one level, a pervasive rationalism can be detected, in the curved volume that precisely defines the ramp to the underground car park, but at another level the architects are engaged in a deliberate play with several geometries that principally obey the rules established by the set of forms chosen.

The *parti* for the new Bankinter building can be seen as a contemporary version of the *parti* for the Mudela villa (fig. 42). Both (as arranged after the addition) are entered from the south, off the drive from Marqués de Riscal, have their principal staircases on the west, project a terrace towards the north, and offer their principal façades towards Paseo de la Castellana. A repetition of the existing nineteenth-century gate in the railings, which is set obliquely on the corner of Paseo de la Castellana and Marqués de Riscal, is placed further along Marqués de Riscal directly opposite the curved granite-paved route down to two floors of underground car park.[3] The entrance drum to the banking hall is set into a 45-degree oblique wall, which slides under the main body of the building above to create a two-storey *porte-cochère*. The five office floors above address the Paseo over the roof of the villa; the plan

---

3   This overt reproduction is a strategy, incidentally, that Moneo was to employ again, more controversially and at a larger scale, in his extension to the Bank of Spain; see pp. 254–5.

42 Rafael Moneo with Ramón Bescós:
Bankinter Headquarters, Madrid, 1972–6.
Ground-floor plan

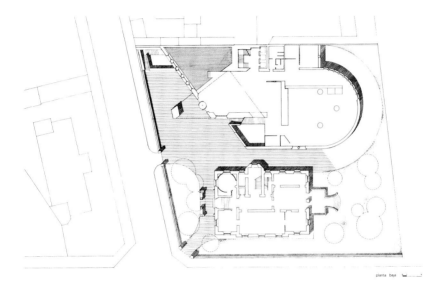

planta baja

is cut back, again at 45 degrees, mildly on the north side, but dramatically on the south façade, accommodating the required rights of light. Then the last two floors, which are treated as a pair on the eastern elevation, are cut back further on the south, creating the grander offices for the president of the bank. The spandrels of the double-height windows are faced with cast bronze reliefs by Francisco López Hernández, whom Moneo had met at the Royal Spanish Academy in Rome; the windows are two bays wide, and the proportions of the openings are double-square overall. This carefully considered crescendo at the top of the building registers across the largest distances, up and down the Paseo. Closer to, the appearance from Marqués de Riscal is much more complex, the dramatic diagonals enhancing the oblique view. And on the rear, the fenestration changes again, with regular strip windows that call to mind the deliberate contrasts that Venturi made between fronts and backs, and even the directness of Adolf Loos.

This broadly tripartite organization of the building, in terms of scale, proves capable of dealing with the different site contingencies and is fundamental to the success of the project. The ground floor accepts the pre-existing building and negotiates the entrances at the scale of the pedestrian by a diagonal

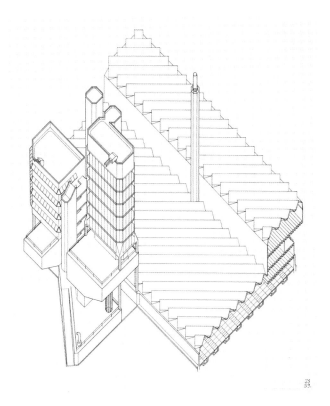

43 Stirling and Gowan: University of Leicester
Engineering building, 1963–6. First-floor plan.
One of many possible precedents for the
composition of Bankinter

deformation of a classical threshold, which creates an ambiguous relation
between frontality and rotation, and between the avenue and the palace. The
blunt curvilinear block meanwhile enables car access, with its logical curved
circulation in the back yard, but can also be seen as a hyperbolic bow window
that addresses the lawn, as in some of Frank Lloyd Wright's houses. Such careful crafting of the building at a domestic or human scale is different from
working with the scale of the office building, and also from that grander metropolitan scale that the building aims to address with the idiosyncracies of
its profile, and the enlargement suggested by a crowning element where the
grander spaces of the bank are located. Yet this complex organization of the
building with different scales and contextual responses is possible because of
Moneo's new-found confidence in 'composition' (discussed below, pp. 202–14)

in ensuring the necessary freedom of these three parts to meet the challenges of the commission.

At a more detailed level, the powerful sculptural quality of the new building is enhanced by the precision of its construction and detailing. Moneo confined himself to two principal instruments in developing a project that needed to be respectful to the pre-existing context, whilst neither imitating it directly nor dissolving itself as an object: its precise geometry already discussed, and the careful choice and deployment of material. In fact it is the quality of material and detail that unites the old and new buildings more than any formal device. He employed a granite base, and a hard red brick as the dominant material, and set the windows well back in the façade, employing thin bronze soffits and cills but a double-brick rebate on plan. The effect is to create sharp modelling and shadows at the heads of the windows, and – because the cills project minimally – a strong emphasis on the wall plane, but a much gentler double frame on the reveals. There are eleven east-facing windows on the principal office floors, and this treatment of the window detailing is sufficient to invigorate the whole elevation and compensate, as it were, for the abandonment of the language of first-floor balustrades, quoins, architraves and decorated entablatures of the villa in front. The bronze panels of the upper floors, seen obliquely, especially from the north where the window system returns for one bay, serve the same function.

Internally there is a similar material reticence and formal discrimination. Oak veneered panelling is used to clad window reveals and some of the walls, and the entrance hall has an abstract stucco mural by Pablo Palazuelo, based on the same 45-degree geometry that orders the building's plan. By incorporating Palazuelo's work, as well as the bronze reliefs by Francisco López, Moneo anticipates a practice that he was to pursue in later projects.

The Bankinter building was recognized immediately as a building of high quality and international importance, primarily because of its ability to defer to its nineteenth-century neighbour whilst being uncompromisingly a building of its own era. In the early 1970s, this was a rare achievement, but it was already clear that the skill to employ such a strategy was going to be essential in coming decades. An architecture that depended for its effect on the demolition of the pre-existing buildings and even street patterns was no longer relevant. In the prevailing uncertainty, when so much of what had been taken for granted in the modernist campaign was under question, including the proscription of decoration, the Bankinter building offered a particularly compelling middle way. It seemed to incorporate the pre-existing conditions without effort, yet had no need to indulge in an ironic pastiche of previous styles in order to demonstrate its sympathy with history. Critics could discover numerous references to Moneo's contemporaries and immediate predecessors. It was indebted to Venturi in the way in which it presented itself, billboard like, to the Paseo de la Castellana: the façade was the generator of the plan, rather than the other way around. The use of the 45-degree geometry might not have been so strictly and consistently applied without the precedent of Stirling and Gowan's 1963–6 Engineering building at Leicester, although the character of the British building is more industrial and hard-edged (fig. 43). Another British precedent was surely the Economist complex in London by Alison and Peter Smithson, where the new offices, bank building and apartment tower, set back from the street, defer respectfully to White's club on St James' Street. Others pointed to the banks by Otto Wagner in Vienna, with their careful control of plan geometry and wall decoration, to the fluid manipulation of building, landscape and terracing in Alvar Aalto's brick Pensions Institute in Helsinki (1949–52), and of course to the decorative cast panels incorporated in the mid-western banks by Louis Sullivan at the end of his career. Others (such as Fullaondo) praised the abstraction of the new building, pointing both to the elementarist compositional technique of early modernists like Peter Behrens and to the clarity of the surreal environments depicted by de Chirico. But all agreed that the most important achievement of the building was its 'respect for the residues of urban history'.[4] Moneo, by resisting the temptation to demolish the earlier building and create his own monument in its stead, had achieved a complex that was both a satisfying solution to the particularities of the brief and site and served as a valuable precedent for future urban interventions.

---

4   José Luis González Cobelo, 'Bankinter, Again' in Fernando Márquez and Richard Levene (eds), *Rafael Moneo 1967–2004: Imperative Anthology*, Madrid: El Croquis Editorial, 2005, pp. 109–11.

The project for Logroño town hall came at a crucial time both in Spanish political history and in Moneo's career. The building was commissioned when Franco was in the last years of his life, and was completed in the first years of the new kingdom of Spain. Behind the commission of Logroño town hall to Rafael Moneo lay a charismatic personality in Logroño's recent history: Narciso San Baldomero. An established politician in Franco's dictatorship, San Baldomero had a number of different responsibilities within the municipal government from 1953. He also held a position in the central Spanish Court. But his views could always be seen as liberal, within the limits of the dictatorship, and in 1957 he supported the cause of the aspiring King Juan de Borbón, Count of Barcelona and father of the Spanish current King Juan Carlos, by signing the Acta de Estoril.[5] The support of the Spanish Royal Family was fundamental later on for the construction of the new town hall, because in 1973, in the final two years of Franco's twenty-year dictatorship, San Baldomero was appointed Mayor of Logroño, a position that he would keep until the first democratic municipal elections in April 1979. He saw his main task as building the new town hall for Logroño, as he claimed the existing building was too small, and his connections with the Royal Family helped ensure a loan of 250 million pesetas from the Banco de Crédito Local. In 1973, San Baldormero offered Rafael Moneo the commission. According to Moneo, it was the fact that his competition submission for Amsterdam town hall, of 1967–8,[6] had been shortlisted, and had been seen as international recognition of the strength of Spanish architecture, that was critical to his selection.[7]For Rafael Moneo, Logroño town hall represents his first public building, after the private commissions for banks and apartments, and in this project he was able to reflect his absorption of the diverse influences of many of his predecessors and

5   The Acta de Estoril was signed by 44 Carlists (see note 1) to support Juan de Borbón as the legitimate heir to the Kingdom of Spain. Some of these traditionalist Carlists had important positions in Franco's government, so the signing of this Acta was the beginning of a certain reconciliation between Franco and Juan de Borbón. As a result, Franco agreed that Juan de Borbón's son, Juan Carlos, could be educated in Spain in the hope that he would 'continue the movemen'. But after his coronation, Juan Carlos initiated democratic elections.

6   Rafael Moneo, 'Ayuntamiento de Logroño', in Francisco González de Canales (ed.), *Rafael Moneo: Una Reflexión Teórica desde la Profesión*, La Coruña: Fundación Barrié de la Maza, 2013, p. 249.

7   Moneo's entry received a lot of attention in Spain and a special display in *Arquitectos*. See, 'Concurso Internacional del Ayuntamiento de Ámsterdam', Arq*uitectura* 124, April 1969, pp. 44–53.

contemporaries: Asplund and Aalto, Rossi and the architects of the Tendenza. The references to Asplund, of course, are not merely formal, but allude to a Nordic tradition, absorbed perhaps in the time when Moneo worked with Jørn Utzon, of a civilized local democracy, and represent an aspiration in the dying days of the Franco regime to reconnect Spain with European civic traditions. The architectural rhetoric is therefore somewhat reticent – cooler and subtler than one might expect – in deference to the political situation in Spain, as much as in acknowledgement of the sophisticated detail of an architect such as Asplund.[8] The site for the town hall, a former military barracks, was at the edge of the old town of Logroño, bordered by a characterful Arts and Crafts institute, which, according to Moneo, was the building 'with the greatest dignity in the area'.[9] Beyond, to the north, the town reaches the river edge, parallel to which is a series of east–west streets, part of the pilgrimage route to Santiago de Compostela. A subsequent urban project by Moneo has established a framework for rebuilding the streets and providing pedestrian routes through to the river. Because the project is located in such a particular position, adjacent to the old city, it acts as a link between the city and its immediate expansion. On one side it faces the entrance to the city proper, presenting itself as a kind of urban gateway; on the other, through the form of the auditorium volume and its location at the end of a public promenade, it relates to the Ebro river. Thus each of the elements has a meaning in relation to the city as a whole as well as to the internal formal composition.

At Logroño, the way that city and building are mediated is by a sophisticated manipulation of fragments. The two major triangles remind one of a Chinese tangram, a puzzle that requires considerable skill to assemble geometric fragments into a coherent figure. The town square itself can be seen as a fragment of a public space. This fragmentary condition, or suggestion of incompleteness, encourages the integration of the building into the city fabric precisely because of its lack of autonomy.

By this means an asymmetrical town square is created, inflected towards the south-west, which is the principal point of arrival, and focused, at the junction of the two wings, on a columned undercroft beneath the auditorium,

8   Moneo, *Remarks on 21 Works*, pp. 81–3.
9   Moneo, in Márquez and Levene (eds), *Rafael Moneo 1967–2004: Imperative Anthology*, p. 127.

that leads to an avenue running northwards to the river (fig. 46). As Juan Antonio Cortés points out, the effect on the square is to elongate the façade of Moneo's building, and reaffirm its presence.[10] The diagonal *parti*, which might be expected to introduce a disjunction or fragmentation of the composition, in fact ties the building to the space, and vice-versa, in a particularly skilful manner. The two wings reach almost to the corners of the square – the south-west wing falling short and privileging access from that direction, while the north-west wing is framed by a giant three-storey high portico. Avenues of trees bind the southern edge of the square, and these were always part of Moneo's conception – indeed in the early sketches there seems to be a greater concentration on the way in which the avenues might be joined or broken than on the behaviour of the building fabric itself. This is an urban project that is completely engaged with its site, as well as being a building of considerable figurative power. Indeed it is the tension between the reading of the building as a spatial container or as the conjunction of three elements that gives the complex much of its interest.

Though the immediate urban context is four or five stories high, the town hall is a modest three-storey building, and gains its civic effect, like Bankinter, by a combination of its powerful geometry and fine materials. The formal *parti* distinguishes the three components of the town hall brief: civic and mayoral functions, office areas and an auditorium. But it does so in a particularly striking way, in placing the rectangular auditorium behind the two triangular buildings linked at their apexes, which contain the civic and office uses (fig. 45).

The two diagonal wings, seen from the square they define, are treated differently, though both are clad in the same Salamanca sandstone, a traditional material choice that distinguishes this building from that of most buildings of the period. Both have colonnades that open towards the square, but one is elongated and the other is compressed (fig. 44 and frontispiece). The colonnade on the eastern wing, containing the offices, reaches the full three-storey height of the building, ending in the portico, and its spindly columns are of white painted steel. The soffit of the colonnade is exactly at the second-floor

10   Juan Antonio Cortés, 'Straightened Obliqueness', in Márquez and Levene (eds), *Rafael Moneo 1967–2004: Imperative Anthology*, pp. 146–8.

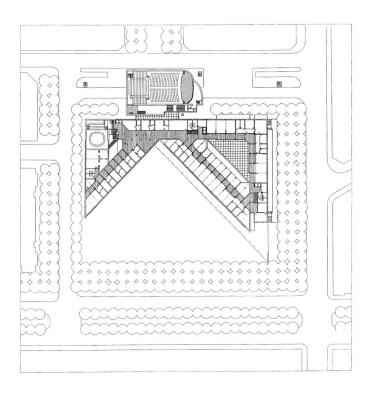

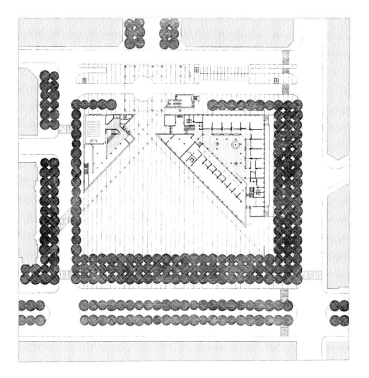

45 (facing top) Rafael Moneo:
Logroño town hall, 1973–81. First-floor plan

46 (facing bottom) Rafael Moneo: Logroño
town hall, 1973–81. Ground-floor plan

47 (following spread) Rafael Moneo:
Logroño town hall, 1973–81. Interior stair hall.
Note the different types of balustrade.

window heads. The western wing, on the other hand, has a colonnade at ground-floor level only, with first-floor openings of the same proportion, and then pairs of windows above. The effect is more domestic, even if repeated across sixteen bays. Shutters are detailed to fold back within the thickness of the wall on the top floor, and lie behind a stone trabeated balcony rail on the first floor.

The drama occurs, of course, at the conjunction of the two triangular buildings, where the different columnar systems come together, at the threshold of the entrances to each wing of the building, and to the auditorium behind, and the start of the route southwards to the river. At this point, a third set of supports is employed in the form of large circular columns. These acknowledge the multiple directions in which people may be moving, in comparison to the linear movement that characterizes the western colonnade, or the visual framing function of the canopy-like metal supports on the eastern colonnade. Seven of these substantial circular columns have mushroom capitals – four of them being twinned, so sharing an elongated capital between two columns. All of the supports fall on the four-metre square centre-line grid, which underlies the whole building; together with the dimensions generated by the diagonal, and the four types of exterior column, enough variety is generated to ensure a rich and expressive repertoire. The auditorium is held entirely on columns; only the staircase entrance connects it with the ground, and its backstage is sculpted in two radiused solid walls, clarifying the difference between the 'front', courtyard side, and the 'rear', whilst, at the intersection with the circular column grid, making for an expressive sculptural drama.

Entry to the two wings of the building fronting the square is from this undercroft; the way to the auditorium is from a separate west-facing lobby via a grand straight-flight staircase. Each of the triangular wings has a naturally lit space at its centre, but of differing characters. The civic wing is centred on a generous staircase, overlooked by a large window from the double-height council chamber. This stair can be seen as an autonomous composition in its own right, and carries a self-conscious association with the noble staircases of medieval town halls. The office wing surrounds a two-storey internal atrium, which acts as the principal point of intersection between the public and the council officers. Both have the character of being semi-external spaces. In the case of the civic stair, this is emphasized by the cladding of the

walls, which is of the same Salamanca sandstone as is used on the elevations (fig. 47); in the public atrium, the materials are internal in character, but the abundant natural light, introduced by a strip of north-facing rooflights, maintains the double reading. The additional height of the office wing facing the square, of about a metre, also contributes to the external character of this volume, which has benches designed by the architect set within the space. The columns around the perimeter are square, on the four-metre grid, whilst the eight double-height columns supporting the roof terrace to the second floor are circular.

If the arrangement of columns, internally and externally, creates one level of detail to supplement and enrich the overall *parti*, a further refinement is supplied by the design of the furniture and fittings. These vary in character in response to local circumstance. For example, balustrades to the galleries overlooking the public atrium are metal, framed with horizontal tubes of a quasi-industrial type; as we shall see they re-occur in the galleries of the Mérida museum. But the later stages of the staircase in the civic building have a refined and somewhat Scandinavian balustrade – closely spaced uprights and a gilded handrail. The columns at either side of the auditorium entrance, and in the centre of the four pairs of double doors, are clad in the same gilded metal. And the auditorium seats represent the first appearance of a design that, with numerous subtle modifications, Moneo employed again and again. The sides of the seat are formed of plywood circular discs, so that the upper portion acts as an armrest. At Logroño, the perimeter is clad in polished chrome, giving an effect that calls to mind 1930s art deco. The freestanding benches in the square outside are another version of the same idea. In all of these small-scale elements, Moneo seems to have abstracted his vocabulary from classical models, and he employs a strict geometry. The effect is less akin to the furniture of the avant-garde than to traditional models, though its abstraction prevents it from being overtly revivalist.

The Logroño town hall results from an eclectic approach, since the set of stylistic references is extraordinarily diverse, from the art deco seats and the Asplund-like balustrades, through to the rationalist architecture of the Tendenza, and the formal inventiveness of Aalto and Stirling. Yet the result is entirely coherent, and unmistakably the product of a single design sensibility.

By Moneo's own account, the architect Dionisio Hernández Gil, at the Dirección General de Patrimonio Artístico, Archivos y Museos of the Ministry of Culture (later Dirección General de Bellas Artes), was responsible for awarding him the commission for the National Museum of Roman Art in Mérida.[11] Hernández Gil, originally from Extremadura, had been the fellow recipient of the Prix de Rome with Moneo in 1962. On their return to Madrid they taught Análisis de Formas at the School of Madrid together, under Professor Adolfo López Durán. However, while Moneo continued his academic career by moving to Proyectos Arquitectónicos and was appointed to the Professorship of Elementos de Composición in 1970, Hernández Gil decided, in 1969, to leave academia to become a public employee of the Cuerpo de Arquitectos in Franco's Ministry of Housing. In the late 1970s, he entered the Dirección General de Patrimonio Artístico, Archivos y Museos as Inspector of Spanish Heritage, becoming Director General de Bellas Artes under the first socialist government from 1983 to 1986.

In 1979, Moneo and Hernández Gil visited Javier Tusell, the Director of Spanish Heritage newly appointed by the first democratic government of Spain. As the senior permanent architect at the office of Spanish Heritage, Hernández Gil convinced both Javier Tusell and José Álvarez Sáez de Buruaga, director of the Roman Museum of Mérida, located at the time in the Convent of Santa Clara, that a major building should be constructed to house a new National Museum of Roman Art, and that Moneo was the ideal architect for the job. The project started modestly enough with a commission to build a retaining wall on José Ramón Mélida Street, which was in danger of collapse because of adjacent archeological excavations. This pragmatic repair work eventually provided one of the guiding principles in the final design.

Mérida was the Roman city of Emerita Augusta, one of the most important settlements of the Iberian peninsula, and the ninth city of the Roman Empire. Its theatre and amphitheatre are both remarkably well preserved; indeed to see equivalently complete examples of late Roman architecture one has to visit what the Romans termed Asia Minor – modern Libya or Turkey. The archaeology of the city itself is still in the process of being excavated and

---

11   Rafael Moneo, 'Museo Nacional de Arte Romano', in Francisco González de Canales (ed.), *Rafael Moneo: Una Reflexión teórica desde la Profesión*, La Coruña: Funadación Barrié de la Maza, 2013, p. 252.

48 (top) Rafael Moneo: National Museum of
Roman Art, Mérida, 1980–86. Sketch of the
museum in relation to the adjacent theatre and
amphitheatre

49 (bottom) Rafael Moneo: National Museum
of Roman Art, Mérida, 1980–86. Plan of the
lower-ground area showing the footprint of the
museum set against the archaeological remains
of the Roman town

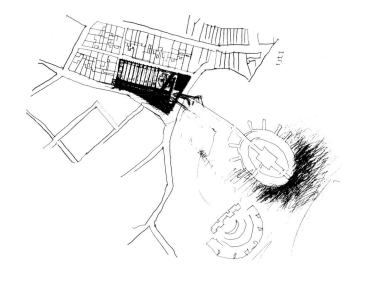

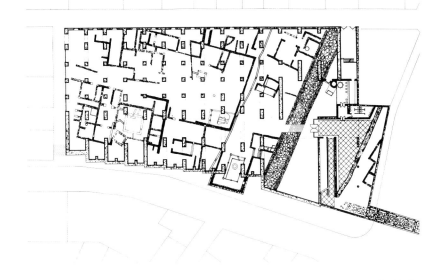

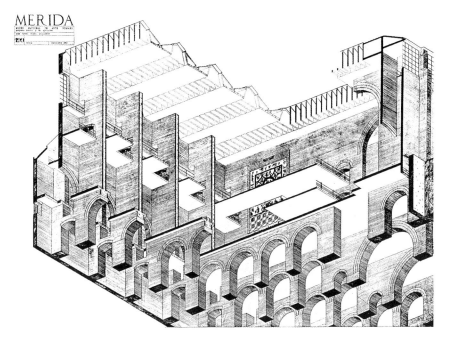

50 Rafael Moneo: National Museum of Roman
Art, Mérida, 1980-86. Upward isometric projection,
using the convention of Auguste Choisy

recorded. As is so often the case, the modern city hardly approaches the grandeur and dignity of its predecessor – it is a modest and unremarkable provincial town. The urbanistic problem for Moneo, therefore, in creating a museum
for Roman antiquities on a site adjacent to the theatre and amphitheatre, was
to relate his building to two quite different scales, and also the grain of two
different city structures (fig.48). There was a further, more general, issue in
1980 when he began work on the design – the question of how to treat a museum space. The collective wisdom of curators would suggest an anonymity
of setting as most appropriate for the display of historic artefacts: a white
or off-white background against which objects could be shown. As Ignasi de
Solà-Morales put it:

> The problem of the material base has almost always been resolved from the
> idea of a neutral unnoticed element. The object and its base were regarded
> as a mere secondary issue – scenography or detail . . . museum architecture
> had always been conceived as the creature of an empty stage . . .[12] Finally,

---

12   Ignasi de Solà-Morales, 'Base, Surface', in Márquez and Levene (eds), *Rafael Moneo 1967–2004: Imperative Anthology*, p. 185.

51 (facing) Rafael Moneo: National Museum of
Roman Art, Mérida, 1980–86. The 'nave'

52 (following page) Rafael Moneo: National Museum
of Roman Art, Mérida, 1980–86. A side gallery

53 (page 133) Rafael Moneo: National Museum of
Roman Art, Mérida, 1980–86. External buttresses

there was the particular issue of the precise location chosen for the museum, which was on top of an already excavated site, where the layout of the previous fabric would be clearly visible in the basement of the new building.

Moneo's answers to these three questions determine the *parti* for his building and inform every detail of it (fig. 49). First, the alignment of the substantial new museum on the contemporary street grid both acknowledges, through its sheer grandeur and scale, the Roman past that Moneo was asked to celebrate while at the same time relating his building to the ordinary domestic surroundings. Then, instead of conforming to an expected anonymity by displaying the artefacts against a white wall, he decided that they would best be shown against textured masonry. And, most courageously and controversially, he determined that the new museum would not tread delicately over the traces of the previous inhabitation of the site, but would establish its own massive footprint in opposition to the previous geometry. Moneo resolved on a quasi-Roman structure, analogous to the structural pattern visible in the remains of the older city, even though it was aligned on the street pattern of the new. Although each of these decisions can be defended on rational grounds, and their objectivity can be seen as a contrast to the idiosyncratic interpretations to which architects are prone in the design of museums – a programme that was quite common at the time – there is no denying that Moneo's approach was personal. It was influenced by the period he had spent in Rome, as well as by the study he had made of Choisy's representations of Roman architecture; this is clear in the axonometric drawings that Moneo's office prepared (fig. 50). The sympathy with Choisy goes beyond the merely graphic, however, in reflecting Moneo's firmly held belief that the forms of ancient architecture, whether Greek (where he admired the interpretation of Roland Martin) or Roman, were bound up with methods of construction.

The museum is ordered in plan in three parts. The main volume is a long four-storey high north–south nave with ten transept-like bays to the east (figs 51, 52); a subsidiary building houses a library and work spaces; a third section contains the main entrance, a ramp down to the undercroft, a lecture theatre and offices. This entrance wing is linked to the main nave by a bridge, constructed and clad in metal, so that the two rectangular courts created between the three wings flow together: through this space runs the main encased Roman aqueduct that served the ancient city. Sectionally, the

undercroft grows higher as it descends the hill northwards, so that at its northernmost edge the building is six or seven storeys high. At the entrance end the building is only four storeys, but, by means of a carefully manipulated section, the appearance is of a relatively modest three-storey structure. The façade of this third section is aligned with the street, thereby further accommodating itself into the surroundings. The south-east corner of the site is still undeveloped, but is designed to contain an auditorium in a future phase.

The straightforward arrangement of the museum makes for clear routes for the visitor. A ramp in the entrance section leads down to the undercroft, which is unenclosed, so that the visitor goes outside, and across a wooden bridge that spans the covered aqueduct, to enter the gradually increasing space beyond. The regular grid of walls is pierced by arches that are themselves usually regularly spaced, though in certain instances the arch is displaced so that its pier can arrive at a more appropriate position in relation to the preserved layout of Roman remains. If these interruptions seem dangerously anarchic, order is retained by the east–west alignment, which is inviolable. A tunnel is located at the half-level of the ramp, which leads below the roadway to the adjacent amphitheatre.

From the entrance, either before or after inspecting the undercroft, the visitor is drawn leftwards across the enclosed metal bridge and into the vast brick nave of the main museum building. Each of the northern transepts contains exhibits, either on the wall, as freestanding objects, or within glass cases. The nave itself can be used for installations of temporary or changing displays. The whole space is naturally lit from above, but windows at the sides are baffled, except at the end bay, where a west-facing window casts light onto the end wall. The final north transept contains the main staircase, and visitors can weave their way back along the first floor gallery to a stair at the far south end, and then return to the second floor, diverting into some or all of the bays along the way. The principal aim of a well-arranged museum is thereby effortlessly achieved, allowing a 'fast' route along the main spaces, or a complete visit by seeing each bay in sequence, or a variety of experiences as choice dictates. The galleries piercing the repetitive walls offer dramatic perspectives both down the nave and diagonally towards the western side. Here there are much shallower transepts or bays, which adjust their dimension according to the street outside.

A Roman-scale brick, made with local clay, is used throughout the building, cladding the concrete structure, as Vitruvius describes in his *Twelve Books*.[13] And the bricks make arches, which is of course the traditional Roman way of spanning openings. But Moneo does not create vaults: the floors that are supported are simple concrete slabs, cast into steel channel sections at their perimeter. This decision is pragmatic and prudent, in economic terms; the project was not well-funded and indeed the initial task was to find sufficient funds for the retaining walls to preserve the archaeological excavations.[14] The scheme that Moneo came up with had to be realisable in discreet phases as funding became available. But this refusal to adopt a whole-hearted Roman form of constructions also has an aesthetic dimension, as will be discussed.

At the undercroft level, the use of a rigorous system of cross walls means that the intersections of the new building with the pattern of pre-existing Roman remains are particularly powerful. This is vividly illustrated in the plan of the undercroft, which is represented on the sliding doors of the entrance. Moneo was involved in some weeks of negotiations with the archae-ologists and museum curators to allow this level of disturbance, since late twentieth-century technology could certainly provide less invasive ways of bringing the loads to rest. But to have resorted to slender steel columns would have been to dilute irreparably the conceptual idea that drove the whole proj-ect, and, provided adequate recording had taken place, the argument was that the large piers did no harm.[15] More importantly, as revealed most clearly in the doorway relief, the formal *parti* is itself particularly Roman. The ruthlessness with which a new order is imposed upon the old is entirely characteristic of imperial practice.

Moneo deliberately avoids any reference in the structure to the orders – that system of 'decoration' (in the sense of 'dignification' of structure) that

---

13 Vitruvius describes *opus incertum* and *opus reticulatum* as two ways in which concrete can be re-tained by bricks either side as permanent formwork. William Curtis is reminded of Vitruvius' *opus reticulatum* by the diagonal patterning of the metal cladding to the bridge link: 'Pieces of City, Memo-ries of Ruins', in Márquez and Levene (eds), *Rafael Moneo 1967–2004: Imperative Anthology*, p. 561.

14 Personal conversation, Nicholas Ray and Fernando Pérez Oyarzun with Rafael Moneo, March 2008.

15 Moneo said that the archaeologists did not need a great deal of persuading that the large columns in-terrupting the ruins would not be too damaging, partly because the remains themselves, in the area of the new building, were not the most important at this extensive site. 'Rafael Moneo: Interview', *Progressive Architecture* 6, June 1986, p. 81.

Rome inherited from Greece. The structural system is more 'modern' since the
absence of vaults stresses the planar quality of the wall plane over the 'carved'
appearance that predominates when walls continue upwards to form vaults.
And of course the very exposure of the bricks relates to a modernist sensibility. Honorific Roman structures would not only employ the orders, but would
also be clad in stone; internally the walls and ceilings would have been plas-
tered and decorated (as indeed several of the exhibits in the museum show).
Some have therefore seen the structure as gothic:

> The complete exhibition space is configured like a modern industrial struc-
> ture or perhaps a gothic factory in which reiteration is the fundamental
> compositional principle.[16]

Although Moneo's inspiration may well be related to his admiration of
Piranesi's *vedute* of Rome, therefore, his pragmatism ensures a building that
is more nineteenth-century neo-gothic than medieval, perhaps like certain
of Viollet-le-Duc's illustrations, though without the heroic and somewhat
clumsy conjunctions of mass masonry and ironwork that his illustrations reveal. The massive external buttresses (fig. 53) reinforce a gothic reading, but
the space is not ecclesiastical – it is more like the medieval 'atarazanes' found
in Barcelona, spaces for ship construction akin to the Arsenale in Venice,
partly because of the even high-level lighting. In 1985, reviewing the building
for the *Architectural Review*, Peter Buchanan found it surprisingly light, and
also empty. He thought it would be a better space if it were crammed with
exhibits, like nineteenth-century museums such as Sir John Soane's house
in Lincoln's Inn Fields, London. But this would be to negate a particularly
twentieth-century character of the building – its intriguing combination of
promenade architecturale and massive static materiality. Buchanan actually
summarised the paradox well: 'Roman in construction yet not at all classical,
archaic in feeling yet thoroughly modern in spirit'.[17] The use of exposed mass

---

16 Solà-Morales, 'Base, Surface', in Márquez and Levene (eds), *Rafael Moneo 1967–2004: Imperative
    Anthology*, p. 187. Solà-Morales also points out how Moneo plays with, but does not slavishly indulge
    in, Piranesian romanticism, and the kind of archaeological correctness that had become *de rigueur*
    since the work of Giovanoni and the Venice Charter.
17 Peter Buchanan, 'Moneo Romana Mérida: Museum, Mérida, Spain', *Architectural Review* 178: 1065,
    November 1985, pp. 38–47. For an extended discussion of Mérida, see *The Charlottesville Tapes: Tran-*

brickwork was not unprecedented of course in 1980 – the most important predecessor in this respect was Louis Kahn. Kahn had always been inspired by the buildings of imperial Rome and, from 1962, he had had an opportunity to employ massive brickwork at a near-imperial scale at the Indian Institute of Management at Ahmedabad, in Gujurat, North India. Famously, Kahn had defended his earlier use of arched brickwork, at the Exeter Library, New Hampshire (1965–71), by explaining that this is how bricks wanted to behave – a beam in brick is an arch.[18] But Kahn's compositional reference point was the teaching of the École des Beaux Arts, inherited in his case through his teacher Paul Cret. Although he was not averse to the expression of a wall of brickwork as a plane (the massive screen walls at his library at Exeter, New Hampshire, are like that), he composed volumetrically, and made use of *poché*, where service zones and staircases are placed in subsidiary volumes that help to define the principal volumes – 'serving' and 'servant' spaces, as he called them. Moneo does not adopt this approach, however, either in the expression of the mass of the wall, or in the way he plans the spaces. As he himself points out, the brick material is emphasized, in a quite un-Roman way, by raking the joints between each course quite deeply, and organizationally the main staircase at the northern end does not sit in a subsidiary space – it occupies the final transept.[19] Furniture and fittings generally are not cased in niches, but are treated as freestanding elements. This makes for an atmosphere that is both more casual (the window cleaning gear, for example, is clearly revealed, as in a factory building), and also more congruent with the *parti* as a whole. One way of reading the project is to see the massive repetitive walls with their arched openings as somehow pre-existing. Lodged into these openings are the 'modern' steel-edged concrete galleries, and sitting over them at roof level is a frankly contemporary flat roof with industrial rooflights. It

scripts of the Conference Held at the University of Virginia School of Architecture, Charlottesville, Virginia, November 12 and 13, 1982, Random House Incorporated, 1985.

18   'You say to a brick: "What do you want, brick?" And brick says to you: "I like an arch". And you say to brick: "Look, I want one too, but arches are expensive and I can use a concrete lintel." And then you say: "What do you think of that, brick?" Brick says: "I like an arch".' Louis I. Kahn during a Graduate Master Class at the University of Pennsylvania, 1971. http://www.youtube.com/watch?feature=player_embedded&v=2CYRSg-cjs4.

19   Moneo, *Remarks on 21 Works*, p. 109.

seems entirely natural that service elements should simply rest against or be attached to the structure in a direct and obvious way. Like the installations that take place in the nave of the building, they inhabit a different timeframe to the masonry structure; as technology moves on they will be replaced. This would be a response to a criticism such as William Curtis makes:

> The tops of the arches come uncomfortably close to the flat concrete soffit in a way that undermines the tectonic strength and presence of the supports. The agendas of the building are extremely rich, but the refinements of language are not always there to support them.[20]

The flat concrete slabs, and their proximity to the arches, in other words, create an entirely intended effect, and Moneo deliberately avoids a reference to a more 'refined language'. The furniture itself, therefore, has at the larger scale a quasi-industrial character, in the handrails to the galleries for example, or the huge metal sliding doors, which close off the bridge entrance to the main gallery. At a smaller scale, Moneo designed more delicate rectangular glass-topped cases for displaying smaller artefacts. They have bronze frames and handrails, and fluted hardwood bases – the flutes being the only concession in the whole building to a language of classical decoration.

The building, so unlike anything that Moneo had built before, clearly illustrates his attitude to the past, which contains a particular mixture of respect and inventiveness. In this context, he rightly determined that the historical remains would have a major affect on his new building, but he also reserved the right to be highly selective in what he chose to reflect and what he decided to ignore. In a lecture given in Chile in 1983, while the museum was under construction, he defended his attitude to the 'memory' of the site. He rejects both a literal repetition of the forms of the past and the notion that a building of the present has to conform to the notion of the *Zeitgeist*. Architects, Moneo believes, have the right to play freely and selectively with memory.[21]

---

20   Curtis, 'Pieces of City, Memories of Ruins', in Márquez and Levene (eds), *Rafael Moneo 1967–2004: Imperative Anthology*, p. 561.

21   Rafael Moneo, 'Arquitectura e Historia', in *CA* 36, 1983, pp. 28–9.

Mallorca, one of the Balearic Islands, lies some 200 kilometres off the coast of Spain, and enjoys a benign Mediterranean climate. Its history, as a Roman colony and under Islamic rule from the tenth century until 1229 when Jaume I took the island, parallels that of Spain. In the twentieth century it was colonized first by writers and artists, and later, from the early 1950s when travel became easier and cheaper, by holidaymakers from all over Europe.

Amongst the artists who settled permanently in Mallorca was Joan Miró. Miró had worked in Barcelona and Paris since the 1920s, associating himself with the Surrealists, but always exhibiting a freer spirit than his contemporaries: he was sceptical of any kind of analysis of painting, and relied on intuition, revealing an apparently child-like delight in characterful abstract forms, whether sinister, cheerful or positively humourous, that still manage to carry associations with human, animal and natural forms. In 1929, he had married Pilar Juncosa, a native Mallorcan, and they holidayed on the island for many years; it had also been their refuge during part of the war, when the Germans occupied Paris. In 1949, Miró commissioned a house from his brother-in-law, Enric Juncosa; built in a traditional style, it occupies the upper portion of a site at Son Abrines, a few kilometres west of Mallorca's capital, Palma, on a south-facing slope with views towards the sea. In 1954, he asked José Lluis Sert (1902–1983) to build him a two-storey studio on the lower section of his land. Sert, who had long been a friend of Miró's, was the foremost Spanish architect of the twentieth century; having worked for Le Corbusier briefly in the 1920s, he ran a practice in Barcelona and, from his office in Paris in 1937, had been responsible for the Spanish Republic's pavilion, which exhibited Picasso's famous *Guernica*, as well as paintings by Miró and sculptures by Alexander Calder. At the outbreak of the war he emigrated to America, where he became the Dean of the Graduate School of Design at Harvard from 1953 until 1969, whilst simultaneously maintaining a busy practice.[22] In this, of course, his career anticipates that of Rafael Moneo. Sert's modest Corbusian building has painted concrete butterfly vaults running north–south, with east- and west-facing rooflights, which have concrete louvres internally. Sert was to reuse these forms in various ways both at the Fondation Maeght at Saint-Paul-de-Vence in Provence (1959–64) and in the later Miró Foundation

---

22 Sert also served as the last CIAM president from 1947 to 1956.

54 (top) Rafael Moneo: Pilar and Joan Miró
Foundation, Mallorca, 1987–92. Plan at entrance
(upper) level

55 (bottom) Rafael Moneo: Pilar and Joan Miró
Foundation, Mallorca, 1987–92. Plan at lower
(gallery) level

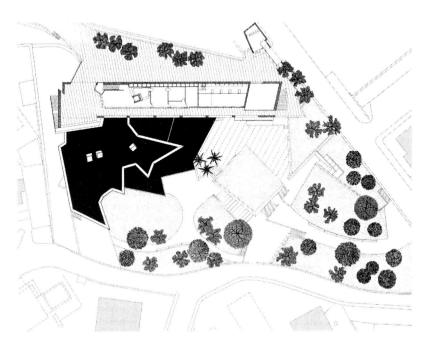

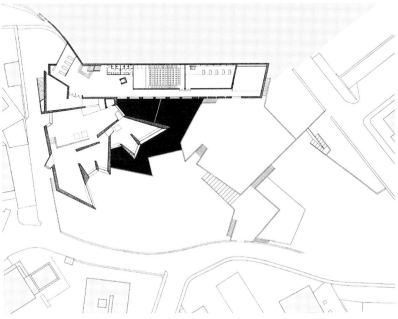

0   5   10m

building in Barcelona (1975). Finally, in 1959, Miró purchased the neighbouring property to the north, San Boter, which had an existing house on it. Thus, in Moneo's own interpretation, Miró 'had both satisfied his family by building their house, and been faithful to his position regarding the avant-garde by erecting his own studio, then paid homage to the past with the purchase of San Boter'.[23]

Joan Miró died in 1983, two years after he and his wife had established a foundation to preserve his legacy, donating the workshops and their paintings and sculptures to the Palma Town Council. In 1985, Rafael Moneo, by then Chair at Harvard, was appointed to design a study centre and gallery for the foundation. It was completed in 1992, three years before the death of Joan Miró's widow, Pilar.

The brief for the study centre envisaged a much larger building than the 1949 house or 1954 studio, and it occupied an area still further down the hill, and closer to the sea. Moneo chose to place most of the accommodation in two contrasting volumes – a long, thin three-storey south-facing block set along the edge of the path leading from the road to the studio, and a jagged-edged freely fashioned single storey building set below it (figs 54, 55). The single-storey building is exclusively a gallery space, while the taller building holds the library, lecture room, bookshop and service areas. But it also contains a double-height exhibition space, and the corridor along the south side of the block can be used for display. Finally, there is a freestanding café and extensive retaining walls in the garden, sharing the same spiky geometry as the gallery. The gallery is partly set in a shallow pool of water, and has a similar pool on its roof, while the café roof has a Japanese gravelled garden; the effect is that only the main study centre building is expressed as an object set on the site – all of the other elements are treated as part of the garden. Yet the expression of the elevations is consistent: painted in-situ board-marked concrete.

The intentions of the design, which Moneo describes as 'a unique, personal interpretation',[24] were to respond both to the particular surroundings – the site that had been so damaged by crass commercial buildings around it (fig. 58) – and to the character of Miró's own work. Thus the long wall of the three-

23   Moneo, *Remarks on 21 Works*, p. 259.
24   Ibid., p. 266.

56 Rafael Moneo: Pilar and Joan Miró
Foundation, Mallorca, 1987–92. Section.
Entrance is at the highest level, opposite the
reflecting pool with its sculptural rooflights

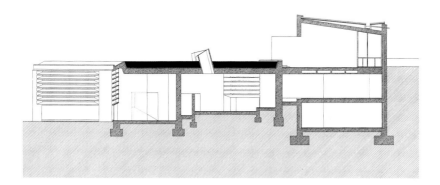

storey block conceals the view southwards entirely until the visitor arrives at
the entrance portico. It is then revealed, but the lower parts, and surrounding
buildings, are masked by the pool of water over the freeform gallery below,
out of which protrude two sculptural rooflights and against which stands a
playful Miró sculpture (fig. 56). Attention is therefore diverted northwards,
towards the relatively unspoilt hillside, with the studio and earlier houses
occupying the foreground. The long wall recalls the naval buildings on the
coast below, and the spiky gallery embedded in the garden is itself resistant,
as it were, to the damaged surroundings, reminding one on plan of fortifica-
tions. But its jagged internal geometry, which contains changes of level as well
as walls at many angles, also provides an appropriate setting for the quirky
and personal art of the painter whose work is on permanent display. Miró-
inspired art work is immovably attached to the building: on a ground floor
wall is a mosaic by María Antònia Carbó, and the cafeteria has a ceramic by
Josep Llorens Artigas, a long-time collaborator with Miró.

Occluding the view of the neighbourhood remains the intention of the
more detailed treatment of the way that light is handled in the gallery space
(fig. 57). Large concrete louvres baffle the direct sunlight, and the high-level
illumination comes through thin sheets of alabaster, or from the few carefully placed rooflights. Only the lowest level of the windows is clear glazed,
in order to direct the eye down to the planting in the immediate foreground.
Artificial lighting is very simply provided by tracks and adjustable spotlights.
As Dean Hawkes summarizes the atmosphere of the building, in responding

57 Rafael Moneo: Pilar and Joan Miró
Foundation, Mallorca, 1987–92. Interior showing
fair-faced concrete soffit and alabaster windows

58 Rafael Moneo, Pilar and Joan Miró
Foundation, Mallorca, 1987–92.
View from the east showing the building
in its compromised context

both to its context and to its requirement to house the work of a particular
and idiosyncratic artist:

> The effect is to render this an intensely internalised building whose exter-
> nal form – 'like a fort' – takes its cues from the topography, both natural and
> manmade, rather than from any abstract and idealised notions about the
> display of works of art. But the nature of Miró's work is such that it pro-
> vokes an original and striking interpretation of both the topography and
> the environment of the art museum.[25] Moneo was to design other galleries,
> notably the Museum of Modern Art in Stockholm (1991–8; fig. 30) and the
> Museum of Fine Arts in Houston (1992–2000; fig. 38), and these indicate a
> similar concern for the quality of light – very different to the more system-
> atic attitude of architects like Herzog de Meuron or Renzo Piano – and also
> respond to their particular context. In Stockholm the building is expressed
> as a number of separate volumes, while in Houston Moneo investigated

25   Dean Hawkes, *The Environmental Imagination – Technics and Poetics of the Architectural Environ-
     ment*, London: Taylor & Francis, 2008, p. 161.

the 'compacted form' of an architect like Scamozzi and produced a building that completely occupied the block. But the overall architectural pattern of such large buildings, with collections that are varied and require the capacity to host visiting exhibitions, nevertheless must maintain a level of generality. With the Pilar and Joan Miró Foundation, the opportunity arose to develop a project that was highly particular, and it was grasped very convincingly.

59 Rafael Moneo: Kursaal Auditorium, San Sebastián, Spain, 1990–99. Aerial view showing the building outside the grid of the city

Rafael Moneo won the limited competition for the Kursaal in 1990. The
entry had been designed in the small office he had established in Cambridge,
Massachusetts, following his appointment as Chairman of the Department
of Architecture at the Graduate School of Design at Harvard, and its design
is indicative of the broadened range of influences to which he had been subjected during his time in America. Back in Madrid, his office was busy with
the San Pablo airport in Seville, L'Illa Diagonal Building in Barcelona, the
Pilar and Joan Miró Foundation in Palma de Mallorca, the Auditorium and
Concert Hall in Barcelona and the Thyssen-Bornemisza Museum in Madrid.
In America he was working on the Davis Museum in Wellesley College, near
Boston (1990–93).

It is instructive to compare the Kursaal design with the Urumea building,
only a few blocks from the site in San Sebastián, constructed some twenty
years earlier in Moneo's career (figs 16–18). That building had interrogated the
typological precedents for apartments, and sought to contribute to the urban
fabric by being discretely inserted into its pattern. In the case of the Kursaal,
it was the larger geographical context that provided the key to the project
(fig. 59).

San Sebastián ('Donostia' in Basque) is now the principal seaside resort of
the Basque country, but its origin was related to commerce and defence: it
was founded in around 1180 by King Sancho el Mayor of Navarra on a remarkable curved bay ('La Concha') dominated by Monte Urgull. The walled city was
subjected to numerous sieges during its lifetime and in August 1813 it was
reduced to ashes when an Anglo-Portuguese army attacked the occupying
French. A major rebuilding effort took place, and further expansion occurred
in the 1860s when the city walls were demolished. By the end of the nineteenth century, the royal family had chosen the Miramar Palace as their summer residence, and casinos had been built to cater for tourists, one of which is
now the city hall. Within this general context, the Kursaal Convention Centre
and Concert Hall is sited in a privileged urban and geographical position – a
triangular artificial piece of land located just at the mouth of Urumea River.
On the opposite side of the river, towards the west, stands the old city beside
the Urgull hill. Beyond, the nineteenth-century 'ensanche', or city expansion,
surrounds the wonderful La Concha bay, culminating in the Ulía mountain.
The 1915 Zurriola, or Kursaal bridge, adorned with the characteristic street

60 Arata Isozaki: entry to the Kursaal
competition, 1990

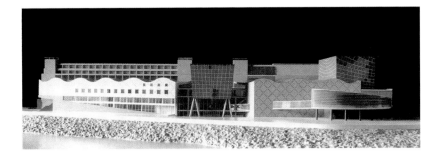

lighting of the period, continues Zurriola Avenue towards La Concha bay. This avenue provides one urban flank of the triangular plot, while the others face the Urumea River and Gros (or Zurriola) beach. The site was always, and remains today, a kind of boundary between very different conditions.

The name of Kursaal, meaning 'cure hall', came from the German name for a typical building found in nineteenth-century resorts, containing a casino, a theatre, and, in the twentieth century, cinemas and other facilities. The original building occupied the site from 1921 to 1973, an imposing eclectic neoclassical structure that became one of the city landmarks and, together with the Zurriola bridge, helped to characterize this elegant resort. But gambling was banned in 1925 and by the late 1960s the building was in a sorry state; according to some, its marble was stripped in the 1970s by Franco to decorate his mansion. Various ideas for the re-use of the site were floated, and there was even a project proposed for it by José Antonio Coderch, but it was not until 1989 that a limited competition was held. The other architects invited, together with Rafael Moneo, were the Japanese Arata Isozaki, the Italian Mario Botta, the Englishman Norman Foster, the Spaniard Juan Navarro Baldeweg and the Basque Luis Peña Ganchegui – who had built the setting for the extraordinary 'wind comb' sculptures, *Peine de los Vientos,* by Eduardo Chillida, at the western end of La Concha beach.[26] Isozaki's project reflected current postmodernist preoccupations (fig. 60), while Foster's office produced an overall structure not unlike Moneo's Amsterdam competition entry (fig. 15).

---

26   The competition was published in *Arquitectura* 283–4, March–April 1990, pp. 24–49.

61 Rafael Moneo: Kursaal Auditorium, San Sebastián, Spain, 1990–99. Plan of the two auditoria. The foyers, the conference centre and a gallery are suppressed within the plinth

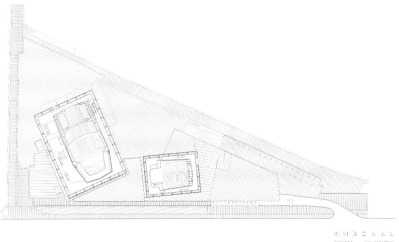

Moneo's concept was announced by the motto for his anonymous entry: 'two rocks beached on the seaside': the tensions and architectural potential of the larger landscape context, rather than the immediate urban setting, were to determine the project. But, as Moneo himself has pointed out,

> The notion of context has been overused in architectural criticism, and architects have eroded this concept by applying a methodology that uses the analysis of the building's location as its basis. Advocates of this method consider architecture to be merely a result of this analysis . . .[27]

Moneo, as will become clear later in the book, wishes to distance himself from this position. An architect's intuition about the site is the starting point, and after that comes a period of intense development that is possible only with 'a profound knowledge of the discipline of architecture'.[28] Equally important for the development of this particular *parti* was the precedent of Utzon's famous Opera House in Sydney, on which, of course, Moneo had worked. There, the two auditoria are expressed under sail-like vaults sitting on the

---

27 Moneo, *Remarks on 21 Works*, p. 387.
28 Ibid., p. 389.

62 Rafael Moneo: Kursaal Auditorium, San
Sebastián, Spain, 1990–99. View down the
frontage facing the sea

solid base that includes all the serving elements. The audience approaches
the auditoria from the stage end, the foyers rising upwards with their rake.
The arrangement at the Kursaal is similar: the two crystalline structures
(auditoria with their attendant foyer spaces) rest on a solid slate-clad base
containing exhibition halls, offices, restaurants and other facilities, and
as at Sydney the foyers rise with the auditorium rake. The podium base
responds to the geometry of Zurriola Avenue, the river promenade and
connection to the beach. Above, the two volumes – the major being 72 by
51 metres and 30 metres high, the smaller one being 42 by 36 metres and
24 metres high – contain the auditoria, and allude in their material and
geometry to the wider landscape [figs 61, 62]. Their apparently casual position-
ing is in fact a careful reconciliation of the requirement to state their own
identity within the local triangular site and to maintain a reference to the
mountains and bay beyond.

The shops in the podium engage with Zurriola Avenue, and the narrowest
point of the triangle, towards the north-east, contains ramps down to basement car parking. On the western façade, cafés and restaurants face the river

63 Rafael Moneo: Kursaal Auditorium,
San Sebastián, Spain, 1990–99.
Interior of the large auditorium

promenade, while the north face is closed and drops down in a series of terraces towards the beach. The podium walls are formed in prefabricated concrete on which a random pattern of slate has been cast.

The two crystalline rock-like forms not only contain an auditorium apiece
but use the space between the auditorium and glazed skin as the foyer in each
case – wooden boxes in glass cubes. Views out are carefully limited, because
the exterior glass skin is mostly opaque. It was the first time that Moneo had
experimented with a fully glazed skin, but it is most unlike the conventional
curtain wall in emphasizing the texture and solidity of the material rather
than its transparency. The external surface is formed of concave horizontal
ribs of opal glass, while the internal surface is translucent, but not transpar-
ent, the effect being that the structure between is perceptible but not domi-
nating.[29] The result externally is that the appearance of the building changes
dramatically in response to prevailing climatic conditions – it sparkles in

29   Only where brackets break through the skin in one or two places, not entirely satisfactorily, is the
structure expressed.

64 Rafael Moneo: Kursaal Auditorium,
San Sebastián, Spain, 1990–99. Foyer
space at the interstice of the opal glazed
skin and the timber-lined concert hall

sunshine, but looks cold and grey in dull weather, and when lit up at night it takes on the appearance of giant lanterns; this effect can be seen most dramatically during the evening when the natural light is fading and the internal lights come on before a performance.

The pattern of the auditoria follows that which Moneo had already adopted in his concert halls for Barcelona, inspired by the acoustic of the Boston Symphony Hall, whose proportions he had come to appreciate (fig. 63). The warmth of the wooden auditoria makes an emphatic contrast with the coldness of the glass in the foyer spaces; here the natural analogy is with the well-fashioned membranes of stringed instruments. After the rocky random-slate clad base and crystalline glass enclosures, wood is the third material in Moneo's carefully restricted palette. Much of the power of the building derives from Moneo's refusal to soften or compromise the formal and material distinction between the parts, but of course this ruthlessness also lends a certain austerity to the foyers, which rely on the activity and colour of the audience to animate the space (fig. 64).

The Kursaal was initially received with some scepticism, and in some instances outright hostility,[30] by the population of San Sebastián – not as familiar as a reproduction of the old Kursaal would have been, nor as obviously dramatic and 'iconic' as Gehry's Bilbao Guggenheim, completed at about the same time – but over the years, unlike the Murcia town hall extension (to be considered in the next section), it has generally become accepted and valued by the citizens of San Sebastián as a distinguished addition to their urban fabric and extraordinary landscape.

30 In the mid-1990s, articles in Basque newspapers revealed open hostility towards Moneo's proposal: 'El Kursaal de Rafael Moneo, Monstruoso. La Plataforma contra el proyecto del arquitecto Navarro se constituyó ayer' ('The Kursaal by Rafael Moneo, Monstrous. The platform against the Navarra architect's Project was constituted yesterday'), in *El Diario Vasco*, 29 January 1995; 'Plataforma ciudadana contra los cubos de Moneo' ('Civic platform against Moneo's cubes'), in *Egin*, 27 January 1995; 'Polémica por el Kursaal. El otro debate. El impacto estético de los cubos se suma a la controversia' ('Polemics about the Kursaal. The other debate. The aesthetic impact of the cubes is added to the controversy'), in *El Diario Vasco*, 7 March 1995; 'Jaque al Kursaal' ('Checkmate to the Kursaal'), *El Correo Español*, 24 March 1995; Alvaro Bermejo: 'Yo no creo en eso' ('I don't believe in that'), *El Diario Vasco*, 27 November 1995.

65 Rafael Moneo: Murcia town hall
extension, 1991–9. View of front faces
showing lowered area

Rafael Moneo was invited to take on this project in 1991 after a competition-winning project by Alberto Noguerol had proved too controversial for the town council. The task was to occupy the site on the west side of the city's main square, which had been left after a baroque town house had been demolished, opposite the cathedral and adjacent to the Cardinal's palace. The problem was therefore quintessentially one of a particular urban context to which the building was required to respond. What makes this relatively small project one of the most important in Moneo's career, however, is the way in which his solution provided a model in subsequent decades for many other architects in its resolution of what might be seen as one of the most pressing problems of twenty-first century urban representation.

Though the plan of this seven-storey building (if we include its basement floor) is subtle and worthy of detailed analysis, it is the public face towards the square that generates the architectural form of the building (fig. 66). The building's façade needed to participate in the public square, but more as a 'spectator, without seeking the status of protagonist held by the cathedral and Cardinal Belluga Palace'.[31] Moneo chose to hold the façade back from the line occupied by the earlier building, and thereby achieved two aims: he revealed the curving prow of the council building, to which his structure was to be an extension, and was able to rotate his frontage so as to address the retable of the cathedral opposite. His own façade then became a secular retable in dialogue with the sacred retable of the cathedral, and the precise proportioning of the openings in this screen became the focus of considerable study, described below. Unlike the cathedral façade, the town hall extension does not contain openings for access; the main entrance is off the end of Frenería Street, opposite Polo Medina Street, just where they join the square. Moneo's retable therefore becomes an abstract play of solid and void, containing in its interstices external terraces that allow the inhabitants to participate in the theatre of the town square. A further level of abstraction – or distancing from the active drama of the square, reinforcing the reading of the building

---

31 'Murcia Town Hall', in Márquez and Levene (eds), *Rafael Moneo 1967–2004: Imperative Anthology*, pp. 338–44.

66 (previous spread) Rafael Moneo: Murcia
town hall extension, 1991–9. View from
square, with the Episcopal Palace on the left

67 Rafael Moneo: Murcia town hall
extension, 1991–9. Perspective from above
showing the relationship to the cathedral
and the Episcopal Palace

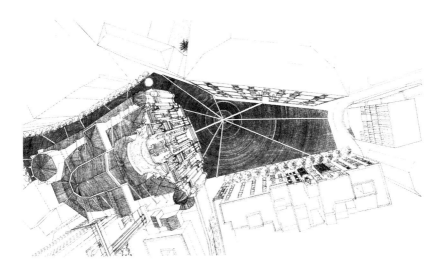

as a spectator rather than active participant – is provided by the curved wall
at the front of the building. This shields a lower level terrace, onto which the
basement cafeteria opens. The low stone wall to the square ensures that the
façade rises out of the ground as an abstract plane, rather than establishing
its own plinth (fig. 65).

The detailed design of the façade has been analysed in detail by Stephen
Smith.[32] Moneo made numerous card models of slightly differently propor-
tioned configurations before settling on a final version. This way of pro-
ceeding – designing by making – may be indebted to Moneo's experience of
students' behaviour in American schools of architecture, as it represents a
different approach to his earlier practice of envisaging everything in small
sketches.

What precedents could Moneo call upon in the design of this façade? An
abstracted classicism had been used by Italian architects of the Mussolini era
– in EUR outside Rome, for instance. Giuseppi Terragni, in his Casa del Fascio
at Como, had played brilliantly with the frame and the wall plane to create
a façade of well-studied proportions. Moneo would have been well aware of

32   Stephen Smith, 'Rafael Moneo', third year dissertation, 2002, retained in the library of the University
     of Cambridge, Department of Architecture.

68 Rafael Moneo: Murcia town hall extension,
1991–9. View from upper floor colonnade back
towards the cathedral façade

68 Rafael Moneo: Murcia town hall extension, 1991–9. View from upper floor colonnade back towards the cathedral façade

Terragni's work through its analysis by Peter Eisenman, by now a friend and colleague. But in Terragni's designs, as well as those of his neoclassical Italian contemporaries, there is a constructional logic behind the creation of frame and panel. In the case of Murcia, this is deliberately negated by avoiding the expression either of a regular frame within the façade, or of placing solids above solids, and void over void, as would be natural in a load-bearing wall. Rather, the placement of openings eschews symmetries and 'is organised as a musical score'.[33] Another precedent may be the *brise-soleil* invented by Le Corbusier. The façade to the plaza faces east, and the disengaged colonnade certainly assists in keeping morning sun off the walls and windows. Especially in his later Indian buildings, such as the Villa Shodhan and the Millowners' Association Building in Ahmedabad (fig. 69), or the capital buildings at Chandigarh, Le Corbusier uses screens as large-scale compositional

33 'Murcia Town Hall', in Márquez and Levene (eds), *Rafael Moneo 1967–2004: Imperative Anthology*, p. 342.

69 Le Corbusier:
Millowners' Association
Building, Ahmedabad,
1951–4

devices, designed to be seen across long distances, and which do indeed come
to have a representative function. But there is no sense that these screens are
also walls. Especially in the use of local (lumaquela) sandstone, the Murcia
façade is more reminiscent of load-bearing walls, such as are seen in vernacular buildings, but without such large openings. In more recent architecture,
one is reminded of buildings such as the two houses that Jørn Utzon constructed for himself on the island of Mallorca. Moneo, as noted, holidays in
Mallorca, and remained friends with Utzon, with whom he worked in 1961–2;
but of course these are small-scale, domestic buildings. Another institutional,
and Spanish precedent was Alejandro de la Sota's Gobierno Civil in Tarragona,
constructed between 1959 and 1963 (fig. 2). This is a frame building, with the
columns held back from the wall face, where voids and large panels of stone
alternate in a sculpturally seductive manner. The freedom that De la Sota ex-
ploited has certainly been influential, but, as a decorated frame, the façade is
not in itself unusual, except for the boldness and confidence with which it is
handled. What Moneo achieved at Murcia was, in fact, a surprisingly new and
almost unprecedented invention, though it seems inevitable and familiar – an
abstraction of the very idea of façade. And this is what has made his invention so compelling to others, to the extent that it is difficult to find a city now
that does not possess a building displaying versions of the screen wall with
'musically' arranged openings. The procedure has become known as 'barcode'
architecture – the random spacing ensuring that some interest is maintained,
compared to the graph-paper façades of previous decades. But it is significant

that, since the circumstances have not warranted it, Moneo himself has not seen it as appropriate to reproduce such a solution himself in other projects.

The sophistication of the façade manipulation might lead one to expect a convoluted and awkward plan to accommodate it. In fact, the reverse is the case. On each floor, the honorific rooms occupy the eastern part of the plan, rotated towards the cathedral, while office spaces occupy the rear, which is orthogonal to the surrounding streets: open plan towards the north, and sub-divided towards the south.[34] The irregular central space serves as the landing and circulation area. On the ground floor, Moneo has arranged a vista right through the building from north to south, located at the half-landing of the staircase, immediately opposite the main entrance. A reception desk is to the left and a pair of lifts immediately to the right. The ground-floor entry area acts as foyer to the raked assembly room, which descends into the basement. A few steps up from what Moneo described as the mezzanine landing, at the turn of the stairs, was a connection by bridge across San Patricio to the main council offices. (This was removed in 2006, in favour of an underground connection.) The first floor proper, above the mezzanine, contains the principal reception room on the eastern side, and this is two storeys high, with a large window back into the square. Appropriately, this is the only element to be allowed to break through the horizontal lines of the east façade and reveal itself to the plaza.

An inspection of the drawings, but more importantly the experience of visiting this compact and powerful building, confirms the widely held view that it is one of Moneo's most successful, as well as (for better or worse) his most influential work, at least amongst architects. The town hall at Murcia remains a controversial building for the inhabitants of the city, however, appearing shockingly bare in comparison with its highly decorated neighbours, and the architects who had been superseded, Alberto Noguerol and Pilar Díez, along with others of their generation, unsurprisingly remained among its most vocal critics.

---

34 William Curtis claims that the depth of the block leads to problems of ventilation and natural light in these offices. William Curtis, 'The Structure of Intentions', in Márquez and Levene (eds), *Rafael Moneo 1967–2004: Imperative Anthology*, p. 573. It seems that assisted ventilation and artificial light are inevitable in any solution that uses the whole block depth; the block is not deep enough to justify an atrium solution.

Rafael Moneo was appointed in the summer of 1996 as architect for the largest Catholic church in Los Angeles, following an international competition; the four other short-listed candidates were the Spaniard Santiago Calatrava, and the American architects Thom Mayne, Robert Venturi and Frank Gehry. One of the methods used to choose the eventual architect was to ask each to propose a memorial sanctuary for Father Junípero Serra (1713–1784), the Franciscan friar who had founded the first catholic mission of an eventual 21, in San Diego in 1769. Moneo proposed an image 'in which he could be perceived either as a saint or a historical figure', by placing a sculpture that was framed in such a way that when seen from inside would become an object of devotion, but from the exterior represented an historical figure.[35] This duality is reflected in the design of the complex as a whole, which is a composition capable of interpretation in a sacred or secular manner. Moneo drew equally on his deep understanding of Catholicism, from the days of his Jesuit education onwards, and on his study of buildings and precincts within a city – in this case the particularly challenging context of the city of Los Angeles.

Although the architectural competition, held in June 1996, had been based on a site next to the damaged Cathedral of Saint Vibiana,[36] by September a new central downtown site had been chosen, adjacent to the Hollywood 101 Freeway. The design task was to make the most of the prominent site, one of the highest areas of the city, and yet to create spaces that could permit the varieties of religious experience that different people might expect. Moneo presented a model to his client, Cardinal Roger Mahony, in Rome in November 1996, to describe the massing of the proposal and much of its sculptural detail, and this remained essentially unchanged in execution (fig. 71). The cathedral itself occupies the highest ground, to the north-west corner of the site, with a lower parish centre and residence for the Cardinal to the south-east, over an underground car park (fig. 72). The plaza formed between is bordered by a continuous cloister on the north-eastern edge, adjacent to and above the freeway, and a bell tower marks the corner. Between the cathedral and the

---

35   Moneo, *Remarks on 21 Works*, p. 509.

36   The Cathedral of St Vibiana had been constructed in 1876, but to a poor standard, and there were plans for its replacement from the beginning of the twentieth century. In 1945, the Holy See approved the name of a new cathedral as the Cathedral of our Lady of the Angels, but the planned construction never took place. The 1994 Northridge earthquake instigated the new project.

71 (top) Rafael Moneo: Cathedral of
Our Lady of Angels, Los Angeles,
1996–2002. Model

72 (bottom) Rafael Moneo: Cathedral
of Our Lady of Angels, Los Angeles,
1996–2002. Plan

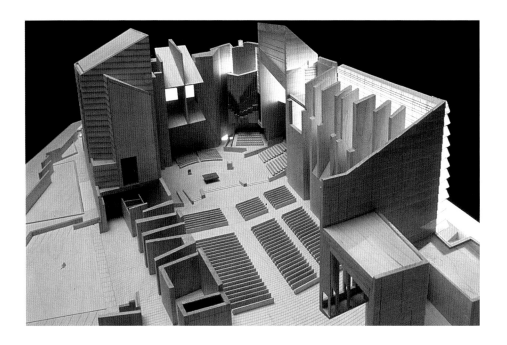

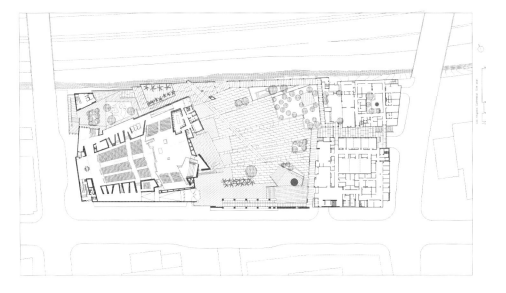

73 (following page) Rafael Moneo: Cathedral
of Our Lady of Angels, Los Angeles, 1996–2002.
View up ascending aisle ramps

74 (page 167) Rafael Moneo: Cathedral of Our
Lady of Angels, Los Angeles, 1996–2002. Interior

extended edge of the precinct is an enclosed garden, onto which its northern aisle, or ambulatory, looks.

Despite the consistent external material, a sand-coloured concrete, the sculptural effect of the complex of buildings is varied depending on the context from which it is seen. From the freeway, the bell tower and monumental mass of the body of the cathedral make a prominent landmark, and it is equally impressive from the north-west, at the corner of Grand and Temple Streets. But the building is set well back from Hill Street, to the south-east, where the scale of the subsidiary buildings is consistent with adjacent blocks. The approach is via the central plaza, rising with the hill, and the cathedral can be entered along the Temple Street edge, or adjacent to the garden. Because the cathedral proper is pushed towards the north-west, highest, corner of the site, and because Moneo has scrupulously respected the tradition of orienting the altar towards the east, entrance in both cases is, unusually, from the altar end. Moneo has capitalized on this unexpected reversal by orienting a number of wedge-shaped chapels along each flank towards the ambulatories, which continue the rising ascent by means of ramps (fig. 73), rather than towards the nave. Thus, the traditional typology of the Jesuit church, based on Il Gesù in Rome, which consists of a central nave with adjacent chapels on both sides, is reversed, so the chapels do not 'contaminate' the sacrality of the central space (fig. 75). At the same time, the complex volume of the cathedral can be seen to have transepts that occupy the depth of the side chapels and are bypassed in the ceremonial approach. The chapels take light from continuous thin alabaster panels that serve to bathe the whole interior, and the profiles of the chapel walls with dramatic slots between them also modulate the light as it penetrates the nave. Moneo consciously aimed to make an architecture that would be amenable to interpretation as traditional cathedrals of different kinds are: as an expression of liturgy, as a dramatic and powerful construction, and as symbolic, through the manipulation of light and atmosphere, of religious experience. A benefit of the relative disengagement of the chapels from the central space has been that they can be appropriated by different Catholic groups, and this has in fact been the case – sometimes with distressingly kitsch results.

With one exception, more literal symbolization is left to the various artworks and sculptural installations in the cathedral, which were provided by

75 Rafael Moneo: Cathedral of Our Lady
of Angels, Los Angeles, 1996–2002. Section
showing independently lit side chapels either
side of the nave and oriented away from it

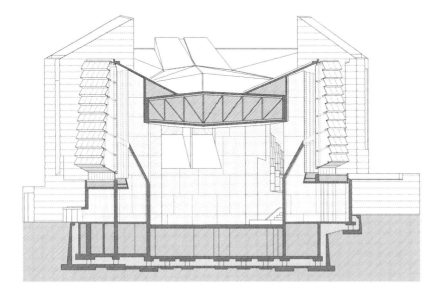

a number of local artists (Moneo's advice on hiring more challenging artists
was not followed).[37] The exception is the huge concrete cross at the east end,
visible, as Moneo's idea for Father Junípero Serra's memorial had suggested,
both from inside where it dominates the liturgical crossing and from outside,
where it acts as a prominent symbol from the plaza, and indeed from the freeway (fig. 70).

By the 1990s, Moneo's practice was international, and realizing complex
buildings in different parts of the world meant collaboration with executive architects as well as numerous specialists. In the case of the cathedral,
a local practice, Leo A. Daly, was appointed, and with their help an enormous
amount of research was undertaken in order to ensure that the client's brief
could be met.[38] Cardinal Mahony asked for a building that would last for five
hundred years – in the context of California, where a philosophy of transience

37 *Rafael Moneo: De la Fundació a la Catedral de L.A. 1990–2002*. Mallorca: Fundació Pilar i Joan Miró a
    Mallorca, 2002.
38 The research undertaken by Leo Daly was described by an associate on the job. Nicholas W. Roberts,
    'Design as Materials Research: Building a Cathedral to Last 500 Years', in *arq* 7: 3, 4, pp. 333–51.

predominates, an unusually demanding request – and that would resist the seismic events from which the region is known to suffer. Moneo chose to create a monolithic building rather than a frame to be clad in facing materials, and much of the quality of the finished work comes from the fact that, as in monumental buildings of the past, the material seen and touched, inside and outside, is the structure of the building itself. Some of the concrete walls are one-and-a-half metres thick, and the first mock-ups indicated that the heat of hydration generated could not escape, which would lead to loss of strength. A low-hydration white cement was therefore imported from Åalborg, Denmark, the walls were cast in the cool of early morning, and water was chilled before mixing, to ensure a quality of concrete that many visitors mistake for stone. To provide earthquake resistance, the whole building structure is isolated from the foundations beneath the crypt on 149 high-damping rubber isolators and 47 slider bearings. Research into the alabaster windows was equally thorough: to maintain its translucency the alabaster needed to be kept cool, and a double-skin arrangement was devised, with a fritted laminated glass outer skin held in a saw-tooth frame protecting the inner alabaster skin. Stack effect in the void between, varying from a metre to two metres in thickness, helps maintain an even temperature. It is noticeable that this curtain wall design combines several solutions Moneo had already used: alabaster at the Miró Foundation, saw-tooth glazing on parts of the Atocha rail sheds, and the principle of double skin explored at the Kursaal, San Sebastián.

The cathedral therefore incorporates something of Rafael Moneo's personal experience, from his Jesuit schooling to the repertoire of forms that he had developed for his architecture over a period of years and for a variety of purposes. It also reflects a deep understanding of the history of ecclesiastical architecture. Whilst referring to no particular stylistic precedents, its understanding of precedent at a conceptual and material level sets it apart from most contemporary building. The purpose of the essays that follow is to demonstrate that this is no accident, but part of Moneo's consistent theory of how architecture should be thought about and composed.

3. THINKING

When, in 1996, Rafael Moneo was awarded the Pritzker Prize for Architecture, the influential Spanish magazine *Arquitectura Viva* published a substantial appraisal of his career entitled 'Professor Moneo'.[1] It seemed to come as no surprise that the central focus of this celebratory article was not on his buildings and projects, but on the way in which his thinking and teaching had shaped an architectural culture and influenced several generations of Spanish and American architects. Teaching, in fact, was for Moneo much more than simply an extension of, or complement to, his professional career. He conceived it as both a social obligation and an intellectual challenge: teaching, writing and practice form a seamless body of work founded on the principle that architecture is a specific way of approaching reality – a coherent discipline, therefore, which can, and should, be thought about, practised and taught.

In Moneo's early years, he was preoccupied with the question of how to approach the teaching of architecture, and his reflections from that period are fundamental to understanding the basis of his architectural philosophy. As described earlier, he had already had some experience of practice with Francisco Javier Sáenz de Oíza and Jørn Utzon, and needed a stable academic position in order to consider one of the most elusive questions in architecture – how to teach design and on what principles to base that teaching. His thinking can be traced back to the important time at the Royal Spanish Academy in Rome (1963–5), and found fulfilment in his programme for the Elements of Composition Professorship at the Escuela Técnica Superior de Arquitectura de Barcelona (ETSAB) in 1970–72. From the 1970s, Moneo appears to have devoted his energies principally to a series of important buildings such as the Madrid Bankinter (see p. 111) and Logroño town hall (see p. 119). But he did not abandon either his teaching or his theoretical engagement with design methodologies, as is evident in the publication during the period of his ETSAB professorship of some of his most important texts, including *Aldo Rossi: The Idea of Architecture and the Modena Cemetery* (1974), and 'On Typology' (1978).[2] Just as it is clear, in any detailed analysis, that buildings such as Bankinter and Logroño closely reflect Moneo's current theoretical concerns, it is also

---

1   Luis Fernández-Galiano, 'Professor Moneo', Ar*quitectura Viva* 63–4, 1997, pp. 194–9.
2   Rafael Moneo, 'Aldo Rossi: The Idea of Architecture and the Modena Cemetery', *Oppositions* 5, 1976, pp. 1–30; 'On Typology', *Oppositions* 13, 1978, pp. 23–44.

possible to see how his teaching, during the period of his Professorship of Architectural Composition at Madrid (1980–85), and later his Chairmanship of the Department of Architecture at the Harvard Graduate School of Design (1985–90), is informed by his own practice. One therefore needs to understand this reciprocal relationship between his teaching and practice to see his contribution completely – a relationship that remained remarkably consistent from the earliest years in the 1960s to his continuing practice, teaching and publications in the twenty-first century.

But to understand fully the context for Moneo's philosophical position, which he developed and refined throughout his career, it is necessary to look beyond the horizon of architectural culture and at his personal encounter with wider ideas. In doing so, we will find that at the back of his thinking lies a profound admiration for the figure of the modern Spanish intellectual, arising out of his formative years in the post-civil war era – an idealized image of a culture that seemed to have been irretrievably lost.[3] The 1940s were particularly difficult years for Spanish culture as many of the most important intellectuals had left the country because of the 1936–9 Spanish Civil War. Once Francisco Franco assumed power, he rigorously pursued surviving leftists and individuals who sympathized or had any relationship with the former Republican government, and ensured they were deported; as a consequence, many intellectuals had to take refuge in France, Latin America or the United States.[4] For Moneo in particular, the figure of the modern Spanish intellectual

3   A comprehensive history of the Spanish intellectual exile can be found in Julio Martín Casas and Pedro Carvajal Urquijo, *El exilio Español, 1936–1978*, Barcelona: Planeta, 2002. On the architects' exile, see VV.AA., *Arquitecturas Desplazadas*, Madrid: Ministerio de Asuntos Exteriores, 2007.

4   Among them were prominent biologists (Severo Ochoa, Enrique Rioja), physicists (Arturo Duperier, Blas Cabrera), chemists (Enrique Moles, Antonio Madinaveitia), mathematicians (Enrique González Jiménez, Ricardo Vinós, Lorenzo Alcaraz), astronomers (Pedro Carrasco Garrorena), oceanographers (Odón de Buen), writers and poets (Manuel Andújar, Rafael Alberti, Manuel Altolaguirre, Max Aub, Arturo Barea, Luis Cernuda, Rafael Dieste, Ramón Gómez de la Serna, Jorge Guillén, Ramon Perez de Ayala, Emilio Prados, Pedro Salinas, Ramón J. Sender), film directors (Luis Buñuel), artists (Aurelio Arteta, Antonio Clavé, Óscar Domínguez, Ramón Gaya, Eugenio Granell, Antonio Rodríguez Luna, Maruja Mallo, Leopoldo Novoa, Manuel Ángeles Ortiz, Gregorio Prieto, Josep Renau, Luis Soane, Alberto Sánchez, José Moreno Villa, Remedios Varo), historians (Américo Castro, Claudio Sánchez Albornoz), philologists (Tomás Navarro), and philosophers (Juan David García Bacca, José Gaos, José Ortega y Gasset, María Zambrano). Those in exile included some of the most important Spanish modern architects of the time, such as José Luis Sert, Félix Candela, Antonio Bonet Castellana, Rafael

was epitomized by personalities such as Miguel de Unamuno (1864–1936), but above all, by José Ortega y Gasset (1883–1955) and some of his followers.[5] These men represented prototypical liberal, independent and critical thinkers, with a broad historical knowledge; they were persuasive advocates of the cultural role of universities, and were deeply involved in the social development of Spain. Moneo, as did many of his young contemporaries, revered and read with passion most of the writings of Ortega y Gasset, the suave and cultivated philosopher and essayist who best represented what a Spanish intellectual should be during this period. It was also around the figure of Ortega that student revolutions broke out in Madrid in the mid-1950s.

Ortega was not only a common reference for the young intellectuals but his powerful defence of the humanities and social sciences was crucial for Moneo, since he was to adopt a humanist position during the 1950s and 1960s in opposition to the predominantly technics-driven professionalization of the discipline.[6] According to Ortega, the natural sciences succeeded in their attempt to make objective descriptions of physical phenomena, and the results have been accepted as the truth by contemporary society. But those sciences were incapable of fully describing the qualities of human experience.[7] As he explained:

> Man does not have a nature, but a history. Man is not a thing, but a drama. His life is something that has to be chosen, made up as he lives it, and making those choices constitutes what it is to be human. Each human being is his own novelist, and though he may choose whether to be an original writer or a plagiarist, he cannot avoid that choice. He is condemned to be free.[8]

Bergamín, Manuel Sánchez Arcas, Germán Rodríguez Arias, Luis Lacasa, Roberto Fernández Balbuena and Martín Domínguez.

5   Amongst these, according Moneo's himself, should be included Xavier Zubiri, Julián Marias and Pedro Laín Entralgo, though they held very different personal positions.

6   Moneo's sympathy for such an intellectual model has been revealed in a number of informal conversations in recent years. The importance of Ortega y Gasset to Moneo's intellectual formation was explored by Valeria Koukoutsi-Mazarakis in 'José Rafael Moneo Vallés, 1965–1985', PhD dissertation, MIT, 2001.

7   José Ortega y Gasset, *El tema de nuestro tiempo*, Madrid: Revista de Occidente, 1981, p. 231 (first published in 1923).

8   José Ortega y Gasset, *History as System*, trans. Helene Weyl, E. Clark and W. Atkinson, San Diego: Academic Press, 1962, p. 19.

'History', in Otega's perception, represents the accumulation of human experience over time, and is the fundamental resource for the recovery of the human sciences. Knowledge therefore acquires an epic character that depends both on the archive of cultural expression, and on the experience of individuals in the way that they construct the narratives of their day-to-day lives. For Moneo, likewise, architectural wisdom cannot be defined merely as a technical skill, but represents both the body of knowledge acquired through the experience of architects in the past, and the experience today of each architect as an individual.

Ortega's position requires a direct confrontation with the realities of a situation – the actual conditions that a person faces in determining his or her own freedom, summarized in this well-known quotation from *Meditation on Quixote*: 'I am myself plus my circumstance, and if I do not save it, I cannot save myself . . . The re-absorption of circumstance is the concrete destiny of man.'[9] The development of Moneo's own position can be described by reference to this particular quotation. It may explain the attraction, as a student at the school of architecture in Madrid, of the eclectic and self-reflective personalities of Luis Moya and more specially Leopoldo Torres-Balbás.[10] His subsequent career can be seen as a manifestation of that requirement to absorb and reflect upon the actuality of the circumstances that engender design: the

9   José Ortega y Gasset: *Meditations on Quixote*, trans. Evelyn Rugg and Diego Marín, introduction by Julián Marías. Chicago and Urbana: The University of Illinois Press, 2000 p. 45 (originally published in Spanish in 1914).

10 In one of his early articles, Moneo praises Torres-Balbás as a professor of an exceptional personality. Rafael Moneo, 'Sobre un intento de reforma didáctica (En la facultad de Arquitectura en Roma)', *Arquitectura* 61, January 1964, p. 45. Antón Capitel, a former student of Moneo in the mid-1960s, also noted that Moneo seemed to be more influenced by the elegant and eclectic personality of Leopoldo Torres-Balbás than by his commonly recognized master. According to Capitel, 'In his school years Moneo chose two exemplary mentors. One was D. Leopoldo Torres-Balbás, who would turn out to be a crucial influence on a few individuals; Moneo aspired to inherit from him not only his passion for historical culture but also his interest in critical depth, and even an aspect of his particular personality, that he may have acquired very privately – that of the moderate and cultivated man, eclectic and brilliant, an analyst of the contemporary and scholar of the ancient. The other, of a very different character, was D. Francisco Saenz de Oíza, his more direct and obvious master, from whom he may well have learned more professionally, but who would have little influence on Moneo's ethos, both personally and in his life's work.' Antón González Capitel, 'Apuntes para un ensayo sobre la obra del arquitecto Rafael Moneo', in *Oteiza – Moneo: Pabellón de Navarra: Exposición Universal de Sevilla*, Pamplona: Caja Municipal, 1992.

contingencies of the site, the client and the programme. His architecture is an interpretation of the conditions of human experience, its relation to social and cultural conditions. And the very fact that Moneo has felt committed to university teaching throughout his career is another testament to his admiration of Ortega, who wrote so compellingly of the *Mission of the University*.[11]

Finally, the trajectory of Moneo's professional career reveals not only his personal response to the circumstances in which he found himself, but casts light on an important period of architectural history, revealed through the lens of one of its most important contributors. From his structural and organicist origins in the 1950s and 1960s, through Italian discourses on form, composition and the city in the 1960s and 1970s, to the theoretical anxieties of the architects of the East Coast of America in the 1970s and 1980s, to his participation in a global star system in the 1990s, Moneo's developing philosophy of design is a story that absorbs, reflects and confronts, throughout his career, some of the most relevant architectural debates of his time, whilst retaining a personal and independent character.

11   José Ortega y Gasset, *Mission of the University*, Princeton, N.J.: Princeton University Press, 1944.

Rafael Moneo began his career in the early 1960s, at a time of particular optimism about the benefits of science and confidence in programmes of modernisation. But, unlike many of his contemporaries, Moneo did not translate this enthusiasm into buildings that celebrated technology and the products of the so-called 'second machine age', but sought instead to absorb new attitudes to knowledge that emerged after the Second World War. While many architectural historians recorded the excitement of new technologies that could be transferred into architecture in the post-war period,[12] Moneo was more interested in the realignment of the disciplines of the human sciences implied by the emergence of structuralism and critical theory. He was therefore attracted to architects such as Robert Venturi, who backed up his arguments with references from psychology, literary criticism and sociology, and Aldo Rossi, who referred to the work of French structuralist geographers and anthropologists as well as German critical theorists,[13] though, as shall be seen, his position is not identical to that of either of these influential architects. Moneo believed firmly that architecture is a form of knowledge, the principles of which can be codified and communicated, and that it is possible to have a rational approach to design that avoids the arbitrariness and personal subjectivity of individual designers. In the compendium of exercises he proposed for the ETSAB course of 1972–3, he wrote,

> We have aimed at stressing the didactic quality of the exercises and linking them as much as possible with the topics discussed in lectures. However, many students misunderstand the training character of these activities and indulge in showing off individual desires that are often completely alien to the topics proposed. This demonstrates once again the strength of the prejudices about the condition of the architect – in this case brought by the students themselves to the School.[14]

---

12   An example would be Reyner Banham's *Theory and Design in the First Machine Age*, which ends with a chapter commending the work of the American engineer Buckminster Fuller. Reyner Banham, *Theory and Design in the First Machine Age*, London: Architectural Press, 1960.

13   Robert Venturi, *Complexity and Contradiction in Architecture*, New York: Museum of Modern Art, 1966; Aldo Rossi, *Architecture of the City*, Cambridge, Mass.: MIT Press, 1982 (originally published in Italian in 1966).

14   Rafael Moneo, *Ejercicios del Curso 1972–3*, Barcelona: Cátedra de Elementos de Composición, 1974, p. 3.

Moneo never succumbed to the temptation of making architecture into a positivistic science, as Aldo Rossi, whom he undoubtedly admired in many respects, was attempting to do in the mid-1960s, though he was certainly influenced by this kind of thinking during his attachment to the Royal Academy of Spain in Rome. During this period he absorbed the teaching of emerging architectural personalities such as Paolo Portoghesi and Manfredo Tafuri, as well as that of more established figures such as Bruno Zevi and Ludovico Quaroni.[15] His interest in Zevi, whose *Verso un'architettura organica* was a major point of reference in Madrid, is particularly significant. During the 1950s and early 1960s the Madrid school was preoccupied with a discussion of organicism, and the work of Nordic architects, especially Alvar Aalto, was revered. Moneo's significant contribution as an intern to the Torres Blancas, Francisco Javier Sáenz de Oíza's masterpiece, can be seen as part of that organic influence, as can his stubborn insistence on working with Jørn Utzon, the new Nordic master, whose winning entry for the Sidney Opera House he had admired in the pages of *L'Architecture d'Aujourd'hui*.[16] But his admiration went beyond merely an attraction to the organic sensibilities promoted by Zevi: what Moneo found in Italy was a commonly shared attitude to the redefinition of the discipline of architecture from within its own traditions. In fact, the Zevi of the mid-1960s was very different from the dogmatic promoter of an organic modernism who was revered in the Madrid of the late 1950s. Zevi was now preoccupied with other issues, such as the reorganization of the architectural discipline after its appropriation for political ends during the period of Mussolini, a recognition of limits in the principles of the modern movement, and indeed his criticism to the Bauhaus teaching model.[17] Zevi exercised an important influence through his professorship at the University of Rome, La Sapienza, but also as a result of his weekly seminars at

---

15 Moneo's personal reflections on the importance of the architectural debate in Italy to his thinking can be seen in Fernando Márquez and Richard Levene, 'Three Step Interview: Spring 1985', in *Rafael Moneo 1967–2004: Imperative Anthology*, Madrid: El Croquis Editoriale, 2005, p. 15. Even though Moneo was to become well known in the Anglo-Saxon academic community for making the work of Aldo Rossi available, his relation with Milanese architects came from a later period in Barcelona.

16 From an interview of Francisco González de Canales with Rafael Moneo, 5 December 2012.

17 Bruno Zevi's attack on Gropius' inadequate understanding of history and its consequences for Bauhaus teaching is first found in Bruno Zevi, 'Architecture', in *Encyclopedia of World Art* 1, McGraw Hill, 1959, pp. 625–93.

the Institute of Architecture, which he held at the Palazzo Taverna, and which the young Moneo attended regularly.[18] In 1964, for instance, the year in which Moneo arrived in Rome, Zevi and Portoghesi curated the polemical exhibition 'Michelangiolo Architetto', which displayed a clear intention to show the work of the renaissance master as relevant and useful for contemporary architects in practice.[19] This exhibition indicated the straightforward instrumentalization of history that was being discussed in Roman circles at the time; in fact it was the Michelangelo exhibition, and the debate around it, that stimulated Manfredo Tafuri's famous critique of operative criticism.[20]

The reason that Moneo was so keen to translate Bruno Zevi's 1964 edition of *Architettura in Nuce* into Spanish is that he was convinced that it was necessary in Spain to fashion an idea of architecture that could transcend historical periods, so that its latent values could be discovered in Greek temples, Islamic mosques, or baroque churches just as easily as in modern masterpieces.[21] His translation appeared in Madrid in 1969, and the book is important both for its methodological stress on the plurality of approaches to architecture and for its insistence that architectural experience derives from the treatment of space and light and construction – an idea to which Moneo was to return repeatedly when he described such buildings as the Hagia Sophia.[22]

18   Ana Esteban Maluenda, 'Sustrato y sedimento', p. 160.

19   The exhibition 'Michelangiolo architetto' was held in commemoration of the four-hundredth anniversary of the death of the artist. Paolo Portoghesi and Bruno Zevi (eds), *Michelangiolo architetto*, Turin: Einaudi, 1964. Zevi's point is quite clear in his introduction entitled 'Introduzione: Attualità di Michelangiolo architetto' (the Modernity of Michelangiolo as an Architect), pp. 11–27. A contemporary discussion of this exhibition can be found in A. Leach, 'Modern Architecture and the Actualisation of History: Bruno Zevi and Michelangiolo Architetto', in *Proceedings of the XXVth International Conference of the Society of Architectural Historians*, Geelong, Australia, 3–6 July 2008, pp. 1–19.

20   Tafuri considered the exhibition to be a deviant instrumentalization of history that obscured the reality of the past in order to justify the actions of the present as projected into the future. See Manfredo Tafuri, *Teorie e storia dell'architettura*, Bari: Laterza, 1968, pp. 165–97.

21   Bruno Zevi, *Architettura in Nuce*, Roma-Venezia: Istituto per la Collaborazione Culturale, 1960. The new 1964 edition of the book had a significant impact, and Zevi received a professorship at the Facoltà di Architettura dell'Università degli studi di Roma 'La Sapienza' while Moneo was in Rome. Moneo's translation was published as Bruno Zevi, *Arquitectura in Nuce, Una definición de arquitectura*, Madrid: Aguilar, 1969 (translation by Rafael Moneo). Note that the subtitle 'A Definition of Architecture' does not appear in the original Italian.

22   See, for instance, Rafael Moneo, 'New Idea of Space', the first lecture at the Harvard Graduate School of Design for the course On Contemporary Architecture, in spring 2006 (Teaching Assistant: Francisco González de Canales). It is difficult not to be reminded of these notions of space when one visits

The Latinism in Zevi's title, 'in nuce', can also be understood as affirming the distinctive role of an architect; this became a recurrent topic in the initial lessons that Moneo was to deliver to his students at Barcelona and Madrid. In one of his course descriptions at Barcelona, for example, he wrote,

> We assume that students have a basic idea about what the profession is, acquired through everyday approaches to professional practice. Whether we like it or not, there is an established idea about the work of architects, usually associated with its well-known features … The conception that the job of the architect is a creative task developed through a project is a generalised way of imagining the profession – at least, compared to the fantastic image usually held by students when they start their training at the School. A closer examination, however, would lead us to question this idea of the 'freedom' of architects. This was precisely the aim of this course: to identify our role within the field of professional practice, that area within which architects can operate independently. It is evident, and important to acknowledge, that the profession is mediated by other realities that architects need to understand, because only from them, or through them, can they comprehend the full scope of the discipline, its specificity and autonomy.[23]

The impact of the debates around Zevi and other Italian contemporaries concerning the reaffirmation of the discipline of architecture is also apparent in one of the first essays Moneo wrote for *Arquitectura* – probably the most influential Spanish architectural magazine at the time.[24] The text, 'On an attempt at Didactic Reform', records and reflects on discussions that took place at a series of meetings in the University of Rome between architectural students and established professors such as Luigi Piccinato, Ludovico Quaroni and Zevi himself, in order to establish the fundamentals of a new academic curriculum for teaching students of architecture. Moneo emphasizes

---

Moneo's own masterpieces such as the National Museum of Roman Art at Mérida (p. 127) or the later Cathedral of Our Lady in Los Angeles (p. 163).

23 Moneo, *Ejercicios de Curso 1972–3*, p. 11.

24 *Arquitectura* is the official magazine of the Colegio de Arquitectos de Madrid. Founded in 1918, it is the oldest periodical in Spain specializing in architecture.

Zevi's understanding of the deeper reasons for student dissatisfaction, and the nature of the crisis in architectural education, quoting Zevi directly:

> The consolidation of the modern movement undoubtedly brought about the collapse of conventional academic didactic methods . . . Since then, the Academy has nevertheless managed to establish a cultural coherence.[25]

Moneo supported the need to reconsider architectural education in the light of the problems that society throws up by arguing for a return to 'reality', thereby avoiding the fantasy and dogmatism into which, according to Moneo, the modern movement had degenerated.[26] The way in which Moneo proposed to engage with this reality was not simply empirical, but by re-establishing, just as Zevi, Quaroni and Portoghesi were suggesting, the central place of architectural history in the education of an architect. In this way, Moneo not only condemned the disgraceful neglect of architectural history in the current curricula in schools of architecture, seemingly forgotten everywhere since the Bauhaus period (witness the teaching at Harvard during the chairmanship of Walter Gropius), but also reasserted its value for designers as a way of bringing the knowledge of precedents to bear on contemporary realities. According to Moneo,

> This contact with architectural reality through history is not as gratuitous as it might seem at first: it reflects a mature cultural understanding of architecture not just as a sculptural entity – the default position that is frequently the result of Bauhaus teaching – but also as a spatial reality in which contemporary social problems are materialized.[27]

History, in this understanding, is not simply to be employed as an erudite postmodern game of references, but is instrumental in bringing design to account, in light of the values that can be found in the tradition of architecture. Such an interest in linking architectural history to its meaningful traditions distinguishes the concerns of architects from those of historians, who may have a merely antiquarian interest in the past, however passionate they may

---

25   Moneo, 'Sobre un intento de reforma didáctica', p. 44.
26   Ibid., p. 45.
27   Ibid., p. 46.

be. For Moneo, architecture as a current discipline and as a culture must be continually regenerated by an understanding of its past. In fact, if we had to define Rafael Moneo's most consistent preoccupation throughout his academic and professional career, it would be his attempt to establish a strong architectural culture, one that would allow practice to be consistent and that could be communicated from the outset of architectural education in the search for methodological principles.

But, contrary to what might be supposed, architectural culture for Moneo is not primarily to be unearthed from books and manuals, where the history of the discipline might be thought to reside, but should be experienced by an encounter with buildings themselves. In his first lecture as Chair of the Department of Architecture at the Harvard Graduate School of Design, he emphasized the physical matter of architecture:

> I believe that in the crude reality of built works one can see clearly the essence of a project, the consistency of ideas. I firmly believe that architecture needs the support of matter; that the former is inseparable from the latter. Architecture arrives when our thoughts about it acquire the real condition that only materials can provide.... Many architects today invent processes or master drawing techniques without concern for the reality of building. The tyranny of drawings is evident in many buildings when the builder tries to follow the drawing literally.... But a truly architectural drawing should imply above all the knowledge of construction.[28]

Moneo was determined to reconnect theory with the actualities of practice, and his article on design methodologies published in 1965 not only referred to the importance of the experience of historical architectural examples, but also related directly to the current demands of architectural students in Madrid, as some of them remember today.[29] The teaching of design at the time was chaotic, highly subjective and quite inadequate as a preparation for the

---

28 Moneo, 'The Solitude of Buildings', pp. 32–40.
29 Interview with Antón Capitel, Rafael Moneo's former student at ETSAM, Madrid, in the late 1960s, London, June 2011. Students were tired of the teaching tradition by which the tutor simply set a brief (site and programme) and compelled students to work without further explanation. They asked for a methodology, a reliable approach to design. An answer to this plea is precisely what Moneo would develop for his Elements of Composition Professorship competition in 1970.

challenges thrown up by society that students would face in practice. Moneo, critical of the progressive independence of theory from design, and wishing to restore its traditional role as a guideline for the practice of architecture, traced this approach back through the Ecole des Beaux-Arts to Bramante.[30] Theory comes after praxis, as it is knowledge derived from experience – the experience of buildings of the past as well as of seeing their own designs realized – that informs better solutions in the future. Theory for Moneo therefore cannot be reduced to the analysis, interpretation and discussion of designs, but is made manifest as a way of designing that is guided by models that have been constructed in the past. This is the theory that architects such as Vitruvius and Palladio taught, as opposed to the types of theory thrown up by modernism: a body of knowledge that gives practical advice to architects as to how they should proceed as designers. Thus the true theorist has also to be a practitioner, because only the practitioner knows about the complexities and constraints of construction. Therefore Moneo swiftly loses interest in those who write about architecture but do not build: real theorists, for him, are Aldo Rossi or Robert Venturi, not Manfredo Tafuri or Charles Jencks. Rossi and Venturi are referential for Moneo because they had a theory about design that they tested through construction.[31]

Clearly, personal experience of construction is not possible in an architectural school, and it is architectural examples in history and the approaches that lie behind them that take its place. In his search for architecture's own specific discipline, Moneo criticizes those who try to establish far-fetched analogies with other arts, and is particularly scornful of visionary and utopian architectures that are excused by the persuasive prose of critics like Reyner Banham:

> The dreamer and utopian architect tells us that he intends to introduce modern technology into his designs but quite often ends up by proposing an a-technical architecture, as I cannot understand how an architecture which forgets prevailing social and economic conditions can be called

30   Moneo, 'Sobre un intento de reforma didáctica', p. 45.

31   The position described emerges in Moneo's writing over a number of years, becoming more emphatic in later texts. See, for example, Moneo, 'The Solitude of Buildings', pp. 32–40.

technical. Such an architect therefore *escapes* by not controlling the reality that surrounds him.[32]

It was in the 1972 programme for the Elements of Composition Professorship that Moneo first set out a coherent method and approach to architecture that undoubtedly established the basis for what would be his architectural philosophy for both teaching and practice.[33] The course was based on a consideration of how architecture is engendered, which becomes the invariable methodological basis for any architect in whom Moneo is interested. This methodology is particularly indebted to Zevi's *Architecture in Nuce*. Interestingly, unlike the holistic – and conclusive – views of Alexander, Norberg-Shulz or Doxiadis, *Architettura in Nuce* does not address the problem of knowledge in architecture by stating an *a priori* set of general principles, but by critically analyzing the plurality of theoretical assumptions that have given rise to different ways in which architecture has been produced over time, and drawing from them a critical knowledge through rational discrimination. A sentence taken from another of Moneo's teaching documents also sheds light on this rational discrimination:

> Critical analysis is, in my view, what gives rise to what might be called theoretical reflection, to the knowledge of those theories that can be understood as the set of criteria and principles that are at the basis of any architecture.[34]

Much like Zevi, rather than assigning value to one architectural approach, Moneo accepts the existence of a plurality of theories that emerge, flow and are transformed over time, just as societies, their cultures and techniques do

---

32 Rafael Moneo, 'A vueltas con la metodología', *Arquitectura* 82, October 1965, p. 13.
33 In actuality, the 1972 document published by the School of Architecture of Barcelona was based on an unpublished manuscript Moneo had prepared for his professorship competition. The 65-page document included his teaching philosophy as well as a sample of 20 lectures that he would teach for the course. Rafael Moneo, *Memoria: Concepto. Oposición a la Cátedra de Elementos de Composición en las Escuelas Técnicas Superiores de Arquitectura de Madrid, Barcelona y Sevilla*, November 1969 (unpublished manuscript).
34 As the Madrid programme for Composición Arquitectónica summarizing the syllabi of the five years of teaching states. Rafael Moneo, *Programas de Curso y Ejercicios de Examen: 1980–1981, 1981–1982, 1982–1983, 1983–1984*, Madrid: Cátedra de Composición II, Ediciones de la ETSAM, 1985, pp. 12–13.

in response to different circumstances. This initial premise shapes the direction of the course. In 1972, he briefly described three steps as follows:

> The first part of the course will be devoted, therefore, to examining how design can be produced, which methodological alternatives are available for projects nowadays – in other words, to examining what we understand by 'architecture'. Thus, we will firstly present the different attitudes towards design that are currently proposed by methodologists and then test their validity by comparing them with reality, by checking on how well they work in actuality, and by explaining the genesis of inhabited spaces, the Architecture. Instead of *assuming* an abstract and *a priori* theory of architectonic composition, our purpose is to *unveil* one, to apprehend it through a continuous observation of the spaces in which people live. To design would be, in a sense, to get to understand both the processes in which the development of the world that surrounds us is immersed today, and the theories that have been proposed throughout history, which are nothing but approaches to this understanding.
>
> Since this is our approach, it is no surprise that we frequently use the past as our starting point. So history becomes something that can be integrated into our research, with the great advantage of perceiving facts from a distance that no doubt acts as a filter to clarify them. It is convenient, therefore, to stress the didactic importance of history, especially if we take into account that history necessarily interferes in a work of architecture: since any landscape is nowadays already manipulated, it presents itself to us as something artificial, as something loaded with history.
>
> If we understand the first part of the course as an analysis of the methodological approaches to the project, filtered through a sieve of reality, the second part will be an attempt to put into practice the method that we have found most valid. Thus, while in the first part of the course we will have carefully examined reality to understand the way in which it was generated, in the second part we study the process of designing, because it is necessary to provide students with a technique, a tool, a set of principles, to enable them to assess the validity of a project throughout its development. While earlier on we focused on the study of reality as architecture, now we will concentrate on the technique of design.

To this end, we will start with the idea of architecture as a language, since that will enable us to analyse the formal results coherently, both in their syntactic and semantic aspects. The idea of architecture as language will allow us to study its connections with society as well as with constructional methods. In addition, a linguistic approach to design will help us to resolve the issue of historic evolution without creating violent discontinuities. Finally, after incorporating the elements of design, it is necessary to verify the validity of the project in which one is working. That is why we need to recover a sense of reality: to inscribe architecture in the wider system of the manipulated environment, the landscape. We therefore identify three steps that help us to approach the project:

a) an analysis of the different projects' methodology;
b) a tool to help us to resolve the design process
c) a reality against which to test it.[35]

Set out in this clear way as early as 1970, these three points have become the cornerstones of Moneo's architectural philosophy.

The first of them, methodology, refers to Moneo's interest in analysing different approaches towards the generation of a design: this is what he considers to be a 'theory of design'. The analysis of other architects' practice in order to discover their 'theory of design' would become a fundamental and consistent tool for Moneo throughout his career. In 1972, his course was structured around the analysis of a series of approaches: functionalist, perceptual, organic, systems-engineering, productive, logical, typological, linguistic, constructivist and so on. In each case he gives examples of architects and theorists whose work can be considered to participate in that methodology – from Christopher Alexander and Kevin Lynch to Rossi and Gregotti. He provides a bibliography ranging from psychology, sociology and semiotics, to biology and cybernetics, but also including classical treatises, classic and newly emerging historians, as well as the familiar modernist masters. Such a broad diorama of architectural history and practice constitutes a body of knowledge that can be useful to architects as guidance when it comes to producing their designs; from such a culture, derived from the works of history as well as of current practitioners, the architect can choose a methodology that better fits his actual needs. Over subsequent decades Moneo continued to enlarge the scope of architectural culture; immediately after the publication of this programme, he was engaged in analysing the theory and designs of those of his contemporaries whose work he most admired – Aldo Rossi and James Stirling amongst them.[36] And while he expanded his area of interest to American architects of the 1960s and 1970s, he simultaneously looked back at past history in articles on the work of Pugin and Viollet-le-Duc and the architecture of the Enlightenment.[37]

The second step in Moneo's three-part process involves choosing the best approach from those analysed to use as a tool to resolve the design. In 1972, as the quotation above reveals, his favoured approach was linguistic – the idea of architecture as a language.[38] This allowed him to make connections later in the course between architecture and social reality (from a semantic position), and between the architectural discipline and its construction (from the syntactic point of view). It also enabled a connection to be made between his Italian and American interests.[39] But this preliminary interest in linguistic theory is supplemented later in his career when he becomes more consistently concerned with establishing relationships between architectural *history*, *composition* and *form*, which will be analysed later in this chapter. History constitutes the body of knowledge that redefines the traditional notion of

36 Rafael Moneo, 'Gregotti y Rossi', *Arquitecturas Bis* 4, November 1974, pp. 1–4; *La Idea de Arquitectura en Rossi y el Cementerio de Módena*, Barcelona, Cátedra de Elementos de Composición, Monografía 4, Ediciones de la ETSAB, 1974 (also Oppositions 5, 1976, pp. 1–30); 'On James Stirling: Buildings and Projects 1950–1974', *Oppositions* 7, Winter 1976–7, pp. 90–92.

37 'Entrados ya en el último cuarto de siglo', *Arquitecturas Bis* 22, May 1978, pp. 2–5; *Comentarios sobre dibujos de 20 arquitectos actuales*, Barcelona, Cátedra de Elementos de Composición Monografía 14, Ediciones de la ETSAB, October 1976 (with Juan Antonio Cortés); *Apuntes sobre Pugin, Ruskin y Viollet*, Barcelona, Cátedra de Elementos de Composición, Monografía 13, Ediciones de la ETSAB, November 1976 (doctorate course taught with Ignasi de Solà-Morales i Rubió, 1975). 'Preface to the Spanish Edition', in Emil Kaufmann, *La Arquitectura de la Ilustración. Barroco y Post-Barroco en Inglaterra, Italia y Francia*, Barcelona: Gustavo Gili, 1974, pp. VII–XXV.

38 Such an interest in language occurs before the 1970s in some early texts such as Rafael Moneo, 'A la Conquista de lo Irracional', *Arquitectura* 87, March 1966, pp. 1–6, where he approaches the notion of language not just as a preoccupation of the generation of Venturi and Rossi, but as one that already was evident in the so-called third generation of modern architects.

39 Moneo, *Programa de la cátedra de Elementos de Composición*, pp. 22–7.

the *canon*; composition is the tool he rediscovered in his academic work, as is reflected in his teaching of Elements of Composition in Barcelona (1971–9), and Composition II in Madrid (1980–85); and form is a particular structuring of architectural space that emerges out of his interest in typology and his study of Luigi Pareyson's notion of formativity (discussed further on pp. 224–5).

The third and final step in Moneo's method involves the confrontation of theoretical ideas with reality. This is fundamental to Moneo's approach and means adopting an attitude that accepts the contingencies of a commission – the site conditions and budgetary constraints for example. Moneo has no desire to mask these everyday realities behind some kind of extreme idealism, whether techno-utopian, socio-utopian, or just indulgently self-referential. On many occasions he has stressed how he enjoys taking on board contingent factors as a stimulus to inventive design.[40] Accordingly, the process Moneo proposes is less a literal prescription of a methodology to be followed, with predictable outcomes, than an attitude towards design that defines a set of concerns from which architecture can arise – a referential field of action, which is insufficient in itself to become a straightforward design tool. For Moneo, though rigour, accuracy and precise performance are essential, real situations demand a certain flexibility – the understanding of different positions and some negotiation between them.

This third step emphasizes two other aspects of Moneo's philosophical position. The first of these is the importance of construction, already referred to, as a way of giving consistency to an architectural proposal. There is a necessary correlation between the ideas embodied in an architectural project, the way that it is constructed and how its material weathers over time. Moneo has argued this forcibly in his teaching over many years, and was especially emphatic when he taught in the United States, where drawing hypothetical projects was more valued than the reality of constructed work. The second aspect that Moneo's insistence on confronting theory with the actualities of practice emphasizes is the necessary relationship of the project to its physical and cultural context – in most instances the European or American city.

---

40   Rafael Moneo, *The Freedom of the Architect* (Raoul Wallenberg Lecture), Ann Arbor: University of Michigan, 2002; *How Difficulties Benefit the Work of the Architect* (Kassler Lecture, unpublished), delivered at Princeton University, 2011.

This entails a close study of the culturally charged landscapes and urban environments that we inhabit, which have to be understood at every level before a responsible intervention can be made. Thus architecture is always not only a response to the realities of its physical construction, but also to the cultural and social conditions within which it is set, to which it will respond, and which in turn it will reveal. How this occurs will be discussed in the final section (pp. 233–57).

Is there a specific knowledge that allows us to speak about our discipline with its own territory and its own laws? I would say 'Yes'. Architects have tried throughout the centuries to establish a body of knowledge which would define their activity like other positive sciences. And yet with the awareness that a systematic approach to the idea of knowledge in architecture isn't possible, I would like to believe that architectural knowledge isn't hopelessly elusive and often can inform the work that we do.[41]

Rafael Moneo

In his lecture, '**Rules for the Human Zoo:** A Response to the Letter on Humanism', Peter Sloterdijk defined humanism as a chain of 'thick letters to friends', creating a kind of 'brotherhood' of *literati* that determines a common territory – a canon.[42] The idea of a canon of shared humanist values, which Sloterdijk attempts to reassess in this lecture, was prevalent in the Europe of the 1950s, where it was called upon to assist in its cultural re-construction after the disastrous cataclysm of the Second World War. Architects such as Ernesto Rogers, who were so influential for Moneo's generation, were well aware of the vivid debate between Jean-Paul Sartre and Martin Heidegger.[43] During that period, humanism was seen both in an instrumental sense, as a way of regaining a solidarity between nations, and historically, as a re-evaluation of that inherited stable body of knowledge that literary critics such as Harold Bloom recognized as a 'western canon'.[44]

---

41   Rafael Moneo, 'Sul concetto di arbitrarietà in architettura', *Casabella*, July–August 2005, pp. 22–33 (republished in English in Manuel Flores Caballero (ed.), *Rafael Moneo: Writings and Conversations in Peru*, Lima: Oficina de Publicaciones de la Universidad Católica del Perú, 2009, pp. 53–131).

42   Peter Sloterdijk, 'Rules for the Human Zoo: A Response to the Letter on Humanism', in *Environment and Planning D: Society and Space* 27, 2009, p. 12, trans. Mary V. Rorty from *Regeln für den Menschenpark: ein Antwortschreiben zu Heideggers Brief über den Humanismus*, Frankfurt: Suhrkamp, 1999 (transcription of a lecture given in Basel, 15 June 1997).

43   Jean-Paul Sartre, 'Existentialism is a Humanism', trans. Philip Mairet, in *Existentialism from Dostoyevsky to Sartre*, ed. Walter Kaufman, New York: World Publishing Company, 1956 (from a lecture originally published in French in 1946); Martin Heidegger, 'Letter on Humanism', trans. Frank A. Capuzzi, in *Basic Writings: Martin Heidegger*, London: Routledge, 1977 (originally published in German in 1949). For one of Ernesto Roger's most important contributions to this debate, see Ernesto Nathan Rogers, *Esperienza dell'architettura*, Turin: Einaudi, 1958.

44   Harold Bloom, *The Western Canon*, New York: Riverhead Books, 1994.

In architecture, however, a discipline that is rooted in many respects in the 'Age of Humanism', the idea of a 'canon' has a very particular implication. It was during the renaissance that a rupture with previous traditions of building occurred that was fundamental to the way in which architecture as a literate form of knowledge was to be transmitted up until the time of the Beaux Arts. The theory of an architect such as Leon Battista Alberti implies not only that the new style (derived from Greco-Roman antiquity, or the *maniera antiqua* as Vasari would have called it) was always to be preferred over the old style (the gothic or *maniera barbara*), but that architectural knowledge was to be found not in the quarry or on the building site, but in books, those 'thick letters to friends' that shaped humanist culture. A treatise such as *De Re Aedificatoria* proposes that architectural knowledge should be consistent and transmittable, so that the architect is a literate intellectual and not a mere builder or mason. Ever since the renaissance, and the recovery of Vitruvius as the foundational basis for the new canon, architecture was taught to each subsequent genera-tion of architects by means of formal compositional and linguistic codes; the theory of architecture in fact consisted in those sets of recommendations that Alberti, Serlio or Vignola had set out in their various treatises. The canon is de-fined and redefined by the way in which buildings embody those recommen-dations, or by successfully reinterpreting and enlarging upon them. In post-war London, the émigré scholar at the Warburg Institute Rudolf Wittkower made explicit the connections between the geometrical forms of renaissance architecture and neo-Platonic philosophy in his book *Architectural Principles in the Age of Humanism,* a study that was to be extraordinarily influential on the architects of the post-war generation.[45] This was the intellectual frame-work within which Moneo and most of his generation were educated,[46] an ap-proach that was quite distinct from the educational system introduced by the Bauhaus, which represents a rupturing of this 'canon'.

---

45 Rudolf Wittkower, *Architectural Principles in the Age of Humanism*, London: Warburg Institute, Uni-versity of London, 1949. His fellow Viennese Ernst Gombrich, working in the field of art history, was equally influential. See Ernst Gombrich, *Norm and Form: Studies in the Art of the Renaissance*, Lon-don: Phaidon, 1966. The 'canon' as an organization of knowledge in the renaissance can be seen to derive from the medieval concept of truth found in Augustine.

46 But, as has been seen, Moneo's position would differ from the neo-Platonism practised by Wittkower and taken even further by his disciple Colin Rowe.

By the mid 1960s, schools all over the world had adopted the Bauhaus paradigm and mostly eliminated the study of the history of architecture from their courses, and had even removed historical texts from their library shelves, as Moneo was later to discover at the illustrious Graduate School of Design at Harvard. Inspired by Ortega's ideas, Moneo was naturally sympathetic to a humanist architectural position that sought to place human experience at the forefront of architecture, rather than understanding it as a predominantly technical discipline. Unusually within his own generation of students in Madrid, he was not so uneasy with the eclectic and historicist work of an older generation of Spanish architects such as Luis Moya, most well-known for his Universidad Laboral de Gijón (1946–56), which clearly opposed the recent 'organic modernist' orthodoxy of the Madrid school.[47] Recognizing how, under the sway of the Bauhaus model, the basis of architectural education had been removed, Moneo's educational aim was to restore history to the syllabus so that it could be used, again, as the basis for its canon.[48] But Moneo's lectures are a constant reminder that he yearns for a history that is not contained in books, but is found in buildings themselves – a nostalgia that recalls Victor Hugo's anxiety that the words in books will come to supersede the lessons that the buildings themselves embody as registers of human experience.[49] For him, history, correctly understood, conveys its lessons through practice – the testing of ideas through actual construction, and the dangers of arbitrariness should be avoided when you build, when ideas are physically realised:

47 Moneo, for instance, supported the publication of an appraisal of Luis Moya's Universidad Laboral in the avant-gardist Barcelona-based *Arquitecturas Bis*. This has to be considered as entirely deliberate, as publishing the work of a fascist architect promoted by Franco's regime in the first years of democracy in Catalonia was not easy to arrange. The essay by Antón Capitel was published at Moneo's (and eventually Luis Domenech's) insistence: Antón Capitel, 'La Universidad Laboral de Gijón o el poder de las arquitecturas', *Arquitecturas Bis* 12, March 1976. Capitel developed his PhD on the work of Luis Moya with Rafael Moneo as advisor.

48 Moneo, 'Sobre un intento de reforma didáctica', p. 44. His position can be distinguished from that of a theorist like Colin Rowe, whose use of historical precedent in his teaching at Cornell was to be highly influential, but did not embrace ideas of construction.

49 Victor Hugo, *Notre Dame de Paris*, usually translated as *The Hunchback of Notre Dame*. See also Neil Levine, 'The Book and the Building: Hugo's Theory of Architecture and Labrouste's Bibliothèque Ste-Geneviève', in Robin Middleton (ed.), *The Beaux-Arts and Nineteenth-century French Architecture*, London: Thames and Hudson, paperback edition, 1984, pp. 138–73.

. . . arbitrariness of form used to disappear in construction, and architecture acted as the bridge between the two. Today arbitrariness of form is
evident in the buildings themselves, because construction has been dealt
out of the game of design. When arbitrariness is so clearly visible in the
buildings themselves, architecture is dead; what I understand as the most
valuable attribute of architecture disappears.[50]

Moneo's notion of history as embedded in buildings themselves is a tool to
assist him in his long-standing fight against arbitrariness in architecture – a
phenomenon that he claims pervades most of the architecture of his time, too
often seduced by the cult of the charismatic personality. As he put it:

It can be said that today the highest goal of any architect is to produce his
or her own language. It seems as if individual experience were only possible through an individual language.[51]

Though it may be inevitable that architecture will be informed by the formal
virtuosity of skilful designers, Moneo understands that architectural culture
should transcend such gestures and be capable of being shared.
While Moneo seeks to prevent arbitrariness in architectural design, he resists
the temptation to see architecture as a positive science or a logical operation.
Thus he has consistently opposed the 'systems approach' that was characteristic of the period, regarding it as extraordinarily naïve to reduce architecture
to a system of problem solving that promised to resolve designs by means
of objective and measurable criteria of efficiency of circulation, ventilation,
lighting or environmental performance. His 1972 course examined the work
of architects who advocated such an approach in order to mount a critique
of their reductiveness.[52] Architecture is fundamentally rooted in social and
cultural interaction, and apparently 'scientific' criteria are insufficient to mea-
sure the way in which a building in a city will affect those who use it or come

---

50 Moneo, 'The Solitude of Buildings', p. 35.
51 Rafael Moneo, 'The Indifference of Anyway', in Cynthia C. Davison, *Anyway*, New York: Rizzoli, 1993,
    pp. 176–83.
52 Moneo, *Programa de Elementos de Composición*, pp. 14–16. He identified Reyner Banham and Chris-
    topher Alexander as representative of this trend. Alexander's *Notes on the Synthesis of Form* set out
    to eliminate the arbitrariness of individual designers. Later work by Alexander reintroduces cultural
    criteria, but either as a kind of checklist (the *Pattern Language*) or in a quasi-mystical way.

across it. So when Moneo was looking for rational reasons to advance one approach rather than another, he tended (just as Robert Venturi or Aldo Rossi did) to turn to the social sciences rather than engineering, since they shared similar problems. Moneo concluded that the only way to validate architectural decisions is through experience – both by practicing architects experiencing their own work, and by taking into account the experience of those that have built before. And he continues to hold this position: as a built reality, architectural knowledge, for Moneo, is inseparably linked to construction and the formal decisions related to it. For him, architecture is 'a form of knowledge which, while allowing construction, needs formal principles in order to exist; without those principles, materialization is impossible'.[53] A reassessment of history that is able to generate a canon of knowledge for Moneo does not begin with ideal principles, but rather with the practice of architecture itself, the act of building. It is this act of building that provides an architect with an understanding of how valid certain formal solutions are in a given context. The aim is that, after a critical analysis of the different theoretical positions presented in each of the lessons of Moneo's course, students can discriminate and acquire knowledge that will justify the formal decisions of their architectural designs and the details of their construction.

And this experience of previous constructions should be the very basis, Moneo believes, of the education of an architect, and the development of the discipline. As he wrote, as early as 1965:

> Experience is barely taken into account in the education of an architect. Furthermore, that which was circumstantial in modern architects has become the norm: architects do not accept the contents of experience and they reject introducing into their own works what other colleagues have previously achieved, seeking originality at any cost – originality for which society patently pays a high price.[54]

This insistence on experience (personal, and mediated through the history of architecture) creates the possibility of fashioning an architectural culture

---

53 Rafael Moneo, 'On Theory' (unpublished manuscript presented at the Institute of Architecture and Urban Studies of New York, 1976), p. 11.
54 Moneo, 'A vueltas con la metodología', p. 12.

that can generate stable canons: guidance for architects, based on experience, on how to proceed. And this notion of canon is Moneo's solution to the problem of avoiding the personally arbitrary. Moneo does, however, accept that the architectural canon may itself originate from something arbitrary. He refers to the example of the Corinthian order:

> ... the most classical element of academic architecture was based on a rather arbitrary choice of those forms able to provide guidelines for construction. When Callimachus, walking in the cemetery, saw a basket with acanthus leaves and transformed it into a capital, he took advantage of a form that was caught in a casual moment. He transformed the basket into an element that has been repeated countless times throughout the centuries. Callimachus needed the form to terminate a column and the basket provided him all the ingredients, ornamental and structural, that he needed. In one way or another, form is essential in order to find the path which will end in a building. This history of Callimachus trying to draw the acanthus is fixed in our minds, and even if it is quite unlikely to be true, has served for many generations to solve an architectural problem, while receiving different interpretations.[55]

Thus, though its origin may be arbitrary, the validity of the Corinthian column is affirmed by its becoming part of a canon that is sanctioned by persistent use over time. According to Moneo, 'architects resist the arbitrary and are delighted when use makes arbitrary form so familiar that its legitimacy becomes unquestionable.'[56] Crucially, this is not an arbitrariness that arises out of the whim of a particular architect, based on his or her own subjectivity and will, which Moneo detects in the work of architects such as Zaha Hadid or Daniel Libeskind.[57] It is the arbitrariness of the collective that establishes a deep convention, or canon.

The canon – a body of knowledge for architects – thus established, can then be freely appropriated in design, and this prevents the necessity of rein-

---

55   *Moneo*, 'Sul concetto di arbitrarietà in architettura', p. 24.

56   Ibid., p. 26.

57   Criticisms of Hadid and Libeskind occurred in Moneo's teaching at Harvard, though in his *Theoretical Anxiety* book he confined himself to discussing those architects he particularly admired; even these are of course subjected to rigorous critical review.

76 Ludwig Hilbersheimer:
Hochhausstadt. An illustration from his
book *City Plan*, 1927

venting architecture from scratch every time one designs a building. Moneo
believes architects should have a deep knowledge of history, and this allows
them to make use of solutions that have already been thought through and
tested by their predecessors. The initial move in a design project is therefore
to select a solution from the history of architecture; architects do not have to
reinvent what has been thoughtfully created already. But this does not mean
that architects cannot invent anything new. The history of architecture is a
living one, but innovations should appear gradually over time, offering new
solutions when they are needed in order to respond to the new demands of
society, which in turn are incorporated into the body of architectural knowledge that forms the canon.

An examination of Rafael Moneo's own buildings reveals numerous elements already 'tested' in the long history of architecture. Moneo appropri-
ates them unashamedly; the validity of his solution depends on his critical
discrimination in choosing an appropriate precedent, and the erudite way in
which he deploys it. Moneo constantly searches for the right elements in the
history of architecture to solve the problems he is facing. Examples include
his appropriation of the rhetoric of Ludwig Hilbersheimer's Hochhausstadt
in his vast metropolitan façade of L'Illa Diagonal in Barcelona (fig. 76), John

77 John Soane: breakfast
room in his house at
13 Lincoln's Inn Fields,
London, re-built
in 1812–13 and showing
the pendentive ceiling

Soane's pendentive domes in the Atocha railway station car park (fig. 77), or Louis Kahn's pyramidal roof system, from the Jewish Community Centre in Trenton (fig. 78), in his Museum of Modern Art in Stockholm (1991–8). So Moneo's buildings could be considered in some respects like museums, or anthologies, of some of the best moments in architectural history.

This recovery of history as a body of knowledge that shapes architecture was crucial for Moneo both in his teaching and practice. History, based on experience, is the only trustworthy form of knowledge for architecture, a discipline that cannot be reduced to a set of quantifiable criteria. Architecture seen through this lens is therefore necessarily eclectic, as it is born from the appropriation of the work of other architects, and for Moneo this is something to be embraced.[58] But architects as individuals still have an important role:

---

58   In a brief description of teaching at the School of Barcelona Moneo precisely reflects on the eclecticism of the schools of architecture at that time. Such eclecticism does not cause him any anxiety, and he is happy to embrace it. Rafael Moneo, 'Designing and Teaching: The Reorganization of the School of Architecture in Barcelona', *Lotus International* 23, 1979, pp. 71–4.

78 Louis Kahn: Trenton
bath house, 1954

This contact with architectural reality through history is not as gratuitous as it might seem at first glance: it represents a state of cultural maturity that understands architecture not only as a mere plastic fact – a default position that was often found in the Bauhaus pedagogy – but as a spatial reality in which all the social problems of a society are materialized – through specific personalities of course.[59]

The process of establishing the correct solution from history is not neutral, and reflects the interests of the particular architect at any given time. Thus, in Moneo's own work of the 1960s, there are traces of the organic architecture from his formative years in the school of Madrid, in the references to the work of Sáenz de Oíza and Utzon that can be detected in the Diestre Transformer Factory, or the Urumea building in San Sebastián, which borrow particular elements from the work of Aalto and Wright. In his projects of the 1970s, such as the Logroño town hall, or the competition for the Colegio de Agentes de Cambio y Bolsa in Madrid (1973), these influences have almost

59   Moneo, 'Sobre un intento de reforma didáctica', p. 46.

completely disappeared. Instead, one finds the attenuated porticos that reflect the architecture of Turin, and show Moneo's interest in the architects of
La Tendenza such as Aldo Rossi and Giorgio Grassi, deriving from his years
in Barcelona. In later buildings, the superimposition of different grids at the
National Museum of Roman Art at Mérida (see pp. 127–38), and the fragmented
composition of the Atocha train station in Madrid, show the effect of Moneo's
contact with American architects of his generation. The accumulation of the
experience of history, therefore, is personal to individual architects, and their
work necessarily takes on something of the character of an autobiography.[60]
If architectural maturity is approached by accepting this autobiographical
component, maturity truly arrives when architects are able to absorb and live
with the many memories they have acquired, without any specific urgency
for the present. In Moneo's career, something of this could be seen in his work
from the 1980s onwards. Here, his reflective practice ignores the prevalence
of any particular time over others, to produce compositions of a multilayered
and ambiguous temporality, elements of which come from many different
periods, conditions and experiences.

---

60 This is the paradox raised by Aldo Rossi in his often poorly understood *Scientific Autobiography*. The
    history of the experience of architecture, even if 'scientifically' addressed, is fundamentally a biogra-
    phy of that experience. Aldo Rossi, *A Scientific Autobiography*, Cambridge, Mass.: MIT Press, 1984.

To understand Moneo's theory of composition, it is necessary to appreciate some of the discussions in the late 1960s and early 1970s about changes in thinking that arose broadly as a reaction to the philosophical consequences of the Enlightenment.

The high esteem in which architects held Gilles Deleuze's notes on Gottfried Leibnitz (written in order to justify their formal experiments in the 1990s),[61] have obscured Deleuze's more substantial work on his contemporary, that other great baroque rationalist philosopher Baruch Spinoza.[62] Deleuze's interest in revisiting Spinoza in the late 1960s can be seen as a discordant but timely initiative that was soon followed by other energetic Marxist thinkers such as Antonio Negri. According to the latter, in the 1970s, Spinoza became an ontological lifeline to whom it was possible to cling amid the crisis of Marxist thinking, presenting an alternative to structuralism and the dead-end that Althusser's critique of ideology had reached.[63] The newly recovered Spinoza offered an ontology that, as Negri remarks, 'reveals itself to be an anthropology', because it refers back to human experience in its most mundane reality.[64]

Within this redefinition of human experience, the body will have a central role for Deleuze, suggesting an understanding of the composition of bodies that can be expanded to assist in the interpretation of other, larger, 'bodies' – such as works of architecture. In Deleuze's reading, Spinoza anticipates and responds to what is to come at the end of the era of transcendental certainty, making him a figure of particular contemporary relevance, because of his special conception of the individual. According to Deleuze:

---

61 Gilles Deleuze, *The Fold: Leibniz and the Baroque*, trans. Tom Conley, Minneapolis: University of Minnesota Press, 1993 (originally published in French in 1988).

62 The work was mainly written in the late 1960s and early 1970s: Gilles Deleuze, *Expressionism in Philosophy: Spinoza*, trans. Martin Joughin, New York: Zone Books, 1990 (first published in French in 1968), and Gilles Deleuze, *Spinoza: Practical Philosophy*, trans. Robert Hurley, San Francisco: City Lights, 1988 (first published in French in 1970, and revised and expanded 1981).

63 Antonio Negri, *Subversive Spinoza: (Un)Contemporary Variations*, trans. Timothy S. Murphy, Manchester: Manchester University Press, 2004, pp. 94–5. On the question of Althusser see Gilles Deleuze, *En Medio de Spinoza*, trans. Equipo Editorial Cáctus, Buenos Aires: Editorial Cactus, 2008, p. 8 (a compilation of Gilles Deleuze's lectures on Spinoza, given at the University of Vincennes, 1980–81, translated from a recording at the National Library of France). It should be noted that Spinoza was already popular in Spain because of the work of Miguel de Unamuno.

64 Negri, *Subversive Spinoza*, p. 98.

> In Spinoza individuals are relationships not substances. There are no sum-
> matories, no additions. There are compositions of relations or decomposi-
> tions of relations.[65]

Elaborating further on Spinoza's theory of individuation, Deleuze adds that compositions are either relations, potentials or gradients, but in every case 'all turns on the same intuition of individuals not being substances'.[66]

The consequences of such an end to the individual as substance are highly relevant in defining the ethos of the late baroque period, and Spinoza's par-ticular position within it, which became so relevant in the 1970s. In other words, at the beginning of the Age of Reason, the individual is not positioned in a transcendental horizon, but in an ethical one. And it is this ethical ho-rizon that provides an existential grounding; within such a framework they can still compose and recompose their own beings as relations, affects and actions, in the effort and enjoyment of their own lives. According to Deleuze's reading of Spinoza, at the beginning of the end of transcendence the individ-ual gains both autonomy and vulnerability, but has an ethical tool to deal with this – namely composition.

Since Ancient Greece, the human body has been understood as the major point of reference for the fashioning of architecture, for its symmetry and systems of proportion. The organic relationship of part to whole so evident in renaissance theory and practice was derived from a certain transcendental understanding of the human body – the body as substance that, in its perfec-tion, relates back to a transcendental infinitude. Deleuze refers to the work of Nicholas of Cusa in discussing this understanding of proportion,[67] a concept that would prove to have a significant influence on the aesthetic theories of Leon Battista Alberti, the most influential proponent of architectural organi-cism.[68] Formal grammatical rules inherited from Alberti clearly survived into

---

65   Gilles Deleuze, *En Medio de Spinoza*, p. 335.

66   Ibid., p. 366.

67   Ibid., p. 367.

68   On the relationship between Alberti and De Cusa, see Giovanni Santinello, 'Nicolo Cusano e Leon Battista Alberti, Pensieri sul bello e su L'arte', in *Nicoló da Cusa: Relazioni tenute al Convegno In-ternazionale di Bressanone nel 1960*, Florence: Sansoni Editore, 1962, pp. 147–83. See also, in English, Graziella Federici Vescovini, 'Nicholas of Cusa, Alberti and the Architectonics of the Mind', in *Nexus II: Architecture and Mathematics*, Fucecchio: Edizioni Dell'erba, 1998, pp. 159–71.

the twentieth century in Le Corbusier's modulor and Frank Lloyd Wright's organic principles.[69] This is why Spinoza's subtle redefinition of the human body, avoiding substance and devoid of transcendental aims, could cause the revolution in architectural conventions[70] that Emil Kaufmann so faithfully pursued in his *Architecture in the Age of Reason* (1995): he needs to return to the baroque to find the basis of rationalist architecture epitomized by a new non-organic composition – a journey that will be traced further below.[71]

Neither Kaufmann nor Moneo quote Spinoza directly in their texts, but his influence is inescapable when the notion of composition is reassessed. In fact, Moneo himself is well-acquainted with Spinoza's *Ethica*,[72] and, when he

69 This issue was so important to Moneo that he devoted two lessons to it in his Elements of Composition course. Rafael Moneo, 'Lección 6: El Modelo orgánico. El Principio de Coherencia', 'Lección 7: El Modelo orgánico: Teoría de las Proporciones', in *Programa de Elementos de Composición*, pp. 10–13.

70 The choice of Spinoza rather than Leibniz (as is more common in German-speaking philosophy in the following centuries) to conceptualize the human body in the baroque period implies a different cultural understanding of the transition from renaissance to baroque, to that canonically expressed in texts such as Heinrich Wölfflin's *Renaissance und Barock* (1888). Such an interpretation, as opposed to the one argued for here, is well explained by Jeffrey Kipnis in the following fragment: 'In *Renaissance and Baroque*, Wölfflin places part to whole effects at the center of the distinction between the two architectural styles, the former calling attention to the parts as they harmonize into wholes, the latter dissolving part into whole. Then, calling upon the power of part/whole to resonate with other discourses, he elaborates the historical-stylistic distinction into what he sees as its deeper cultural consequence: two simultaneous but incompatible understandings of the human body. Renaissance architecture produces the body as an ensemble of parts in orderly relation to one another, the baroque as an indivisible, fluid whole.' Jeffrey Kipnis, 'Cincinnati Impressions' in *Morphosis IV*, New York: Rizzoli, 2006, p. 17.

71 The link that Kaufmann wanted to establish between Ledoux and Kant, as part of his search for rational founding principles for the discipline of architecture, has been frequently stressed. It is particularly clear in his well-known *Von Ledoux bis Le Corbusier*, first published in 1933. (See, for instance, Anthony Vidler, 'Neoclassical Modernism: Emil Kaufmann', in *Histories of the Immediate Present: Inventing Architectural Modernism*, Cambridge Mass.: MIT Press, 2008, pp. 17–60). However, young Italian architects such as Aldo Rossi were the first to notice that Kaufmann's central concern in his search for a rationalist architecture was more evident in his reading of the neoclassical baroque; he therefore valued *Architecture in the Age of Reason: Baroque and Post-Baroque in England, Italy and France* (1995) more than his work on Ledoux. These origins of rationalist architecture, to be found in the baroque and late baroque, are closer to the thought of philosophers such as Spinoza than to that of Kant, as is so often claimed, when discussing Kaufmann's work. Emil Kaufmann, *Architecture in the Age of Reason*, Cambridge, Mass.: Harvard University Press, 1955.

72 Moneo knows Spinoza mainly from the interpretation of Miguel Unamuno, as Spinoza's *Ethica* is central to Unamuno's *The Tragic Sense of Life* (1913). According to Moneo, Unamuno's book was one of most important for him during his youth and early intellectual formation (from an interview with Rafael Moneo conducted by Francisco González de Canales, 5 December 2012). Miguel de Unamuno,

sees the excesses of some Dutch architects in Portugal, he likes to remind us
that this is not the proper way to repay Spinoza's gift from Portugal to the
Netherlands.[73]

Even though debates about architectural composition had occurred in
post-war academic circles in Europe, Moneo was unusual, in the late 1960s,
when he prepared for his candidacy for the Elements of Composition professorship, in taking composition seriously as a discipline that ultimately
derived from the Beaux Arts. With the easing of restrictions under Franco's
dictatorship from 1956, the academic tradition of architectural education
was generally regarded as obsolete. From the inauguration of the Escuela
Técnica Superior de Arquitectura (Superior Technical School of Architecture)
in Madrid the following year, the attempts to update architectural education
to address the issues raised by the modern movement were fragmentary and
on an individual and somewhat incoherent basis. The various Beaux-Arts inspired courses therefore still retained their titles. It might have been expected
that an architect of Moneo's generation, trained as he was in the core of the
new School of Madrid under Sáenz de Oíza, with its aim of renovating architecture to accord with the principles of post-war modernism, would use his
first years as a teacher as an opportunity to update the syllabus, and thereby
address the new social, economic and political conditions in Spain with an
overt celebration of modern architecture. But Moneo ignored that assumption and decided to accept the syllabus he inherited. In this way, he sought to
re-examine the potential virtues of the Beaux-Arts tradition from a contemporary viewpoint.

Moneo's interest in composition as a design tool was not a transient phenomenon concocted in response to the Elements of Composition competition, but remained a consistent interest throughout his career. It is characteristic that the only two books for which he provided prefaces in the early
1970s and 1980s were related in some way to the question of composition:

The Tragic Sense of Life, trans. J. E. Crawford Flitch, New York: Dover Publications, 1954 (originally
published in Spanish in 1913).

73   The statement by Moneo has been recorded at least twice: in November 2002 during the II Encuentro Luso-Español held at Salamanca; and in the lecture 'Casa da Musica. Rem Koolhaas', as part of
his course On Contemporary Architecture (Harvard Graduate School of Design, Cambridge, Mass.,
spring 2007).

79 Jean-Nicolas-Louis Durand: illustration from his *Précis des leçons d'architecture données à l'École royale polytechnique*, 1809

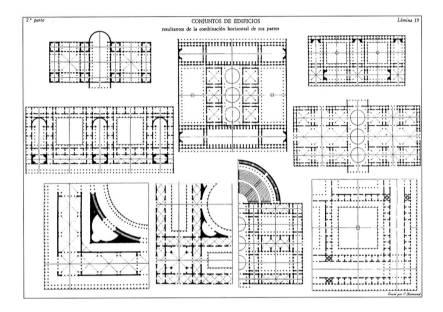

Emil Kaufmann's *Architecture in the Age of Reason*, and Jean-Nicolas-Louis Durand's *Précis des leçons d'architecture* (fig. 79). Both appear within the bibliography of Moneo's Elements of Composition course, together with other canonical texts of the Beaux-Arts such as Julien Guadet's *Éléments et théories de l'architecture*.[74]

Moneo's recuperation of Durand, or Quatremère de Quincy, in the mid-1960s was part of his aim of establishing a specific territory for architecture as a discipline that could be seen through the lens of reason, an attitude that was prevalent in Italian architects of 'La Tendenza'. As Moneo stated, if Wittkower's *Architecture in the Age of Humanism* was mandatory reading for architects in the Smithsons' circle in the 1950s, Kaufmann's *Architecture in the Age of Reason* would be fundamental to the architects around Aldo Rossi in the 1960s. Kaufmann's book is an attempt to identify, through a study of the late eighteenth century, how the discipline could be formed that derived not from a transcendent order, which presumed a relationship between the whole

74 Moneo, *Programa de Curso de Elementos de Composición*, p. 2.

and the parts that was derived eventually from divine authority (as did the architecture of the renaissance and baroque periods), but from the exercise of human reason. If architectural history is a body of knowledge that provides architects with a repertoire of solutions that have been previously tested – a way of incorporating the experience of others into their designs – architects require an instrument to integrate this repertoire into their projects. A theory of composition is required for an architecture that is made of many parts.

As Moneo understood his aims, Kaufmann tried to prove that 'architecture is voluntarily established by men from what constitutes the authentic core of the discipline, composition.'[75] What is at stake in this redefinition of composition is not only the independence of architecture from naturalist principles, but also its liberation from the eschatological ideas that ensnared it in a tyranny of the whole. Kaufmann's investigation into the compositional methods of the eighteenth century showed how the independent autonomy of a building's elements negated Alberti's famous definition of beauty as 'that reasoned harmony of all parts within a body, so that nothing may be added, taken away or altered, but for the worse'.[76] The freedom of Piranesi's composition in his reconstruction of the Campo Marzio plan, or the way in which Lecqueu understands façade as collage, are examples of a new attitude, the origins of which Kaufmann traces back to the late baroque in England, Italy and France. Buildings made up of different parts that respond to different compositional needs can be seen in the work of an architect like Nicholas Hawksmoor, whose Christ Church, Spitalfields, in London (1714–29) can be understood as a rebellion of the individual parts over the whole. It is with Durand, however, that this idea finds its fulfilment, since, according to Moneo, he is the 'great populariser of the new *maniera*', whilst he clearly strips the architecture of classicism of any of its transcendental aims.[77]

It was precisely for this reason that Durand came to be seen as representative of all that architecture should not be – namely devoid of transcendental aims – by those who wanted the discipline to be re-fashioned within

75 Moneo, 'Prólogo a la edición española', in Kaufmann, *La Arquitectura de la Ilustración*, p. ix.
76 Leon Battista Alberti, *De Re Aedificatoria: On the Art of Building in Ten Books*, trans. Joseph Rykwert, Robert Tavernor and Neil Leach, Cambridge, Mass.: MIT Press, 1988, p. 156 (book vi, chapter 2).
77 Moneo, 'Prólogo a la edición española', in Kaufmann, *La Arquitectura de la Ilustración*, p. xxiv.

a phenomenological frame of reference. Joseph Rykwert, for example, explained that Durand, as the most influential teacher of the discipline in his day, achieved his aim of making architecture a rational science at the expense of 'sacrificing most of the matters which were the meat of architectural theory before his time'. Rykwert continues:

> For his part, he was able to formulate, once and for all time, the permanent principles of architecture framed in terms of both structural analysis and geometrical composition. His formulae were widely applied, and his pragmatic teaching methods are the source of many of our troubles today.[78]

Alberto Pérez-Gómez, discussing in particular Durand's use of geometry, is even more explicit in blaming him for a reduced vision of what architecture involves:

> In Durand's theory, number and geometry finally discarded their symbolic connotations. From now on, proportional systems would have the character of technical instruments, and the geometry applied to design would act merely as a vehicle for ensuring its efficiency. Geometrical forms lost their cosmological reverberations; they were uprooted from the *Lebenswelt* and their traditional symbolic horizon, and they became instead signs of technological values. This in turn led to the geometry of the Bauhaus, the International Style, and the Modern Movement, which was essentially the undifferentiated product of a technological world view. As part of a theory that cast off metaphysical speculation, the simple and anonymous geometry of most contemporary architecture speaks only to a technological process, not to the world of man.[79]

But, as shall become apparent, Moneo's view is more charitable. For him, Durand's methodology is useful, but of course it is not in itself sufficient. Many other factors are involved in creating architecture, so as a complete answer it is quite inadequate.

---

78   Joseph Rykwert, *The First Moderns: The Architects of the Eighteenth Century*, Cambridge, Mass.: MIT Press, 1980, pp. 469–70.

79   Alberto Pérez-Gómez, *Architecture and the Crisis of Modern Science*, Cambridge, Mass.: MIT Press, 1983, p. 311.

Durand embraced this instrumental notion of an architecture made by an assembly of parts in order that it could respond to new programmatic requirements. 'Composition' allowed architecture to be freed from the necessity of being conceived as a whole, so that in turn it could become a tool to enable the construction of emerging institutions such as the hospitals, prisons, schools, arsenals, warehouses and ports that were needed in a post-revolutionary France. Liberated from closed traditional types, the combination of parts can deal with any particular need. Durand's pragmatism, his ambition to respond to current social and economic conditions rather than submit to conventional ideals and traditions, stimulates his most important contribution to architecture – the organization of parts and elements of a building as an ordering system that supersedes a global or unitary conception.

Clearly an architecture that is composed of parts allows the legibility of the individual elements that are to be manipulated. For Moneo, these elements are not *a priori*, as in the neo-Kantian approach of Colin Rowe in his essay *The Mathematics of the Ideal Villa*, which was to be so influential on the compositional procedures of some of his pupils, such as Peter Eisenman.[80] As Moneo wrote:

The 'Elements of Composition' cannot therefore be today's starting point *a priori*. It is rather the reverse: the analysis of reality will enable us to discern what the 'Elements of Architecture' are and, once these are known, to propose a methodological basis for their use.

Durand discovered his elements in architectural history. As a taxonomist, he attempts to break with the idea of *maniera* by systematically and scientifically listing architectural precedents.[81] Just as Moneo was to do, Durand believed that the lessons of history should be judged worthy of incorporation

80   Colin Rowe, 'The Mathematics of the Ideal Villa: Palladio and Le Corbusier Compared', in *The Architectural Review* 101, March 1947, pp. 101–4 (subsequently reprinted in *The Mathematics of the Ideal Villa and other Essays*, Cambridge, Mass.: MIT Press, 1976).

81   In one of his most polemical and well-known etchings, Durand shows St Peter's in Rome as an example of an error in architectural references and the way of appropriating them: the basilica and the cloister had not been used in a rational way, and Durand argues provocatively that this arbitrariness caused wars and calamities in Europe. J.-N.-L. Durand, 'Example des funestes effets qui résulten de l'ignorance ou l'inobservation des vrais principes de l'Architecture', in *Précis des leçons d'architecture données à l'École Royale Polytechnique* (1802–5), facsimile edition, Paris: L'Ecole Royale Polytechnique,

according to how well they were applied to designs in the past. Moneo quotes approvingly from Durand's *Précis*: 'It is necessary to study the ancients through the lens of reason, instead of, as is frequently done, suppressing reason under the authority of the ancients.'[82]

But though Moneo celebrates Durand's pragmatism and clear-sighted rationalism, he criticizes his attempt to make architecture an entirely rational science, and his stripping of the architectural language of any reference to the material conditions of construction.[83] Once again, Moneo stresses that the true knowledge of architecture arises not out of paper projects of successful designs, but from the physical experience of the buildings themselves in all their material presence.

In this sense, the way in which architecture is engendered, according to Moneo's view of 'composition', runs contrary to the traditional modernist notion of 'the project' as a design method. Whilst composition relies on the architect's experience and knowledge, the term 'project' implies what is foreseen, and is based on speculation. The 'project' always aspires to some ideal that is yet to be realised and thus is eminently characteristic of modernity – literally attempting to 'project ideas into the future'. 'Composition', on the other hand, is content to make use of pre-existing elements, however transformed they may be to accommodate present circumstances. This idea of composition, and suspicion of gratuitous invention, was prevalent in the thinking of Aldo Rossi, a formative influence on Moneo from the late 1960s, as remarked, especially following his contact with Manuel de Solà-Morales and his appointment to the professorship in Barcelona in the 1970s. Some of Moneo's most important texts dealing with contemporary architects were concerned with the study of the Milanese architect, just as he was publishing on Durand. At that time, Rossi described the architecture of the city as made of parts, which was congruent with his fundamental political agenda, and he communicated this idea through his teaching at the Swiss Federal Institute of Technology (ETH) at Zurich from 1972–5, where the notion of composition became central.

1819, p. 71 (English edition: *Precis of the Lectures on Architecture, with Graphic Portion of the Lectures on Architecture*, trans. David Britt, Los Angeles: Getty Research Institute, 2000).

82 Rafael Moneo, 'Prólogo', in *Compendio de lecciones de Arquitectura: Parte gráfica de los cursos de Arquitectura*, Madrid,: Pronaos 1981, p. vi.

83 Ibid., pp. vii–viii.

One result of this teaching was 'La Città analoga', an exhibition at the 1976
Venice Biennale in collaboration with some young Swiss architects (fig. 80).
'La Città analoga' is entirely a matter of composition: a city that develops and
grows by taking up and transforming elements of its own past. Again, this is
an architecture based more on a knowledge of its past than speculation on an
uncertain future. Moneo is similarly critical of approaches that participate
in the modernist myth of utopia and revolution, proposing a radical techno-
cratic architecture,[84] and instead embraces the discipline of 'composition' as
a way of generating an architecture that could deal with real conditions, real
problems and real contexts. That this is a firmly held ethical position is clear
in the following statement:

> To recover the authentic dimension of design is, to our minds, necessary
> in the current situation, in which the profession oscillates dangerously
> between an absolutely degraded pragmatism, based on a dubious profes-
> sional institutionalization, and a utopianism expressed in highly diverse
> ways, ranging from personal escapism to the most ludicrous and credulous
> dreams of a redemptive technology.[85]

'Composition', or the possibility of an architecture made from different parts,
is what provides Moneo with the essential flexibility that was not permitted
in organic functionalist models of the 1960s. If composition for Durand was
the necessary freedom to respond to the diverse programmes of nineteenth-
century society, for Moneo in the twentieth century it provided the possibility
of incorporating existing reality and, more importantly, history and context.
A shift away from the 'modern organicism' of the school of Madrid can be
seen in Moneo's work by the end of the 1960s. By that time, the systematic
nature of designs such as those for the Diestre Transformer Factory and the

---

84   Two very important critiques were to be made, from opposite positions of the techno-utopian and
     technocratic architectures of the 1960s and 1970s – one neoliberal, from Colin Rowe and his pupils, and
     the other Marxist, from Manfredo Tafuri. A sense of each can be gained from Colin Rowe, 'Introduc-
     tion' in *Five Architects*, New York: Wittenborn, 1972, and Manfredo Tafuri, 'Design and Techno Utopia'
     in Emilio Ambasz, *Italy: The New Domestic Landscape*, New York: MoMA, 1972. The critique of uto-
     pia was later expanded by both in Colin Rowe and Fred Koetter, *Collage City*, Cambridge, Mass.: MIT
     Press, 1978, and Manfredo Tafuri, *Architecture and Utopia, Design and Capitalist Development*, trans.
     Barbara Luigi La Penta, Cambridge, Mass.: MIT Press, 1976 (originally published in Italian in 1973).
85   Moneo, 'Prólogo', in *Compendio de lecciones de Arquitectura*, p. ii.

80 Aldo Rossi, with E. Consolascio,
B. Reichlin and F. Reinhart: illustration
from 'La Città analoga', exhibited at the
1976 Venice Biennale – a city of composition

Amsterdam Town Hall Competition, or the restrained yet organic designs for the house at La Moraleja or the schools at Tudela, had been replaced by work that attempted to respond to the complexities of urban context and contemporary programmes by a composition of separate parts: paradigmatic amongst these was the Bankinter headquarters in Madrid (pp. 111–17), Moneo's masterpiece of the 1970s.

From the 1970s onwards, Moneo's compositional flexibility enabled him to incorporate a plural experience of history, and to recycle architectural elements that have been successfully used in the past in carefully considered compositions to meet the needs of the present. This unprejudiced eclecticism, avoiding modernist dogmas, including the organicism of Moneo's own formative years, became a leit-motif of his subsequent career. As numerous published examples illustrate, any analysis of his work recognizes the motifs from history that Moneo has appropriated and reinterpreted.[86] The Soanian domes at Atocha have already been noted – they also occur at Don Benito. Kahn's lantern is quoted in Stockholm, and again in Houston. The inside-outside condition of the equestrian figure in Scarpa's Castelvecchio appears in the cathedral at Los Angeles with its cross-like skylight above the altar, and late Le Corbusier is referenced at the portico of the LISE at Harvard (fig. 81). The Asplund-influenced balustrades and Terragni elementarism in Logroño, and the Sullivan-like ornamentation and Aaltoesque brickwork at Bankinter have aleady been noted, together with elements from the contemporaries that Moneo most admired such as Rossi, Stirling or Venturi.

More importantly, compositional freedom according to Moneo allows the architect not only to incorporate historical and contemporary motifs, but any of the other constraints imposed by clients who expect solutions to their complex programmes, the intricacies of particular sites, municipal regulations, relationships with urban conditions, cultural factors and the disciplines of construction and budget. Composition should allow that freedom to meet all these necessary commitments without betraying the rationale of the design. According to Moneo it is crucial for architects that such contingent conditions are not neglected, but grasped as creative opportunities. One of the most important aspects of the Bankinter project was that it represented the first time that Moneo's reflections on the role of composition reached their full potential. If Hawksmoor's Christ Church in Spitalfields finds, in its unrestrained superimposition of different architectural elements, a way to deal with the scales of the mundane and the divine through its tripartite structure, Bankinter can be said to articulate the overlaying scales of the human,

86   Two early reflections on Moneo's appropriations, among many that would come later, can be found in Daniele Vitale, 'Rafael Moneo, Architect: Designs and Works', *Lotus International* 33: 4, 1981, pp. 67–70, and Antón Capitel, 'Apuntes sobre la Obra de Rafael Moneo', *Arquitectura* 236, 1982, pp. 9–17. But the first author to notice the characteristic was Juan Daniel Fullaondo, in his 'Notas de Sociedad' written for the *Nueva Forma* monograph on Moneo in 1975: Juan Daniel Fullaondo, 'Notas de Sociedad', *Nueva Forma* 108, pp. 2-13.

81 Rafael Moneo: LISE building, Harvard, 2000–7. The treatment of what are in fact large rooflights to the space below references the late work of Le Corbusier

the building itself and the context of the city, through a masterful composition of parts within a coherent entity.

Such compositional freedom (and indeed virtuosity) was to be an integral component of Moneo's future work. Even buildings that seem to depend on a more cohesive overall formal strategy, such as the National Museum of Roman Art at Mérida, L'Illa Diagonal building in Barcelona, or the Kursaal in San Sebastián, rely on a mastery of composition. The way in which each relates to different scales, urban or landscape conditions, or differing layers of historical fabric, as at Mérida, is always by means of a composition of parts. Nevertheless, Moneo resists the temptation to indulge in an excess of fragmentation – he recognizes the need for a certain consistency, and a structuring of the building as a whole in a way that can establish its identity within the city. This was a problem that Durand also faced, as the foremost exponent of composition as the expression of the principles of the Enlightenment. He solved it by the use of an undifferentiated grid – the precedent, as Rykwert lamented, for all the modernist grids – proposed as a primary ordering device for all other elements. But a grid *per se*, as an endless isotropic extension of modernity, while it might be an instrumental diagram to enable the architect to lay out architectural elements freely, also erases the relational consistency of architectural form, the interior/exterior division of space, and the hierarchy and order of any structured formal entity, and makes little contribution to its understanding on a human scale. These drawbacks finally forced Durand to recommend that his students adopt axial baroque principles for the organization of their buildings. Moneo explains eloquently how it must have created a 'resigned and melancholy sadness' for his advocates, such as Kaufmann, who acknowledged 'that the great populariser of Neoclassicism in architecture, Durand, distant and strange father of so many modest provincial Works, was forced to admit, and even to recommend, those compositional criteria typical of the "baroque" system, against which he had valiantly fought across an entire century'.[87]

87   Moneo, 'Prólogo a la edición Española', in Kaufmann, *La Arquitectura de la Ilustración*, p. xxv.

By Formalism I do not mean what the term is usually taken to describe: belief in the availability of a deductive or quasi-deductive method capable of giving determinate solutions to particular problems of legal choice. Formalism in this context is a commitment to, and therefore also a belief in the possibility of, a method of legal justification that contrasts with open-ended disputes about basic terms of social life, disputes that the people call ideological, philosophical or visionary.[88]

Roberto Mangabeira Unger

In one of his famous lectures at Harvard University, the political theorist Roberto Mangabeira Unger identified more than seven different types of 'formalism'. In a careful analysis, Mangabeira Unger dismantled the claims of those who believe that is possible to conceive of form as an *a priori*, impersonal and neutral structure of discrimination, highlighting the plurality of ways in which this notion of form might be understood, by pointing to the different ideological, philosophical and cultural positions to be found in its subtext.[89] In this aspiration to conceive an immanence of form – dismantled here by Mangabeira Unger – it is not difficult to see a reference to those social scientists who followed the path of anthropologist Claude Levi-Strauss in the 1950s and 1960s, and whose ultimate aspiration would be, in his own words:

the elaboration of a universal code capable of expressing the common features of specific structures. Such a code could be legitimately applied both to a single system and to the totality.[90]

The implications of this social thinking cannot be underestimated in other fields. In architecture, the investigation of this 'code' went beyond an interest in revisiting the architecture of the Enlightenment,[91] and eventually resulted

---

88 Roberto Mangabeira Unger, *The Critical Legal Studies Movement*, Cambridge, Mass.: Harvard University Press, 1983, p. 1.

89 We would like to thank Juan Luis Rodríguez for this reference to Robert Mangabeira Unger's speech at Harvard.

90 Claude Lévi-Strauss, *Structural Anthropology*, London: Penguin, 1968, p. 71.

91 Aldo Rossi was not only interested in revisiting Quatremère de Quincy, Durand and other architects who became relevant to the debates of the period for the definition of a universal and scientific architecture. He was also particularly interested in Boullée. A clear example of this notion of immanence

in a debate about whether certain building typologies could be discerned as ahistorical structures in the city. In the early 1960s, this approach was openly embraced and promoted, as noted above, by the group of young Italian architects known as 'La Tendenza' (Aldo Rossi, Giorgio Grassi and Carlo Aymonino), who were to prove so influential on Moneo.[92] Having 'de-composed' his architecture into separate elements, Moneo still faced the same problem as Durand – how to give an internal consistency and order to a design made of diverse parts.[93] He sought for such a consistency in formal explorations that represented his own approach to the notion of typology from the late 1960s. However, his understanding of architectural form was personal and went beyond the debates on typology typical of the times, as he later made clear in his celebrated essay *On Typology*. For Moneo, in general, form is not merely the figurative appearance of a building, but is the structure of those relationships that are inherent in any design, and serve to articulate its spaces and define its character not only internally but also in the context of the city.

Debates on form during the 1960s and 1970s were heated in the light of the perceived inadequacies of modernism, and two predominant trends can be identified. On the one hand there was the group of young Italian architects mentioned above, including Rossi, Grassi and Aymonino, who intensified

of form occurs in one of the quotations by Boullée to be found in Rossi's *Architecture of the City*: 'A sphere, at all times, is equal only to itself; it is the perfect symbol of equality.' Rossi adds: 'The symbol of the sphere thus can sum up an architecture and its principles; at a same time, it can be the very condition for its being constructed, its motive. The sphere not only represents – or rather, does not represent, in itself – the idea of equality; its presence as a sphere, and thus as a monument, is the constituting equality.' Rossi, *The Architecture of the City*, p. 114.

92   In his 1972 course Moneo reveals a substantial knowledge of all the relevant publications on the topic, including among others, Carlo Aymonino's *Aspetti e problema della tipología edilizia* (1964) and *La Formazione del concetto di tipología edilizia* (1965); Aldo Rossi's *Aspetti della tipología residenziale di Berlino* (1964), *L'Architettura della Città* (1966), *Raporti fra la morfologia urbana e la tipología edilizia* (1966), and Georgio Grassi's *La construzione lógica dell'architettura* (1967).

93   Having rejected Durand's recommendation to employ axes and symmetries, Moneo had to follow a different path. In the late 1960s and early 1970s, in common with a number of other architects, Moneo became interested in the linguistic analogy whereby the grammar and syntax of architecture could be described, illustrations of which can be found in the work of the New York Five. Linguistic coherence could be a way to give this consistency to the parts, but language was only of temporary use to Moneo as an aid in understanding the overall coherence of design, and he soon searched for alternatives. Rafael Moneo, 'Lección 14. Arquitectura y Lenguaje: La analogía Arquitectura Lenguaje: ventajas que ofrece', in *Programa de Elementos de Composición*, p. 22.

and radicalized the work of their predecessors, Giuseppe De Finetti, Ernesto Nathan Rogers, Rogelio Samonà, Ludovico Quaroni and Saverio Muratori. Their interest in form was predominantly in the way it survived through time in the city, in the complex dialectical relation between building typology and urban morphology. On the other hand there were those architects who took up the challenge of Colin Rowe, whose analysis concentrated on the 'flesh', as it were, of modern architecture, while abandoning its 'morality'. These would include, in different ways, James Stirling, Peter Eisenman and other members of the so-called 'New York Five'. Moneo, characteristically, was interested in both attitudes in relation to architectural form, and made particular studies of the work of Rossi, Gregotti, Stirling, Hejduk and Eisenman. But he refused to align himself with either position, and remained critical of aspects of Rossi's and Eisenman's stance.[94] In his practice he absorbed only those elements of their work that were useful and relevant to the problem at hand.

The background to Moneo's position on form, as for other issues, was his reflection on how the discipline of architecture should have been absorbing new ideas that emerged in the human sciences after the Second World War. Amongst those ideas, the most influential was probably structuralism, which attempted to reconstruct a scientific epistemology based on diachronic invariables. Applied to architectural problems, it suggested that it was possible to find relevant historical precedents for contemporary practice. Based as it may have been on principles of dialectical opposition derived from Marx, structuralism sought to explain complex socio-cultural issues.[95] Even though the methodology emerged from linguistics, particularly the work of Ferdinand de Saussure, Claude Lévi-Strauss was responsible for popularizing it in his social and anthropological studies, and it was sociology and anthropology rather

94 Moneo was also critical of those younger Spanish architects who tried to follow either of these approaches in a literal and unreflective way.
95 The French anthropologist Claude Lévi-Strauss' *The Structure of Kinship* (1949) can be said to have initiated structuralism by appropriating Saussure's structural organization of language into the social sciences. For Lévi-Strauss, social sciences needed models capable of revealing those underlying and immanent mechanisms that order social life. A clear introduction to the basis of Lévi-Strauss' thinking can be found in Vincent Descombes, *Modern French Philosophy*, trans. L. Scott-Fox and J. M. Harding, Paris: Minuit, 1980, pp. 77–109 (originally published in French in 1979).

than linguistics that most attracted young architects such as Aldo Rossi.[96] Since Moneo was attracted intellectually to the kinds of dialectical tensions that structuralism investigates, he was more sympathetic theoretically to the formal positions of the young Italians such as Rossi than to the neo-Kantian or neo-liberal approach represented by the followers of Colin Rowe, which is not to say that he would not borrow from them in his own architectural compositions.

Moneo's attraction to the thinking of Aldo Rossi, from the late 1960s onwards, is revealed in his teaching and a series of writings that show a deep assimilation of the work of this Milanese architect and of the ideas of La Tendenza.[97] The influence of his friend and frequent collaborator Manuel de Solà-Morales can also hardly be exaggerated: from the time that they first met in 1968 onwards, Solà-Morales' interest in the city enlarged Moneo's own view considerably.[98] Moneo had not engaged as much with Rossi's theories during

96   In 'The Structure of Urban Artifacts', the first chapter of *The Architecture of the City*, Rossi credits Claude Lévi-Strauss as his inspiration for a new way of looking at urban experience, and also quotes the works of sociologist Maurice Halbwachs (specifically notions such as 'collective memory' that he had coined earlier on) as arising out of it. It is therefore neither architects nor historians, but Halbwachs, followed by other social scientists such as the human geographer Max Sorre, who turn out to be the most cited authors in *The Architecture of the City*. See Rossi, *The Architecture of the City*, p. 33.

97   His most well-known text on Rossi emerged from his teaching in Barcelona, 'La Idea de Arquitectura en Rossi y el Cementerio de Módena, Barcelona: Cátedra de Elementos de Composición', *Monografía* 4, Ediciones de la ETSAB, 1974 (English edition: Aldo Rossi, 'The Idea of Architecture and the Modena Cemetery', *Oppositions* 5, 1976, pp. 1–30). Amongst many later reflections on Rossi are those in local Barcelona journals such as 'Gregotti y Rossi', Arq*uitecturas Bis* 4, November 1974, pp. 1–4, and 'La obra reciente de Aldo Rossi: dos reflexiones', in *2C Construcción de la Ciudad* 14, December 1979, pp. 38–41; the postscript for the first full monograph on Rossi: *Aldo Rossi: Works and Projects*, New York: Rizzoli, 1985, pp. 310–17. More recently, in the 1990s, his lecture on Rossi at Harvard GSD appeared as a chapter in his *Theoretical Anxiety and Design Strategies in the Work of Eight Contemporary Architects*, Cambridge, Mass.: MIT Press, 2004.

98   It was during Moneo's examination in Madrid for the ETSA of Barcelona Professorship in Urbanism. Solà-Morales was a similar age to Moneo and like him had been in Rome, but he had also studied at the Harvard GSD under the Catalan exile Josep Lluis Sert. In Spain, Solà-Morales continued the traditional Barcelona–Milan axis already established by previous generations of Catalan architects, and became interested in the theories of the young Milanese architects such as Vittorio Gregotti and Aldo Rossi, whose most important books, respectively *Il Territorio dell'Architettura* ('The Territory of Architecture') and *The Architecture of the City*, were both published in 1966. Vittorio Gregotti, *Il Territorio dell'Architettura*, Milan: Feltrinelli, 1966. The book was never translated into English. However some excerpts can be found in: Vittorio Gregotti, 'Architecture, Environment, Nature,' in Joan Ockman (ed.), *Architecture Culture 1943–1968: A Documentary Anthology*, New York: Rizzoli, 1993, pp. 399–401; 'The Form of the Territory,' trans. Walter van der Star, in *OASE* 80: *On Territories*, Spring, 2010,

his first stay in Rome, when he was principally influenced by his contact with the ideas of historians such as Bruno Zevi and the young Manfredo Tafuri. In 1968, the year they met, Solà-Morales founded the *Laboratori d'urbanisme* at the ETSAB, which reinterpreted many of the ideas coming from Milan for a Spanish sensibility. Both Solà-Morales and Moneo avoided a direct appropriation, and therefore distanced themselves from the more militant followers of Rossi in Spain.[99] Moneo frequently criticized the work of Rossi's followers as mimetic of his buildings and their imagery, but unfaithful to his ideas, which were not fully understood.[100] In contrast, Moneo stressed that architectural form was to be seen not 'as an enjoyable object or an expression of the formal will of a period, but as a definition of the rules that govern the relationship between elements' – a system of relations that, as has been demonstrated, relates to the structuralist theories of the period.[101] In fact, Rossi's most profound concept in his *Architecture of the City*, the notion of *locus*, can be seen to be indebted to the way in which structuralists sought to shape a discipline such as human geography: any particular element of a structural system could have no meaning in itself and would be understood only in relation to the system as a whole.[102] To apply such an epistemology to the city, the first task for Rossi was to propose a distinction in types of space from which formal entities can derive: he divided the city into what he called 'urban artifacts', separate elements that compose its structure. Moneo describes his procedure as follows:

pp. 7–22; 'Territory and Architecture' in Kate Nesbitt (ed.), *Theorizing a New Agenda for Architecture*, New York: Princeton Architectural Press, 1996, pp. 338–44.

99   This was a younger generation of architects such as Salvador Tarragó and Carlos Martí in Catalonia, Antonio Barrionuevo and Francisco Torres in Andalusia, and Cesar Portela in Galicia. Their work is evident in *2C: la Construcción de la Ciudad*, a magazine directed from Barcelona between 1972 and 1985 by Salvador Tarragó and Carlos Martí, and which was mostly devoted to the promotion of Rossi's ideas. Rossi himself chaired the SIAC (Simposio Internacional de Ciudad y Arquitectura / International Symposium of City and Architecture) in Santiago de Compostela in 1976, and in Seville in 1978.

100 Moneo lamented how 'mimetically and monotonously the architecture of La Tendenza had been reproduced until now' in 'Gregotti y Rossi', p. 4.

101 Moneo, 'Gregotti y Rossi', p. 4.

102 While Rossi's thinking is derived from Lévi-Strauss' structural anthropology, it is also supported by particular aspects of the geographer Max Sorre's theory of the division of space, and the notion of 'collective memory' proposed by sociologist Maurice Halbwachs. The work of both is leant on more explicitly by Rossi in *The Architecture of the City*, pp. 103ff.

Rossi begins his description with the elements from which the city is constructed. Once the elements have been established it is possible to grasp the laws by which they are composed and through which they create a more complex reality – the city. For Rossi, the experience of the city is what permits the discovery of these elements, an identification of them as urban artifacts, as an 'unicum', having a value in the whole as well as individually as form in a particular place. These elements are intelligible through memory, not through remembering.[103]

Such a notion of the city made up of distinct formal elements echoes a similar idea found in Kaufmann's analysis of the composition of buildings – in this case transposed to the notion that just as buildings are composed of elements, cities are composed of buildings. This understanding was as important for Moneo as it was for Rossi, and contrasts with the notion of a city that is dissolved into its region as a network or continuous infrastructural system, which prevailed in most of the master-planning projects in Spain in the 1960s and 1970s, and was epitomized in the studies and projects commissioned from Constantinos Doxiadis. From the late 1960s, Moneo consistently opposed such a systematic position, and embraced the distinctions proposed by Rossi, though, as will be seen, the meaning for the two architects is not identical. Rossi argued that the understanding of a city was dependant on its architecture (which he described as 'urban artifacts'), not on its infrastructure (services and transportation). It both receives its significance and communicates its meaning by means of the collective memory of its citizens as they practice their everyday lives. Rossi used the example of the Roman Catholic Church taken from Maurice Halbwachs:

Let us consider for a moment the space of the Catholic religion. Since the Church is indivisible this space covers the whole earth . . . Even in this total and undifferentiated framework, where the idea of space itself is nullified and transcended, 'singular points' exist; these are the places of pilgrimage, the sanctuaries where the faithful enter into more direct communication with God . . . Through their visible parts they signify or indicate the

103 Moneo, 'Aldo Rossi: The Idea of Architecture and the Modena Cemetery', p. 4.

invisible grace that they confer; and because in signifying it they actually confer it, they are potent signs.[104]

Hence any particular Roman Catholic chapel comprised, in its own fragmentary form, the whole body of the Church, understood as the universal Catholic congregation.[105] In a similar way, the formal integrity of any urban artifact is fundamental in aiding the definition of its role in the understanding of the city, which is the congregation of citizens. Hence, in Rossi's theory of *locus*, architecture and the city are structurally interrelated through politics, in its deepest sense: there is an endless dialectical relationship between architectural form, as a stable system, and the citizenry, as an informal and autonomous group of individuals with the capacity for plural and contradictory forms of life. This interaction, between a stabilizing unity and plural diversity, proved to be a potent issue in Moneo's own approach to urban design.

Even though Moneo understood the city as composed of defined urban artifacts, and thus agreed in many respects with Rossi, he never subscribed to such a political reading of the city. Nor did he believe that the architecturally schematic and dogmatic architecture that frequently emerged was the only possible interpretation of Rossi's analysis.[106] And Moneo's architecture distinguishes itself from Rossi's rational idealism and elemental procedures in being always rooted in the material reality of its construction, and the contingencies of the design process. Moneo's political commitment arises out of this necessary compromise with the realities of practice, and can be seen as an ethical stance that prohibits architecture's subjugation to the radical ideas and inflexible ideology of the architect.

Moneo's typological approach first becomes evident in the Urumea building in San Sebastián (1968–71), and morphological approaches to the city deriving from it can also be seen in urban proposals such as the competitions for the refurbishment of Zaragoza city centre (1969–70; fig. 82), which was undertaken with Manuel de Solà-Morales and was awarded second prize, and for the Éibar city centre refurbishment (1972–3; fig. 83). As ever he pursued

104 Aldo Rossi, 'Urban Artifacts', in *The Architecture of the City*, p. 103.

105 Ibid.

106 As he put it, 'Rossi's (architecture) is not the only and inevitable paradigm of his theories, and these have other possible manifestations'. Moneo, 'Gregotti y Rossi', p. 4.

82 Rafael Moneo: second-prize-winning
competition entry with Manuel de
Solà-Morales for the refurbishment of
Zaragoza City Centre, 1969–70

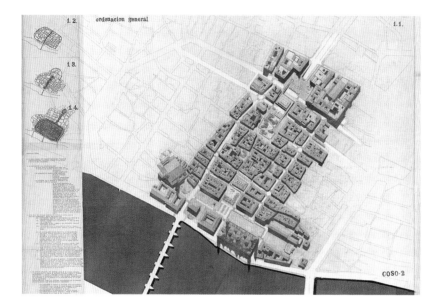

his own design investigations while also teaching and publishing papers that
reflected on questions of composition, the strengths and weaknesses of the
free plan and, in particular, on typology.[107]

By 1978, Moneo was able to summarize most of his reflections on form in a
long essay in which he calls typology the 'essence of the work of architecture',
a definition that indicates its central position in Moneo's search for the re-
establishment of the principles of architectural form.[108] This text is a late contribution to a debate that had been conducted with significant contributions
from Giulio Carlo Argan, Alan Colquhoun, Aldo Rossi and Carlo Aymonino.[109]

107 Rafael Moneo, 'On Typology', Oppositions 13, 1978, p. 23–44; 'La Vie de bâtiments: extensions de la
      Mosquée de Cordoue', DA Informations 62, 1979, pp. 23–45 (translated in this volume on pp. 266–83),
      and 'Sobre el concepto de planta libre', in Programas de Curso y Ejercicios de Examen, 1980–1981, 1981–
      1982, 1982–1983, 1983–1984, Madrid: Cátedra de Composición II, Ediciones de la ETSAM, 1985, pp. 17–21.
108 Ibid., pp. 23–44.
109 Giulio Carlo Argan, 'On the Typology of Architecture', Architectural Design 33: 12, 1963, pp. 564–5
      (reprinted in Theorizing a New Agenda for Architecture, pp. 242–6; Alan Colquhoun, 'Typology and
      Design Method', Perspecta 12, 1969, pp. 71–4 (first published in Arena 33, June 1967, reprinted in Essays
      in Architectural Criticism, Cambridge, Mass.: MIT Press, 1981, pp. 43–50. Apart from Rossi's reflection

83 Rafael Moneo: first-prize-winning
competition entry for the refurbishment
of Éibar city centre, 1972–3. The influence
of the debates in Italy at the time is clear

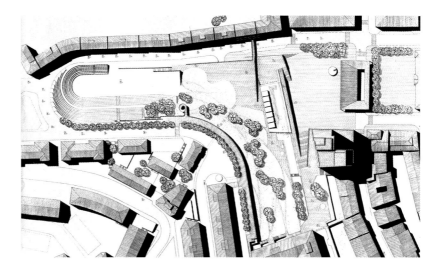

Moneo's essay reveals that he continued to share Rossi's understanding of typology as a product of structuralist thinking, defining it as 'a group of objects characterized by having the same formal structure', and explaining that it is:

> …neither a spatial diagram nor the average in a series. The notion of typology is fundamentally based on the possibility of grouping different objects using those structural similarities which are inherent to it.[110]

Typology in his understanding is therefore a formal structure found diachronically in other designs yet integral to the design under consideration, a reflection of immanent form and not of the methodology for producing such

---

on typology in the *Architecture of the City*, his and Aymonino's texts on this subject have not been translated into English. Aldo Rossi's include *Contributo al problema dei rapporti tra tipologia edilizia e morfologia urbana*, Milan: ILSES, 1964 (reprintend in Aldo Rossi, *Scritti scelti sull'architettura e la città*, Milan: CLUP, 1975, pp. 253–60); 'Considerazioni sulla tipologia edilizia e la morfologia urbana', in IUAV, *Aspetti e problemi della tipologia edilizia*, Venice: Cluva, 1964, pp. 15–32 (reprintend in Rossi, *Scritti scelti sull'architettura e la città*, pp. 209–25, and 'Tipologia, manualistica e architettura', in IUAV, *Rapporti tra la morfologia urbana e la tipologia edilizia*, Venice: Cluva, 1966, pp. 67–82. Carlo Aymonino's contributions include 'La formazione del concetto di tipologia edilizia', in *La formazione del concetto di tipologia edilizia*, pp. 67–90, and 'La formazione di un moderno concetto di tipologia edilizia', in *Rapporti tra la morfologia urbana e la tipologia edilizia*, pp. 13–52.

110 Moneo, 'On Typology', p. 24 .

forms. Moneo resists the notion that it can act as a form-finding device for a performative functional architecture, just as he was later to resist hypercontextual and parametric approaches. Typology is not simply 'a mere geometric abstraction', but, 'as a formal structure is intimately linked with reality, with a wide range of concerns from social activity to construction'. Such an integrated consideration of architectural form is characteristic of Moneo, always concerned to reconcile the different aspects of architecture; in the rest of the essay, equally characteristically, he moves typology on from the well-established territory of the debates on Quatremère de Quincy and Durand to an analysis of more recent contributions from Mies van de Rohe, Le Corbusier, Kahn and Ernesto Rogers, and the contemporary work of Rossi, Léon Krier and Robert Venturi. Typology is liberated, as it were, from being a revisionist and academic term to one that Moneo would continue to use for many years.

More recently, Moneo has frequently quoted the Italian philosopher Luigi Pareyson, who described a theory of form based on the ideal of 'formativity' ('formatività'):

> To give form means to invent the work, and, at the same time, the way of making it. There are those moments in which we foresee the inevitability in all genuine works of art. Pareyson has expressed this concept with clarity and I quote him: 'Every work fulfilled seems – to the artist – once it has been achieved, the only one which could be done, but it was mandatory that it was done and only by doing does he come to know it: before it was one among many possibilities. Once it is done, it becomes the possibility he was looking for.[111]

Luigi Pareyson (1918–1991) both trained and taught at the University of Turin, and amongst his pupils were Gianni Vattimo and Umberto Eco. His early work was in the field of existentialism, under the influence of Kierkegaard, and he ended his career with a number of quasi-theological meditations, but most well-known, and most important for Moneo's own thinking, is his work on

---

111 Rafael Moneo's Royal Gold Medal lecture. Royal Institute of British Architects: Royal Gold Medal 2003 presented to Rafael Moneo, London: RIBA, 2003. www.architecture. com/go/Architecture/ News_2938.html.

interpretation. So far from claiming that 'everything is text' and subscribing to a pessimistic relativism, Pareyson was deeply concerned with truth, but believed that it could be approached only through a series of interpretations. Refreshingly, in contrast to some within the phenomenological tradition, he acknowledged that those interpretations would necessarily be subject to debate in the philosophical arena, by an appeal to reason, and that conclusions could only be provisional. His procedure is dialectical, positing oppositions that move towards a resolution. Thus, for him, interpretation has two aspects, an active and a passive one, and they alternate. In an active phase, according to this theory, we attempt to interpret and cannot yet name the thing that is to be interpreted – we can only fashion a hypothesis. But at the same time forms emerge as images, and eventually image and form coincide, and this should result in mature contemplation. Knowledge, and therefore proper interpretation, is 'the insuperable synthesis of receptivity and activity'.[112] Similarly, an act of invention is always a singular product of action, but also an expression of the totality of a person and his or her own biographical experience and potential. Pareyson compares the 'cult of mystery' ('depth without evidence') with 'the cult of evidence verging on superstition'. A proper respect for mystery, on the other hand, together with the careful evaluation of evidence, are essential ingredients in any balanced interpretation.

Pareyson, as a philosopher, naturally expresses himself rather abstractly in comparison with Moneo, who is always concerned to illustrate his point by reference to the work of particular architects. The concept of 'typology', for Moneo, maintains those two aspects suggested in Pareyson: it has a poetic aspect, revealed in the writings and drawings of an architect like Rossi, but it can also be a framework for a rigorous form of analysis that is conditioned by historical knowledge. An architect of the twentieth century, who serves as an illustration, is Louis Kahn, who believed, poetically, that particular institutions 'wanted' to have a specific character – that every building had its own will, its own aspiration to become something that is particular to itself. Form

112 Luigi Pareyson, *Existence, Interpretation, Freedom: Selected Writings*, ed. with an introduction and notes by Paolo Diego Bubbio, trans. Anna Mattei, Aurora, Colo.: The Davies Group, 2009, p. 106. At present this is the only English-language selection of Pareyson's writings.

therefore arises to serve an institution. Another such example, of course, was Aldo Rossi, who dreamt of the liberation of the formal structure of the city from functional criteria to live independently as 'urban artifacts' and recipients of collective memory.

The thinking of Kahn and Rossi went against the grain of earlier twentieth-century ideas. Moneo talks of Mies van der Rohe and Le Corbusier as architects who, in their own way, understood the free plan of modernism as very particular articulations of a continuous Cartesian grid.[113] But the immanent and integral character of the formal structures that Moneo sought is inimical to that kind of freedom, or the dream of the 1960s and 1970s that saw architecture as a light infrastructure sustained by technology within an unqualified open lattice, thus promising an infinite flexibility of individual actions, and adaptability over time. Such a fantasy is the opposite of Moneo's understanding of form as a regulated and contained structure. Change is inevitable, but that does not mean that architecture should be reduced to a diagrammatic and characterless grid. His essay on the Great Mosque of Córdoba (appended in full on pp. 266–84) is as clear an expression of his position as any:

> Change, continuous intervention, is the fate, whether one wants it or not, of architecture. Architects' concern to take into account continuous change, thus ensuring the work of architecture answers adequately to the passage of time, has led to the introduction of the concepts of flexibility and multi-functionality. These concepts are born from the implicit idea that the eternal youth of a building, its resistance to the passage of time, would be achieved through an 'open project', permitting a continuous adaptation to a reality which is necessarily changing. The architect would enable her

---

113   In his Composition course in Madrid, Moneo discussed the notion of free plan very fully, using one whole semester – half the course. For Moneo, the free plan was a very particular spatial understanding, conceived by modernist architects, which sought specific formal arrangements. This understanding goes beyond the generally assumed idea of the free plan as providing abstract compositional freedom within the Cartesian grid, originating with the freedom that is gained by the independence between building structure and building layout, and capable of providing buildings with open spaces and flexible organizations. Moneo criticizes a similarly naïve way of understanding an open and flexible building in his lecture on the Córdoba Mosque. Rafael Moneo, 'Sobre el concepto de planta libre', in *Programas de Curso y Ejercicios de Examen: 1980–1981, 1981–1982, 1982–1983, 1983–1984*, pp. 17–21; 'La Vie de bâtiments: extensions de la Mosquée de Cordoue', pp. 23–5 (translated in this volume, pp. 267–84).

> or his work to withstand the passage of time, provided the project could qualify as 'open'. But experience shows that the life of buildings manifests itself through the permanence over time of a building's most distinctive formal characteristics and, therefore, its life does not reside so much in the project's process as in the autonomy that the building acquires once built.[114]

It is the building's formal structure that provides it with the necessary autonomy that allows for change and transformation; confronting with its pre-existing architectural integrity the social values of successive ages, it filters them and sediments their implications in its evolving form. The internal rules of a building such as the Mosque of Córdoba transcend the subjectivity, moreover, of any particular architect. For Moneo, a design without such internal rules or structuring logic risks becoming unintelligible: the so-called open plan cannot articulate differences and offers a false sense of freedom, and therefore the behaviour of people cannot be mediated by the buildings they experience and becomes subsumed in an amorphous continuum that is social as much as spatial. The accommodation of difference and plurality requires rules, which in the sphere of architecture means the internal structuring of architectural form; it is this structuring to accommodate diversity that resolves the difficulties that Durand had in characterizing the isotropic continuities of the modernist grid.

From the 1970s on, it is clear how such an internal formal logic, integrating spatial organization, the potential for activity and constructional disciplines, begins to show itself in Moneo's buildings. This is a logic that is attached neither to specific functional or programmatic requirements nor to a stable spatial diagram, but maintains a dialectical relationship between the particular spatial and organizational character of each building and the activities that it has the potential to support; crucially, it can be manifested only in the material reality of its construction. Moneo explains that a building such as his town hall at Logroño, composed as it is in different parts, acquires in this way its own cohesion:

---

114   Rafael Moneo, 'The Life of Buildings'; see pp. 266–84 below.

The supporting structure (of Logroño) thus became a constant frame of reference in the project with the clear intention of helping to unify the diverse elements. The design of the structure went beyond solving its strictly load-bearing function to reveal the formal logic behind it, which is based on geometrical relationships. The dialectics between the wall architecture and the grid – part of the essence of the city hall's architecture – was reflected in the design of its structure, which can easily be seen as an alternative to the way Le Corbusier used this notion through his *plan libre*. Therefore, one could claim that the structure of the Logroño City Hall offers a response to all the architectural questions posed in the project. It is not a regular, homogenous grid that must be imbued with meaning; instead, the structure reveals and anticipates in its placement and layout what the architecture will be. The structure solves the critical problem addressed in the project: how to integrate autonomous parts to form a cohesive whole.[115]

As Alan Colquhoun has already pointed out, sometimes Moneo takes an existing and known typological/formal structure that he then deforms and manipulates. Since pre-existing formal models no longer need to maintain the traditional functions that they once housed, their appropriation can result in surprising inventions.[116] This is the case at Mérida, which takes the Roman Basilica as its principal type, or Seville Airport, which refers to the tradition of the Mosque type for the general layout of the building. In others cases, the appropriation might be considered more evident, as in the Cathedral of Our Lady in Los Angeles, where the formal structure is derived from the tradition of Jesuit churches, stemming from Il Gesù in Rome. In none of these instances, however, is the spatial structure directly assumed, as it is in its original model, but it is intelligently and deliberately transformed and manipulated by the architect for his own purposes. In the case of Los Angeles, as noted above, the structure of the traditional Jesuit nave is inverted, and the chapels are turned around to face the long side arcades, thus controlling the contamination by these lateral chapels of the central liturgical space. In other

115   Moneo, *Remarks on 21 Works*, p. 79.
116   Alan Colquhoun, 'Between Type and Context: Forms and Elements of a Unique Architecture', *A&V* 36, 1992, p. 8.

cases, such as Mérida, the manipulation is far more complicated and appears as a cross-breed of several structural organizations. In fact, one could say that Mérida reveals a superimposition of three structural systems overlapping the same space. The first structure is a vertical internal ordering, evident in the dimensions of the bays as well as the external buttresses, and is more 'gothic', as in the medieval architecture of the industrial 'atarazanas' found in Seville or Barcelona, or an orthogonal systematization of traditional medieval urban fabric. The second structure, crossing the previous one, can be understood as a reinterpretation of the Roman basilica, which underlines the central, processional and scenographic space of the building. Finally, the third spatial structure is made of concrete – the bridges that traverse both of the other structures. Intricately interrelated, the three structures together could be considered as a particularly dense and complex composite formal system, which gives meaning to the building as a whole.

Such autonomy of the internal logic of form as a structuring principle not only applies to a building's internal arrangement but also to the way in which it is seen in the city, its independence as an entity from the rest of the urban fabric. This quality can be appreciated in the Bankinter building, which whilst being composed of three different parts does not lose its individual definition and integrity: a human scale at its base (the zone of everyday interaction, similar to that advocated by Ernesto Rogers), a discourse with the immediate townscape in its expression of repetitive windows, and finally a metropolitan magnificence at its crown. Bankinter, Logroño, Mérida, and indeed all Moneo's buildings from then on, exhibit this consideration of form.

In 1998, in an article in the *Harvard Design Magazine*, Moneo described how he learned to look with 'less indulgent eyes' on the aspiration for the 'immanency of form', which derived from those typological approaches that had inspired him in the 1970s and 1980s. But, while acknowledging the impossibility of reducing the results of the creative process to structural formal archetypes, he still argued that it was an inescapable requirement of any work of architecture that form was produced, confronting the more recent tendency of those who tried to 'dissolve their architecture' as 'a formless construction'.[117] According to him:

> The exercise of freedom cannot happen in a world without form . . . Architecture can be manipulated with freedom, avoiding both a fortuitous and indiscriminate fragmentation and the flat landscaped architecture that seems to be the aim of those who currently pursue a 'formless' world. In other words, we can attempt an architecture which is neither forcibly fragmented nor reduced to a new topography. There is room for an architectural world liberated from symmetries, partis, authoritarian axes, and all those devices which Beaux-Arts theoreticians tried to fashion into an articulated body of knowledge; so that architects can enjoy freedom within the boundaries of the principles of the visual discipline that we call architecture.[118]

Moneo is also critical of the search for abstract form, systematized during the 1970s and 1980s by means of complex notation systems, and evident in such projects as Eisenman's Cannaregio competition entry or Bernard Tschumi's *Manhattan Transcripts*.[119] In these projects, form is engendered, and justified, entirely self-referentially – an approach that was to prove seductive to a younger generation of architect-theorists in the 1990s, such as Greg Lynn, Patrick Schumacher, Jesse Reisser, Alejandro Zaera Polo and Ben Van Berkel.[120] Moneo is not interested in the justification of form as an index of the complex process that has generated it, but in the performance of form itself – how well it succeeds in articulating interrelated spaces and conditions. In contrast to his (qualified) admiration for the work of Rossi or Stirling, Moneo has been fiercely critical of these new 'indexical' positions:

---

117   Rafael Moneo, 'Recent Architectural Paradigms and a Personal Alternative', *Harvard Design Magazine*, Summer 1998, pp. 71–5.

118   Ibid. Because of a number of inaccuracies in the English translation as published, we have amended the text slightly to recover the meaning of the Spanish original.

119   Eisenman's indexical processes develop from the Cannaregio project for the Aronoff Centre, while Bernard Tschumi's work in the *Manhattan Transcripts* is realised at the Park de La Villette.

120   For an interesting reading of the later evolution of the architectural debate on form, and its devaluation into a discussion of shape (that is to say a form which is not a structural articulation of relations but pure figure), see the paradigmatic text by Robert Somol '12 Reasons to Get Back in Shape' in *Content*, ed. The Office of Metropolitan Architecture and Rem Koolhaas, Cologne: Taschen, 2004, pp. 86–7.

> Two camps that appear so different – those that base their work in arbi-
> trariness and those who consider their architecture to be a result of deci-
> sive circumstances – coincide in rejecting any commitment to the creation
> of form.[121]

In this essay he also proclaims an interest in 'compactness' and the possibility
of designs being seen as distinct objects that are internally cohesive and in a
dialectical relationship with the city.[122]

Even though Moneo has accepted that the typological approach falls short
of being the only basis for design, he still conceives of each building as being defined by form, and as an entity capable of receiving signification from
the city. Formal consistency, compactness, the ability of architecture to frame
and delimit a space of its own through form remains fundamental for Moneo,
and this view is still indebted to the vision of the city articulated by Rossi,
who had asserted that: 'urban artefacts often coexist like lacerations within
a certain order; above all, they constitute forms rather than continue them'.[123]
Such a notion can be seen in radical form in L'Illa, the gigantic building on the
Diagonal Avenue of Barcelona, which maintains its character as an independent piece of the urban fabric even though it occupies more than 400 metres
of frontage. But its individual presence does not make it alien to the city, as
it adapts itself to its immediate context through fragmentation and the differing orders of its fenestration, thus integrating the diverse realities of the
situation into its inherent formal structure. At L'Illa, as elsewhere, Moneo
ensures the building demarks its own territory. In some cases this could be
seen as idiosyncratic, as when, at the Cathedral of Our Lady in Los Angeles, he
created a building within a city that apparently understands itself purely as
an infrastructure for automobiles. Moneo delights in displaying this isolated
architectural piece, standing proud of its fluid and amorphous context; one of
the duties of such a project is to manifest itself as a solid entity in the midst
of a disjointed city, criss-crossed by the endless flow of vehicles. In a mature

---

121 Moneo, 'Recent Architectural Paradigms and a Personal Alternative', pp. 71–5.
122 Ibid.
123 Rossi, *The Architecture of the City*, pp. 113–16.

project by Moneo, form may have lost its archetypical immanence, but it is still capable of giving consistency to the parts, the effect being that the work of architecture can stand out without being dissolved into an urban condition of 'fragmentation', or an unmediated context of flow and 'continuity'.

Though we have repeatedly emphasized the importance of material realization to Moneo in each of the preceding sections (on the canon, composition and form), it is important to investigate this crucial aspect of his design
philosophy in greater detail. From the time of his 1972 teaching course in
Barcelona, Moneo stressed that a 'confrontation with reality' was the necessary culmination of the design approach he advocated. Such a confrontation
confirms two important strands in his thinking: first, the pre-eminence of
construction and materials, and second, the fundamental relationship that
a design should have with its context – context understood in its deepest
sense as an anthropologically charged landscape. Moneo's anti-idealist stance
is deeply rooted in a particular Spanish tradition, evident in the thinking of
intellectuals such as Miguel de Unamuno or José Ortega y Gasset. Because of
their commitment to the realities of Spanish culture and society, Moneo was
always attracted to these thinkers. In their view, only by a thorough understanding of Spain and its recurring myths, rather than a superficial, romantic
or idealized appreciation, could the deep social, cultural and political crises
that prevailed there since the eighteenth century be overcome. Anti-idealist
and materialist intellectual positions, even adopting atavistic and primitiv-
ist tones, were influential in Spain from the 'generation of 98' to the 'generation of 27'.[124] A reciprocal dialectic between existing landscape and material

---

[124] The so-called 'generation of 98' and the 'generation of 27' were the two most influential and celebrated
intellectual movements in Spain from the end of the nineteenth century to the mid-point of the
twentieth. The 'generation of 98' was shaped by the moral, social and economic crisis after the Spanish defeat in the war against the United States in 1898, and the loss of Spain's last remaining colonies
(Cuba, Puerto Rico, the Philippines). Relevant members of this generation were Miguel de Unamuno,
Ángel Ganivet, Ramón María del Valle-Inclán, Pío Baroja, Antonio Ruiz 'Azorín', Ramiro de Maeztu
and Antonio Machado. The group shared a pessimistic attitude that denounced Spanish social, economic, cultural and political underdevelopment. They were obsessed with Spanish identity, and confronted the false idealized 'official' vision of Spain, with a miserable, crude and anachronistic reality,
while maintaining a fascination with Castilian landscape, its archaic language and the spontaneity
of its traditions. The term 'generation of 27' is mostly used to refer to a group of poets who gathered
together at the Seville Ateneum in 1927 in honour of the baroque poet Luis de Góngora. The 'generation of 27' includes poets such as Jorge Guillén, Pedro Salinas, Rafael Alberti, Federico García Lorca,
Luis Cernuda, Vicente Aleixandre, León Felipe and Miguel Hernández, but also related artists such as
Luis Buñuel, Salvador Dali, José Caballero, Maruja Mallo, José Moreno Villa and Alberto Sánchez. This
generation introduced Spain to the current European artistic avant-gardes, especially surrealism,
but filtered it through a delight for vernacular, popular and traditional Spanish cultural expressions,
which also included the recovery of the greatest personalities of Spanish artistic tradition from the

and cultural practices developed across it was promoted by Unamuno and other members of the Spanish 'generation of 98', and permeated through the works of Ortega y Gasset to the 'generation of 27' in the works of poets such as Federico García Lorca and sculptors such as Alberto Sánchez.[125] Strongly rooted in Spanish intellectual culture, this kind of thinking especially affected the young Moneo during his high school education in the 1940s and 1950s, following the devastating Spanish Civil War of 1936–9.

Moneo's 'commitment to reality' was already visible in his earliest projects, such as his proposal for the Plaza del Obradoiro in Santiago de Compostela, the project that won him his two-year tenure at the Royal Academy of Spain in Rome. Professor Luis Moya, one of the jurors for the prize, jested that the architecture that Moneo designed seemed older than the pre-existing architecture in the square.[126] Moya's provocative remark underlines how this early design indicated Moneo's remarkable sensitivity to urban context, with buildings that were carefully aligned and given particular set-backs, and were thoroughly understood in terms of material and structure. Even though the design shares some of the organic formal mannerisms typical of the School of Madrid at that time, in a period dominated by a militant and dogmatic modernism it demonstrated an unusual sensitivity to material fabric and context.

During the 1960s and 1970s, Moneo's preoccupation with the confrontation with reality (at least in his writings) remained in the background, being displaced by the debates on architectural language, typology and compositional method discussed earlier. It is not until the 1980s, during the American years, that this focus reappeared as a major component of Moneo's thinking, and this was most probably as a reaction to the abstract tendencies of American architectural schools. He found that, as an architect with a Spanish background,

renaissance and baroque. Such a concern for establishing a relationship between vernacular and avant-garde culture is also very clear in Spanish architecture of this time, as can be observed in the thinking of Josep Lluis Sert in the 1930s, which is shared with the generation of Spanish architects of the GATEPAC group. For an interesting analysis of this relationship, see Antonio Pizza (ed.), *J. Ll. Sert and Mediterranean Culture*, Barcelona: COAC, 1996.

125   Of special influence would be Ortega's *La España Invertebrada* ('The Invertebrate Spain'), a collection of essays published in the newspaper *El Sol* from 1917 to 1921. This text bridges the interests of the 98 and 27 generations, while also retaining a very strong reference in the 1940s and 1950s. José Ortega y Gasset, *Invertebrate Spain*, trans. Mildred Adams, New York: Howard Fertig, 1974.

126   'Premios de Roma 1962', Arqu*itectura* 50, 1963, pp. 18–26.

he could contribute a properly articulated reflection on the importance to architecture of its relation to a material and cultural context that was relevant
to the international debates then current at the Harvard Graduate School of
Design. From this time, when addressing students, he concentrated on the
'confrontation with reality', rather than on those questions of typology or
construction that were being discussed in Italy and the United Kingdom.[127]

As Moneo has written, 'By accepting conditions and limits and negotiating
with them, through the act of construction, architecture becomes what it really is.'[128] Architecture in its full sense can be achieved only if it is conceived
intrinsically in relation to its means of construction. If Moneo's recovery of
pre-modern principles is emphasized in his stress on the canon, in relation
to the use of materials and their tectonic veracity his beliefs show continuity with those of the modern movement, in contrast to his contemporaries.[129]
In the 1960s, unlike many of his closest colleagues such as Aldo Rossi, John
Hejduk, Peter Eisenman and Robert Venturi, Moneo was interested not so
much in the break with modernity, but in discovering ways of improving it, in
finding a truer and more *realistic* modernity.[130] Such an emphasis on 'honest

---

127 Moneo's *Hispanism* was reinforced by his encounter with the community of Spanish emigré intel-
     lectuals, from the time of the Civil War, on the East Coast of the USA. Especially remarkable is his
     relationship with the Guillén family, descendants of exiled poet of the 'generation of 27' Jorge Guillén.
     The Guillén family also proved to be useful patrons, as they were instrumental in securing Moneo's
     first commission in the US, the David Museum at Wellesley College, where poets Jorge Guillén and
     Pedro Salinas had taught after the Spanish Civil war. Teresa Guillén, daughter of the poet, was also a
     regular attender at Moneo's lectures at the GSD.

128 *The Solitude of Buildings*, p. 30.

129 In this respect his concern was similar to that of Kenneth Frampton, who saw the way to redeem
     modernism was to put a special emphasis on tectonic culture: Kenneth Frampton, 'Reflections on the
     Scope of the Tectonic' in *Studies in Tectonic Architecture, The Poetics of Construction in Nineteenth-
     and Twentieth-century Architecture*, Cambridge Mass.: MIT Press, 1995, pp. 1–7.

130 Such a search was common amongst young architects at the time. Some followed Reyner Banham
     and relied on technology itself for a redefinition, but Moneo was closer to architects who looked
     for inspiration to new directions in the social sciences, though each had rather different spheres of
     interest. Rossi sought a scientific architecture based on social sciences such as structuralism; Hejduk
     was interested in the rediscovery of the spatial consequences of architecture in modernist paintings;
     Eisenman saw true modernity as being rooted in the inescapable relativity of the modern – in its
     post-humanist stance; Venturi explored the linguistic capacity of architecture, inspired by the com-
     municational needs of modern democracies. Moneo, however, believed that the correction of the er-
     rors of modernity, or the discovery of a true modernism, would come through the recovery of reality
     and of experience.

construction', which Moneo retained throughout his career, was directly indebted to his formative years at the School of Architecture in Madrid, which
emphasized the role of the architect as a builder, and as a technically compe-
tent professional. Young architects were trained to build, at the expense of
more theoretical study of aesthetics or history – subjects that many professors at the school, as well as students, regarded as secondary, if not entirely irrelevant.[131] This spirit, of architects as constructors, appears in Moneo's
work as an apprentice to Francisco Javier Sáenz de Oíza and Jørn Utzon. Even
though he questioned the organic tradition of the school of Madrid, and its
compliance with the dogmas of the modern movement, he had a great respect for Oíza and shared his interest in construction, agreeing with him that
'good construction guarantees beauty'. During his time with Utzon, Moneo
was faced with the problem of building the incredibly ambitious design of
the Sydney Opera House. As an intermediary between Ove Arup's London office and Utzon's in Hellebaek, Denmark, he came to realise the importance of
structural integrity for that project – an experience that left an indelible impression on him.[132]

Moneo's stress on the importance of construction is evident not only in
the work of his own practice, but also in his critical writing. During the 1960s,
he traveled across Europe many times, and reviewed the work of the modern masters after experiencing their buildings first-hand. Moneo has often
stated that he would only talk about buildings he had already visited, since
personal experience was fundamental. Amongst his many reviews, that of
the Villa Savoye in 1965 can be regarded as paradigmatic. In his short text
for *Arquitectura*, Moneo recorded his distress at the state of decay of Le
Corbusier's celebrated and most idiosyncratic villa, one that he had frequently admired in photographs for its unadulterated cleanliness. He clearly identified the deficiencies in Le Corbusier's understanding of construction as the
cause, and talks about the extreme naïvity represented by his attempt to be
true to his dogmatic principles. The most interesting part of the text in many

---

131   In one of the first articles he wrote about the school of Madrid, Moneo described his pain at discover-
      ing how students were quite uninterested in the lectures of one of the greatest architectural histori-
      ans at the time, Leopoldo Torres-Balbás. Moneo, 'Sobre un intento de reforma didáctica', p. 45.

132   Moneo defended Utzon's approach – where theory succeeds practice, because it arises out of con-
      structional experience – in his essay 'Sobre el escándalo de Sydney', Arq*uitectura* 109, 1968, p. 53.

84 Ignazio Gardella: House on the
Zattere, Venice, 1954–8. A building
admired by Moneo for its constructional
consistency and its engagement with
the local context

ways is his comparison of Villa Savoye with Ignacio Gardella's house on the Zattere, Venice, a building that is conventionally regarded as a mannerist and rhetorical exercise that strays well beyond the boundaries of modernism (fig. 84). But, Moneo pointed out, Gardella's house was in a perfect state of preservation some nine years after its completion because it was built in accordance with the constructional tradition of the city. Thus, for Moneo, this house on the Zattere, which accommodates the realities of construction as its architect had understood them, is a better model for current architecture, representing as it does a more 'realistic' modernity than the dogmatic and irresponsible villa by Le Corbusier at Poissy.[133] This period of Moneo's early career must be understood not only as a reaction against acknowledged modern masters, a necessary parricide that the young in each generation perform, but also a construction of his own position; later, in the mid-1970s, Moneo did not shrink from severe criticism of other revered work of the 1920s and 1930s, such as the

133 Rafael Moneo, 'Una visita a Poissy. (Villa Saboya, Francia)', Arq*uitectura* 74, 1965, pp. 35–6.

housing blocks by Josep Lluis Sert in Barcelona. He was particularly scathing about the apparent lack of concern amongst architects of that period for the constructional durability of their buildings, and saw it as a symptom of a lack of commitment to the real conditions of the time, and ultimately therefore to their society.[134] In contrast, Moneo has always been sympathetic to the work of Antoni Gaudí, an architect conventionally ignored by modernists, as an example of how exuberant creativity can be derived from the knowledge of constructional technique.[135]

Moneo's concern for construction, and insistence on the reciprocity between architectural concept, expression and technique, was in some sense an inheritance from the origins of modernism.[136] He may have admired Bruno Zevi as the model of a historian who showed that architecture could be understood from multiple viewpoints, but he also respected the work of Auguste Choisy, who encouraged the understanding of historic works of architecture through an analysis of their construction. Under Choisy's influence, Moneo studied Greek temples not from a linguistic or compositional point of view, but as an evolution of constructional technique.[137] Moneo's willingness to study architectural history à la Choisy, from the Greek temple to Gaudí and Gardella, was in contrast to the attitude of most of his American colleagues, some of whom he certainly admired. Robert Venturi emphasized the contradictions between his chosen language and tectonics; Peter Eisenman claimed his architecture was merely the physical notation of a conceptual process, and

134 For Josep Lluis Sert in Barcelona, see Rafael Moneo, 'Si te dicen que caí [Sobre las últimas obras de J. Ll. Sert en Barcelona]', Arquitecturas Bis 6, 1975, pp. 10–11. Moneo's concern does not mean to say that, in an extraordinarily prolific career, some of his own buildings have not suffered from inadequate construction. An extreme instance is the residence for the Spanish Ambassador in Washington, USA (1995–2002), which the Spanish Ministry of External Affairs described as being 'in a state of ruin' only ten years after its construction. Major repairs were necessary also at the Stockholm Museum, because of interstitial condensation, though it seems the responsibility for this problem lay with the local executive architect (correspondence with Professor Johan Mårtelius, 27 December 2013).

135 In the 1960s, he used Gaudí as the ultimate reference of the true fulfillment of the aspirations of the third generation of modern architects, and also wrote a panegyric article: Moneo, 'A la Conquista de lo Irracional', pp. 1–6; 'Sobre Gaudí', Arquitectura 75, 1965, pp. 9–14.

136 As just one reference close to Rafael Moneo's formative years in Madrid, one could cite Sigfried Giedion's Space, Time and Architecture and its chapter 'The Demand for Morality in Architecture', Cambridge, Mass.: Harvard University Press, 1982, pp. 291–332 (first edition 1941).

137 Rafael Moneo, 'Notas sobre la arquitectura griega', Hogar y Arquitectura 59, July–August 1965, pp. 67–82.

happily defined his buildings as 'cardboard architecture'; John Hejduk's ideas were never even intended for construction.[138] Even his European colleagues, such as Aldo Rossi, fall short in this respect, because, according to Moneo, for Rossi 'to construct is simply to act on the basis of reason, not, as one might think, to materialize thought'.[139] In these terms, only the buildings of James Stirling seemed to live up to Moneo's criterion of constructional veracity, though he also found some support in the projects of the Krier brothers. Leon and Rob Krier sought to recover the language of classicism not merely for se-miotic reasons but because it represented a system of construction that had been tested for more than 2,000 years.[140] However, Moneo would never go so far as the Kriers in re-embracing the classical language, as he remained firmly convinced that architecture could not return to the classical after the indus-trial revolution.[141]

The concern for construction was clearly evident in Moneo's writing and teaching in the 1980s, when he felt it most important to distinguish his po-sition in the light of international debates. At a time when postmodernism reached the zenith of its popularity, and when emerging talents in other man-ners were principally concerned with buildings as abstract extensions of the drawing board – Zaha Hadid's Hong Kong Peak (1983) or Daniel Libeskind's Chamber Works (1984) being good examples – Moneo's campaign for the

---

138 Moneo has frequently praised the work of John Hejduk, which particularly undermines Moneo's belief in the necessary consistency between architectural ideas and their construction. Hejduk's architecture was confined to drawings, and he resisted its transformation into a built work al-most until the late 1970s, when he became less 'Hejduk-like' for Moneo. Because Moneo paradoxi-cally believed the built works by Hejduk betrayed the spirit of his architecture, he can claim that Hejduk, without building anything, was the most profound and complete architect of those considered under the group of the New York Five (which comment was made in a lecture at Harvard Gradu-ate School of Design on 'The Loss of Objecthood and the Death of Organicism', for the course On Contemporary Architecture, Spring 2006). Rafael Moneo, 'The Work of John Hejduk or the Passion to Teach', *Lotus International* 27, 1980, pp. 64–85.
139 Moneo, 'Aldo Rossi: The Idea of Architecture and the Modena Cemetery', p. 4.
140 Peter Eisenman and Léon Krier, 'Eisenman and Krier: A Conversation', in Cynthia Davison (ed.), *Eisenman-Krier: Two Ideologies: A Conference at Yale University School of Architecture*, New York: Monacelli Press, 2004, p. 31 (originally published in *Skyline*, February 1983).
141 As an inheritor of some aspects of the modern movement tradition, Moneo has often quoted in his lectures Walter Benjamin's *The Work of Art in the Age of Mechanical Reproduction* to stress the im-possibility of going back to the classical language as it was, and the need to assume an architecture that starts from a reflection on industrial production.

importance of construction, the durability of materials and the necessity for drawings to reflect the future realization of a project in technical terms, became even more vocal. And this was to be the central argument in his acceptance lecture as Chairman of the Department of Architecture at the Harvard Graduate School of Design in 1985.[142] In this lecture, Moneo used three of his own projects (Bankinter, Logroño and Mérida) as evidence that it was possible to develop a theoretical position out of the particularities of practice, and as a call for architecture to rediscover the traditional relationship between drawing and construction:

> Many architects today invent processes or master drawing techniques without concern for the reality of building. The tyranny of drawings is evident in many buildings when the builder tries to follow the drawing literally. . . . But a truly architectural drawing should imply above all the knowledge of construction.[143]

Moneo's position was consistent with one of his very first essays, for *Arquitectura*, where he praised the builders of antiquity – modest stonemasons who sought to deepen their understanding of construction and record their architectural ideas by means of drawings, which, crucially and inevitably revealed their knowledge of how to build.[144] And later, during the 1970s when he put together a selection of drawings by contemporary architects, accompanied by a commentary, Moneo proclaimed that his interest was to demonstrate that 'architectural representations contain already, if in a reduced form, the future reality'.[145] In the 1980s, as Chair of the Department of Architecture at the Harvard Graduate School of Design, indicating that typological understanding may be necessary but in itself was insufficient, he described construction as the ultimate test for architectural ideas:

> Consistency relates to the existing coherence between built form and image that is conveyed in the art of construction, rather than in the imitation

---

142 Moneo, 'The Solitude of Buildings', pp. 32–40, and Rafael Moneo, 'The Idea of Lasting: A Conversation with Rafael Moneo', Perspecta, 24, 1988, pp. 147–57.

143 Moneo, 'The Solitude of Buildings', p. 34.

144 Moneo, 'A vueltas con la metodología', p. 11.

145 Moneo and Cortés, *Comentarios sobre dibujos de 20 arquitectos actuales*, p. 2.

of known models of architectural types . . . My wish is to give buildings a consistency that derives from their materiality.[146]

At a philosophical level, Moneo's attempt to rethink the problem of constructional honesty relates to Luigi Pareyson's notion of formativity ('formatività'), to which we have already referred, since, for Pareyson, material and form were inseparable. Expanding on this idea, Moneo wrote:

> Architecture is the mediator between form and construction, and the work of architecture is the outcome of this mediation, the tangible reality that makes theoretical reflection possible. And from this we can say that to make architecture is to invent, or to accept, the formal conventions that make construction possible.[147]

From such an understanding, Moneo is able to attack what he believes to be the fundamental problem of contemporary practice: the arbitrariness of form. For Moneo, this arbitrariness evaporates when there is proper connection between the architectural idea and its materialization; when architects were committed to a way of constructing their buildings, 'arbitrariness of form disappeared in construction'.[148]

Naturally, this insistence on the confrontation with the actual materialization of buildings not only is evident in Moneo's writing and teaching, but is a fundamental concern in all of his buildings. Thus the Bankinter building in Madrid (pp. 111–17), as Moneo has described it, can be seen as an example of how a certain discipline in the use of brick can advance the idea of the architecture.[149] The precision of its crafting, indebted as it is to the organic tradition in America evident in the work of Richardson, Sullivan and Wright, is a clear example of Moneo's confidence in construction as a discipline that could be experienced and learned from. This attitude pervades all his work: the visual expression of the building always coincides with its constructional method. So, if the architectural idea is of a dome, as is the case in Moneo's Seville air terminal, the domes will work structurally as domes, not as false plaster domes –

146 Moneo, 'The Idea of Lasting', p. 147.
147 Moneo, *Programas de curso y ejercicios de examen, Cursos 1980–84*, pp. 11–12.
148 Moneo, 'The Solitude of Buildings', p. 35.
149 Moneo, *Remarks on 21 Works*, pp. 44–57.

the building's geometry and structure is at one with the phenomenological experience. Buildings such as the Auditorium at Barcelona, or the Kursaal in San Sebastián (pp. 147–54), have a façade language that is a straightforward reflection of the structure that supports it, delicately manipulated to exploit appropriate rhythms and degrees of transparency.

One of the most paradigmatic and complex explorations of this issue is undoubtedly Moneo's National Museum of Roman Art at Mérida (pp. 127–38), where the method of construction takes a pre-eminent role in mediating between past and present. By reappropriating a particular type of brick, and constructing the walls and arches in a manner directly indebted to Roman techniques, Moneo aligns himself with tradition, whilst the flat concrete slabs are both more 'modern' and more industrial in character. This is a cross-breed between Roman splendour and the laconic modern factory. It is no accident that the beautiful pencil drawings, produced after construction, used Choisy's technique of worm's-eye axonometric to reveal the correlation between material and form, perfectly articulating Moneo's view of how construction, form and experience come together to make a work of architecture (p. 129; fig. 50).

> Critical to my understanding of the role of the site is my conviction that architecture belongs to the site, that architecture should be appropriate to the site, should recognize in some way the site's attributes. The architect's first move when starting to think about a building should be to decipher these attributes, to hear how they manifest themselves.[150]
>
> Rafael Moneo

The site, understood as a reflection on the context in its fullest sense, is the ultimate, and inescapable, argument on which Moneo bases his idea of a non-arbitrary architecture. The architect is required to listen to 'the murmur of the site', as he memorably described it.

> I believe that learning to listen to the murmur of the site is one of the most necessary experiences in an architectural education. To discern what should be kept, what could permeate from the previously existing site into the new presence and emerge after the substantial immobile artifacts built, is crucial for any architect. Understanding what is to be ignored, subtracted, erased, added, transformed, etc., from the existing conditions of the site is fundamental to the practice of architecture.[151]

The context fully considered not only embraces the particular urban or rural landscape in which a building is situated, but also includes the geometrical constraints of the location, its legal and technical constraints, the building's budget and the clients' aspirations – in fact the whole way it responds to specific cultural and social conditions. The multitude of factors that arise out of the specifics of a commission are circumstances the architect has to accept and make use of in order to create a realistic architecture. Intellectually, Moneo's insistence on the prime importance of the circumstances shows his debt to the ethos of Ortega y Gasset's motto: 'I am myself plus my circumstance.'[152] It is out of these constraints that architects are able to embrace their own free-

---

150 Rafael Moneo, 'The Murmur of the Site', in Cynthia C. Davison (ed.), *Anywhere*, New York: Rizzoli, 1992, p. 48.
151 Ibid., p. 48.
152 Ortega y Gasset, *Meditations on Quixote*, p. 45.

dom – an idea that some of the most talented of those architects influenced by Moneo, such as Emilio Tuñón and Luis Moreno Mansilla, have since elaborated upon.[153] Moneo emphasized the point in lectures given in the first decade of the twenty-first century, stressing that limitations form the real opportunities for inventive design, and are in fact a necessary pre-condition for freedom.[154] In his submission for the Prado competition, he quotes the Socrates of Paul Valery's *Eupalinos or the Architect*, and his affirmation that 'the greatest freedom is born of maximum rigour'.[155] Accepting the conditions in which one has to work sometimes has unfortunate consequences, however: one of Moneo's least successful and most controversial recent projects was the reconstruction of the central square around the Mercado Grande, Ávila, with a number of luxury housing blocks, and raises the question of the extent to which Moneo's philosophy of accepting the given conditions is always right, since it eliminates architects' responsibility to criticize the reality that they inherit, as well as undermining Moneo's own discourse, in this case, of acute sensibility towards the site.[156]

---

153 In the late 1990s, Emilio Tuñón and Luis Moreno Mansilla established a working system based on a common agreement amongst the design team regarding certain selected design restraints. The architects produced an elementary description of their approach in 'Start and Oscillation [on funnels and showers]', to accompany the publication of their recent work in *El Croquis*, 2001, pp. 106–7. A paradigmatic text of that time, explaining and supporting Mansilla's and Tuñón's approach (though it does not directly reference the practice) can be found in Carles Muro, 'Hacia una arquitectura potencial', *Circo* 97, 2002. Muro wrote: 'the architect can get more freedom in his work by an apparent limitation of that same freedom. A potential architecture that works with systems of self-imposed constraints, specifically elaborated for each project.' Finally, a fuller description of Mansilla's and Tuñón's design approach by that time can be found in *2G* 27, 2003, with texts by Luis Díaz Mauriño, Carles Muro, Luis Rojo and Rafael Moneo himself.

154 In lectures such as 'The Freedom of the Architect' or 'How Difficulties Benefit the Work of the Architect', Moneo supports his point by presenting his own work and discussing his experience as a practicing architect. Moneo, *The Freedom of the Architect*; Moneo, *How Difficulties Benefit the Work of the Architect*.

155 See Luis Fernández Galiano 'El Prado, suma y sigue', Arqu*itectura Viva* 63, November/December 1998, pp. 67–9.

156 Moneo received the commission directly from the municipality in 1991, but the brief changed several times, most unfortunately after 1998 when a special plan for Santa Teresa Square permitted an increase in building volume in order to generate increased private subsidy for the public works. One of the most common criticisms of the buildings is their actual size, and it is clear that they are too large for their delicate historical context. As might be expected, the Ávila housing attracted a similar opposition from the public as other controversial works (the Kursaal, Murcia town hall and the Prado extension), but the UNESCO World Heritage Committee also registered their concern, in a note to the

Amongst these creative limitations, context is the most powerful. The origins of Moneo's attitude towards this can be found in the various influences he absorbed at the beginning of his career. On the one hand, he favoured Scandinavian examples – the work of Aalto, Asplund, Lewerentz, Jacobsen, Utzon and Pietilä – which we could understand as a search for a gentler modernity, more suitable for the climate and culture of northern Europe than the central European context within which modernism arose. On the other hand, he embraced some Mediterranean influence in the projects of Ignazio Gardella, Dimitris Pikionis, Antonio Coderch and even some of the early work of Alejandro de la Sota.

It is important to see this in the particular cultural and political context of post-Franco Spain. From about 1955 onwards, the heroic national-Catholic historicism of buildings such as El Valle de los Caidos (1940–58, Franco's iconic monument) or Luis Gutiérrez Soto's Ministerio del Aire (1940-51) was gradually superseded by an apparently neutral modernism. The 'School of Madrid', as mentioned earlier, looked to figures such as Paul Rudolph and Eero Saarinen amongst second-generation modernists, and resulted in buildings such as the Torres Blancas (1961–9; fig. 3) or Banco Bilbao Tower (1971–8), both by Francisco Javier Sáenz de Oíza.[157] Even though this 'clean' international modernism became the orthodox language for luxurious private or institutional buildings, and was promoted in architectural schools, architects were searching for a kind of modernity that was suitable for the specific Spanish context. During the 1930s, however, as is clear from some of the GATEPAC projects, such as Josep Lluis Sert and Josep Torres Clavé's houses in Garraf, there had been an

---

municipality of Ávila, that the project could cause damage to the town's historic centre. Moneo has claimed it was only a matter of explaining the project correctly to them (Patricia G. Robledo, 'Rafael Moneo: Habré Podido no acertar pero he respetado la monumentalidad de Ávila', in ABC, 3 September 2003). But the project remains one of Moneo's less well-known and least published works in his recent career, referred to only when journalists seek to redress the balance when the work of Spain's most famous architect is being discussed.

157   Although Oíza was sensitive to the revision of modernism through vernacular culture in the early 1950s, as can be seen in his Santuario de Nuestra Señora de Arántzazu (1950–54), in which he collaborated with the sculptor Jorge Oteiza, from the mid-1950s on, when Moneo worked in the office (1956–61), he championed a more purist and international architecture.

85 Gunnar Asplund: Law Courts and city
hall extension, Gothenburg, completed in
1937 after a twenty-year gestation period

attempt to integrate modernism and popular Spanish culture.[158] And it was
this other kind of modernity that interested Moneo, rather than the militant and a-critical style that represented the mainstream. His admiration for
Gardella's house on the Zattere has already been noted; as well as appreciating

158 GATEPAC (Grupo de Artistas y Técnicos Españoles para el Progreso de la Arquitectura Contem-
poránea) was the Association of Spanish Modern Architects active in Spain between 1930 and 1937,
recognized as the official Spanish delegation of the Comité International pour la Résolution des
Problèmes de l'Architecture Contemporaine (CIRPAC) since 1932. GATCPAC (Grup d'Artistes i Tècnics
Catalans per al Progrès de l'Arquitectura Contemporània), led by the Barcelona-based architect Josep
Lluis Sert, was the only branch of the GATEPAC that worked as a group, and produced some notable works. Members of the GATCPAC group were acutely interested in local Mediterranean culture,
which can be seen in the pages of the GATEPAC official magazine A.C. The number 18 of the magazine was entitled 'The Popular Mediterranean Architecture' ('La arquitectura popular mediterránea'),
while A.C. 21 was devoted to 'Popular Architecture in Ibiza' ('La arquitectura popular in Ibiza'). The
most remarkable architects from this group, aside from Sert, were Sixt Illescas, Germán Rodríguez
Arias, Josep Maria Subirana and Josep Torres-Clavé, who was the director of A.C. For information
on the relation between the GATCPAC and the vernacular Mediterranean culture see Pizza (ed.),
J. Ll. Sert and the Mediterranean.

its construction, Moneo also showed how he engaged with the site.[159] Moneo denied that this building represented a departure from modernism and in its place a regressive historicism, as was commonly claimed by critics. In the same text, Moneo referred, amongst other examples, to Asplund's Gothenburg Law Courts extension (1917–37; fig. 85), a building that would become a paradigm for Moneo's thinking and practice, and the influence of which can still be seen in more recent projects such as the extension to the Prado Museum. Ultimately he found in the work of Gardella and Asplund a modernist manner that was able to enter into a dialogue with the existing built context – an exemplar for contemporary architecture.

As has been discussed, Moneo was as influenced by theoretical discussions at the time as he was by built examples, and one writer in whom he took a significant interest was Ernesto Nathan Rogers, editor of the Milan-based magazine *Casabella*, which Rogers had deliberately re-christened *Casabella Continuità*. By 'continuity', Rogers referred not only to the fact that the magazine had survived the war, but also, in a more ideological sense, that the traditional disciplines of architecture that had been disrupted by the modern movement would be reinvigorated. This was a fundamental issue in a country such as Italy, where modernism had a unique place in view of the many monuments of past cultures that survived.[160] 'Continuity' entailed not only the recovery of the history of architecture as a relevant source of knowledge and reinforcement of the autonomy of the discipline, but also the relationship between architecture and the pre-existing urban context. One of Rogers' most important concepts, which he called *preesistenze ambientali* ('pre-existing

159 Rafael Moneo, 'Una obra de Ignazio Gardella, Casa en *La Zattere*, Venecia', Arquitectura 71, 1964, pp. 43–50.

160 The thinking of Ernesto Nathan Rogers had little impact on the Anglo-Saxon architectural scene. This was mainly due to Reyner Banham's forceful criticism of Rogers' position, represented by Rogers' office BBPR's buildings such as Torre Velasca (1954–8) or Ignazio Gardella's House Apartment at Zattere (1953–8). For Banham, these 'continuist' efforts were no more than deplorable historicist regressions that indicated Italy's lamentable abandonment of Modern Movement principles. Reyner Banham, 'Neo-Liberty: The Italian Retreat from Modern Architecture', *Architectural Review* 125: 747, April 1959, pp. 231–5. Rogers replied to Banham with his article 'L'evoluzione dell'architettura: risposta al custode dei frigidaires,' *Casabella-continuità* 228, pp. 2–4 (English version, 'The Evolution of Architecture: Reply to the Custodian of Frigidaires', in Joan Ockman (ed.), *Architecture Culture 1943–1968: A Documentary Anthology*, New York: Rizzoli, 1993).

86 Ernesto Rogers, of BBPR: Torre
Velasca, Milan, 1957–60. An illustration of
his theory of 'preesistenze ambientali',
promulgated in *Casabella*, of which
Rogers was editor

surroundings'), appeared in *Casabella* articles in the 1950s. According to
Rogers:

> In order to combat cosmopolitanism, which works on behalf of a universal
> feeling which is not yet sufficiently rooted, and which erects the same ar-
> chitecture in New York, Rome, Tokyo or Rio de Janeiro (in the countryside
> just as in the cities), we should try to harmonize our works with the pre-
> existing surroundings, be they natural or historically created by human
> ingenuity.[161]

Rogers's thinking was illustrated by some of the buildings designed by his
office, such as the Torre Velasca, which provoked a major controversy at the
time (fig. 86). However, the tower acted as a manifesto for the *continuità* that

161 Ernesto Nathan Rogers, 'Las preexistencias ambientales y los temas prácticos contemporáneos', in
Experiencia de la Arquitectura, Buenos Aires, Nueva Visión, 1965, p. 34, our translation.

Rogers advocated: architecture should be built with contemporary technology, and should function efficiently, but it also has a duty to integrate itself with the pre-existing urban context and architectural conventions. In the 1980s the Torre Velasca was one of the case studies that Moneo particularly emphasised in his lecture series 'Introduction to Design and Visual Studies in Architecture', which he taught during his chairmanship at the Harvard Graduate School of Design.[162] Moneo acknowledges Rogers' importance and uses his notion of continuity as a way of discussing the relationship between the pre-existing urban context and the architecture that is created within it. In one of his contributions to the *Any* debates of the early 1990s he stated:

> The materiality of the city testifies to the action of a mechanism that enables continuity to emerge in constructed form. Since it is through architecture that cities come to life, I would like to believe that this mechanism is architecture. Architectural continuity is the product of the interaction with the constructed world, a world that connotes recognition of the past as well as anticipation of the future. Architecture emerges from the dialogue that we maintain with our surroundings. We need to look around in order to act. Continuity, which has nothing to do with plain conservatism, is a key to intervention in cities. To be aware of continuity is the first step toward proper construction.[163]

Moneo was attracted not only to Rogers, but also to his disciples and to younger contributors to *Casabella* such as Vittorio Gregotti and Aldo Rossi, the work of whom he analysed intensively, particularly during his time as a lecturer at Barcelona. If he took most of his ideas on the uses of architectural history and the autonomy of the discipline of architecture from Rossi's *L'architettura de la citta*, he also absorbed the notion of 'place' from Gregotti's *Il Territorio della Architettura*, with its distinct Heideggerian ethos.[164] Moneo referred to this more ambivalent notion in his 1972 Elements of Composition course, in which

---

162 Subsequently Moneo explained that it was necessary to use two lectures to explain this important example: Rafael Moneo, 'New Idea of Space', first lecture at the Harvard Graduate School of Design in the course On Contemporary Architecture, spring 2006 (Teaching Assistant Francisco González de Canales).

163 Moneo, 'The Indifference of Anyway', p. 176–83.

164 Moneo, 'Gregotti y Rossi', p. 2.

he declared that the way in which a building meets the existing 'landscape' represents a fundamental test.[165] Moneo describes Gregotti's interest in the connection between architecture and its surroundings – how it is 'increasingly more difficult to make a project independently from its context',[166] and quotes this statement:

> This idea of landscape as a total environment, in which I have tried to situate architecture, forces us not to conserve or reconstruct specific natural qualities, but to recognise the materiality of the anthropo-geographical environment, as a field in which architecture operates, and continues to convey meaning; and to acknowledge its importance as something indispensable, which can be understood as a structural principle of the environment, even outside the existing cultural model.

Gregotti's thinking about the relationship between architecture and the existing landscape became more refined and sophisticated with the concept of *modificazione* ('modification'), which became a central focus of the debate in the pages of *Casabella* during the 1980s while Gregotti was editor. Using the concept of *modificazione*, Gregotti rethought the idea of context in an interesting way, exploring the link between 'belonging' and 'otherness', a concept derived from the reflections on 'the other' initiated by post-war Jewish thinkers such as Emmanuel Levinas. Gregotti found several examples of Mediterranean architecture that served as a sensitive modification of landscape, most prominently in the work of Alvaro Siza.

A strength of *modificazione* as a design procedure was its ability to integrate alien material from the pre-existing context, such as local geometries or material fragments, into a project; instead of homogenizing these elements within some internal design logic, differences – the 'otherness' – could be highlighted. According to Gregotti:

> The notion of belonging develops transverse relationships for which project design primarily represents a process of modification: one that attracts

---

165 Rafael Moneo, 'Hacia una comprobación del diseño: El encuentro arquitectura-medio/Lección 18: La arquitectura como sistema: El paisaje', in *Programa de Elementos de Composición*, pp. 28–9.

166 Moneo, 'Gregotti y Rossi', p. 2.

and organizes the debris contained in context, and that constructs from those pieces asymmetry, varying density, and the values of diversity.[167]

Modificazione can recreate a sense of belonging, not by an imitation of the landscape condition but by revealing the radical 'otherness' of the land, the material and cultural specifics of the context. The project becomes the material expression of this encounter, or dialogue, between two different realities, and the knowledge of how to operate this difference arises out of the traditions of the architectural discipline.

Moneo was highly aware of this debate, and shared an interest in relating architecture to the site, which is reflected in his writings from the 1990s. But Moneo distinguishes between context (the immediate environment) and site, which for him involves not only a comprehensive understanding of the physical environment but also the anthropological landscape, historically and culturally charged. This understanding prevents the possibility of fantasizing about a site as 'intact' or 'virgin'. Instead, its necessary artificiality leads us more naturally to talk about its 'contamination' as a result of time, and the 'manipulation' of a pre-existing situation. The site does not dictate a particular approach; rather it is the task of the architect to learn how to interpret and decipher the clues embedded in it:

> There can be no automatic, determined response to a site in the construction of a building. . . . Architecture emerges out of the inevitable dialogue between a site and the act of building on it.[168]

This debate on the nature of the site encouraged Moneo to look for contemporaries who were engaged in the problem and, in the late 1970s, when the debate on typology appeared to be exhausted, led him to the work of the Portuguese architect Álvaro Siza. From that time, Siza was a stable reference in helping him to articulate his theory of architecture and the site. Moneo found Siza to be the most successful architect of his generation in re-validating modern

167 Vittorio Gregotti, 'On Modification', in *Inside Architecture*, trans. Peter Wong and Francesca Zaccheo, Chicago and Cambridge, Mass.: Graham Foundation and MIT Press, 1996, p. 68 (originally published in Italian in 1991).

168 Rafael Moneo, 'The Murmur of the Site', op. cit., p. 49. The usual English translation has been amended by the authors to convey the sense more accurately.

architecture. As he put it, Siza's 'knowledge of modern architecture transcends strict information and allows the incorporation of the formal patrimony of the modern tradition into his work with an instrumental character'. Siza's uncompromising modernism comes up against the specific material and cultural context of any of his commissions in order to create the architecture:

> Siza's non-style is a response to the real, the concrete. The formal motifs, the architecture, appear from the understanding of both the programme and the place.[169]

This is a tension that interests Moneo, and in his descriptions of Siza's architecture he often seems to be referring to his own. Siza's example encouraged his reluctance to be seduced by an architecture derived merely from an unmediated concern for the local context, which could become absorbed in the analysis and manipulation of pre-existing motifs as its genesis; Moneo was always concerned to recognize a certain autonomy of architectural form that would enter into dialogue with the context.

Such a definition of the site, as the anthropo-geological environment with which architecture enters into a dialogue, became more important during the 1980s and 1990s. Although he had been critical of Christian Norberg-Schulz's popular *Intentions in Architecture*,[170] which he found to be a reductive and deterministic way of establishing a design methodology, he recognized in his later Heideggerian books, such as *Genius Loci*,[171] an attempt to reconsider the notion of place. Heidegger's thinking was influential in Spain, as it offered a way to define a cultural practice in relation to one's own regional context in early democratic Spain.[172] Following Heidegger, Norberg-Schulz understood

---

169 Ibid., p. 4.
170 This critique is expressed in his 1972 Elements of Composition course. Rafael Moneo, 'Lección 5 – La arquitectura desde el nivel perceptivo: Nuevas aproximaciones al problema / Intentos totalizadores: Norberg-Schulz', p. 8 ('Architecture from the Perceptive Point of View: New Approaches to the Problem / Totalizing Attempts: Norberg-Schulz').
171 Christian Norberg-Schulz, *Genius Loci: Towards a Phenomenology of Architecture*, New York: Rizzoli, 1980. Also important was Christian Norberg-Schulz, *Louis I. Kahn: Idea e Imagine*, Roma: Officina Ed., 1980.
172 An intellectual predilection for Heidegger in the Spain of the 1980s emerged in the first years of the democracy, when it was necessary for the new political status of the regional autonomies to theorize an art of the land, such as those developed by Jorge Oteiza and his disciple Eduardo Chillida (in

that there was a need for a principle of reciprocity between architecture and the site, namely that architecture should not be imposed on the site, but should help in the understanding of the site, reveal its latent nature and its particular logic, whether as landscape or an urban structure. In this sense, it is architecture that constructs the site, as the act of human construction unveils it. Moneo followed this kind of intellectual discourse very closely, and it is as common to see in his lectures and articles illustrations from Norberg Schulz's *Genius Loci* as those from Rossi's *The Architecture of the City*, as he stresses the dialectical relationship between site and construction.[173]

From the mid 1980s onwards, most of Moneo's critical writings stress questions of context, as for instance in his discussion of Peter Eisenman's Wexner Centre for the Visual Arts, Frank Gehry's Walt Disney Concert Hall and Robert Venturi's Hall for the Philadelphia Orchestra. In comparing the latter two examples, Moneo modified the idea of context by invoking the notion of 'appropriateness', which he claimed would be 'more open, giving more leeway to intervention, to dialogue, without dictating a formal decision'.[174] Sometimes it is necessary to challenge the site, to negate it. This is the case in his 'Projeto Biccoca' competition entry for the Pirelli industries in Milan. Moneo understood that the site was located in such a degraded urban environment that the industrial complex should be generated without regard to any pre-existing context, as an independent city fragment to be shaped by large urban infrastructural decisions.[175] In the Miró Foundation the negation of the site is more careful. Moneo decided to use his own building to mask the

relation to the Basque region) or by Antoni Tapies (in relation to Catalonia). Among the intellectual promoters of Heidegger in Spain, perhaps the most remarkable is Professor Félix Duque from the Universidad Complutense de Madrid, who was also interested in the criticism of artistic practice. Also instrumental in the diffusion of Heideggerian thinking in the 1980s was Felipe Martínez Marzoa, professor at the Universidad Autonoma de Barcelona.

173 See for instance Rafael Moneo, 'Indifference Towards the Site', slides 1–3, *On Contemporary Architecture, Session 4*, Harvard Graduate School of Design, Spring 2006 (T.A. Francisco González de Canales).

174 Rafael Moneo, 'Reflecting on Two Concert Halls: Gehry versus Venturi', Walter Gropius Lecture, Harvard University Graduate School of Design, 25 April 1990, published in *El Croquis* 64, 'Rafael Moneo 1990/1994', February 1994 pp. 156–75; 'Unexpected Coincidences', in *Wexner Center for The Visual Arts, Ohio State University: A Building Designed By Eisenman/Trott Architects*, New York: Rizzoli, 1989, pp. 52–61.

175 A commentary on the competition can be found in Oriol Bohigas: 'Notas sobre el concurso Bicocca', Arq*uitectura* 260, May–June 1986, pp. 9–13.

low quality constructions in the immediate context, and to encourage views towards the further horizon and the sea (see pp. 139–46).

Moneo's most comprehensive definition of the concept of site occurs in his 1992 speech to the *Any* conference entitled 'The Murmur of the Site':

> Architecture relates to the real presence of the building on the site. It is there – on the site – where the specific kind of object that a building is achieves its only mode of being. It is on the site where the building acquires its necessary uniqueness; where the specificity of architecture becomes visible and can be understood as its most valuable attribute. It is the site that allows the establishment of the due distance between ourselves and the object we produce. The site is so completely inevitable that even those architects who claim to reject the idea of the site and ignore the concept of context are forced to include it in their work and, as a result, are obliged to invent a site.
>
> Architecture, by virtue of the indispensable site, then allows men and women the pleasure of transferring their individuality into objecthood. The site is the first stone we use in constructing our outside world. It provides us with a distance that allows us to see in it our ideas, our wishes, our knowledge. And then with architecture – as with many other human activities – it demonstrates for us the possibility of the transcendence of men and women.[176]

Naturally, Moneo's interest in the site is not confined to his teaching and writing, but is frequently exemplified in his own work. Already at Bankinter, one of his early masterpieces, the building reflects its particular context, from the retention of the existing Marquez de Tudela palace to the dislocations of the building form, its division into separate sections and the punctuations of its skin. All derive from his understanding of the context – the geometry of the two streets, the negotiation of the formality of the entrance, and the autonomous character of the main elevation as a dignified and somewhat abstract background to the Tudela palace. His approach is close to that of Gregotti's later theory of modification: the deformations of the logical language of the

---

176 Rafael Moneo, 'Substantial Immobility', in *Contra la Indiferencia como Norma*, Santiago: Ediciones ARQ, 1995, pp. 36–8.

87 Rafael Moneo: Bank of Spain
Competition entry, 1979. As eventually
constructed, in 2006, the detail is slightly
different, but the principle is the same

building reflect the contingencies of the site just as much as his choice of material – the deeply carved brickwork, which is sensitive to the texture and colour of the palace – without overtly mimicking it.

While most of Moneo's buildings respond in some way to the specifics of
their site, one of the most controversial was his prize-winning entry for the
extension to the Bank of Spain in Madrid in 1979. With this proposal Moneo
showed that he was quite prepared to challenge the accepted modernist dog-
ma that contemporary architecture should never replicate the styles of the
past, a premise that is even more emphatic when extending historic buildings,
since in modernist conservation practice old and new should be clearly distinguished. In this case Moneo decided to extend by employing a classical language, arguing that the circumstances of the project – the reality of the site
– demanded such a response (fig. 87). His approach contrasted with that of
most competitors, including those who attempted a version of Moneo's own
Bankinter building (fig. 88). The original building was in an eclectic classical
manner, inspired by renaissance models, by Eduardo de Adaro and Severiano
Sainz de la Lastra in 1891. Moneo considered the scale of the extension so

88 Corrales and Molezun: Bank of
Spain Competition entry, 1979 (second
proposal). This project seems to refer to
Moneo's Bankinter building

small in comparison with that of the block as a whole that it was better to follow the pattern of an earlier extension (in 1927, by José Yárnoz Larrosa), which
had already employed a slightly simplified classical style. He argued that this
was the most appropriate solution, since introducing another architectural
language would disrupt the overall coherence of the building.[177] The project
was delayed for decades, but was finally realised in a slightly different version,
while following the same principles, in 2006.

If in the Bank of Spain classical mimesis was the answer, at Murcia town
hall Moneo's approach was quite the reverse (pp. 155–62). The fact that the
building would have a presence in the square as a discrete entity persuaded
Moneo that an abstracted language was more appropriate, while the dignity

177   Rafael Moneo, 'A mi entender', Arquitectura 228, 1981, pp. 54–6.

of an institutional building was maintained by the use of materials and the subtle ordering of openings on the façade. The paving design in the square was also crucial, integrating the Episcopal palace, the baroque cathedral and the new town hall extension. And later, as already mentioned, the policy adopted at the Prado extension, somewhere between these two extremes, can be seen to refer back to the inspiration of Asplund's Law Courts extension at Gothenburg.

At another level, Moneo's attitude to context can examined by observing the way in which he integrates several urban conditions in a single work. At the National Museum of Roman Art at Mérida (pp. 127–38), the formal structure refers both to the immediate site but also to three different urban conditions that are brought together in the building: the repetitive cross-walls of a housing block, the flat concrete slabs and metal balconies of the industrial city, and the central nave of a Roman basilica. Each condition is modified by its conjunction with alternative models to form a coherent whole. The process is different in each example, so that in L'Illa Diagonal at Barcelona, Moneo realised that the formal strength of the site could absorb a powerful block whose repetitive façades of window and wall would recall the rationalist metropolitan dreams of the architects of La Tendenza.

In his Kursaal project at San Sebastián, Moneo confounds architectural preconceptions in his treatment of the building. Moneo saw that the demolition of the previous structure had left the nineteenth-century blocks of urban fabric complete in themselves, so that the new building could be conceived of as part of the geographic condition of the shore, rather than an extension of the city fabric – responding to the beach of La Concha and the Urumea river and taking on the appearance of two massive rocks on the shore. And at the Pilar and Joan Miró Foundation, Moneo's attitude to the landscape referred to the picturesque tradition, where views would be hidden and disclosed so as to make the most of a landscape that had already been badly damaged.

In each of these works, Moneo has acknowledged the particular circumstances of the context but transformed them by what he has made. His deep understanding of the interconnectedness between context and design could be considered his most important contribution to the architectural debates of his time, permeating his teaching and influencing subsequent generations of Spanish architects. In 2006, an exhibition of Spanish architecture at MoMA, New York, was entitled *On Site*. The first image was of a floor-to-ceiling photograph of Moneo's Murcia town hall extension – a tribute to the legacy of Moneo's teaching. Not only can Moneo's built work be understood as the result of a career spent considering the importance of site and context, but perhaps more importantly the ideas that he has taught and illustrated in his buildings can act as an inspiration to future generations: his own students and younger Spanish architects who have lived through a period when the last attempts at universal values of type, or architecture as a transmitted body of knowledge, have lost their authority and are now occupying a diverse and complex culture built out of the specifics of difference – in gender, culture, race, ethnicity or site.

In architecture, as in other disciplines, those who adopt an extreme position may be rewarded by a short-term notoriety, and even ensure a reputation for themselves that endures in later historical surveys. Three examples from the last quarter of the twentieth century would serve to illustrate the point. First would be the group of architects whose theoretical projects in the 1960s were published under the name 'Archigram'. Their work fetishized technology and promoted an uncritical view of the exciting world to come. It was widely published and influenced 'high-tech' architects all over the world, and because some of the group's members taught at schools of architecture, their approach was disseminated to a younger generation. Another version of an extreme approach would be that espoused by Peter Eisenman. Moneo has remained on close and friendly terms with him throughout his career, but Eisenman promulgated a rigorous formalism that disregarded questions of specific sites or contexts for buildings, and the effect that buildings might have on their occupants, in favour of an exclusive concentration on architecture as a language.[1] The reverse position is represented by dogmatic phenomenologists, who tend, under the influence of Heidegger and post-Heideggerian philosophy, both to be suspicious of technology *per se*, and to be sceptical about the idea that architectural form can, or should, be studied independently of questions of meaning. Thus these three factions can find each other's attitudes to be so wrong-headed as to be hardly worthy of discussion. But Moneo has shown interest in each of these positions. He put their writings on his students' reading lists and made sure they were aware of the strengths as well as weaknesses of each approach. He discusses alternative approaches in his own writings: he insists on the importance of technical understanding in any rounded appreciation of architecture; he has advocated the close attention to the writings of a 'formalist' such as Durand; and repeatedly he underlines the crucial importance of the specifics of the site. In his own practice, he absorbs positive lessons from each attitude to the subject.

---

1   For a recent debate in which this position is articulated, see Peter Eisenman and Mark Wigley, moderated by Enrique Walker, 'The Cat Has Nine Lives' (fourth lecture of the Wobble Series), Columbia GSAPP, 12 September 2012. www.youtube.com/watch?v=Gu4-ErX6hDA&playnext=1&list=PLhRIxbhj2GOO-eSO6aEVL_XAuRKwtPeXQ&feature=results_video. Eisenman's work does often respect context, as it happens, although he likes to claim that this is of no concern to him.

Such liberalism in theoretical and pedagogic approach, and eclecticism in practice, can lead to a lazy pragmatism in the hands of lesser talents. Much studio teaching in architectural schools is undoubtedly undertaken without any theoretical underpinning. Most architects in practice are content to absorb diverse influences in their buildings as a response to immediate pressures from client or budget, or as a result of the latest publication they happen to have seen. But Moneo has shown himself to be an extraordinarily thoughtful kind of liberal. His 'theoretical anxiety', to use his own term, has been translated into design principles that are neither constrained by an unrealistically limited position nor merely pragmatic. It seems also that his position has changed over time. In a period when architectural theorists such as Christopher Alexander or Christian Norberg-Schultz (in his earlier writing) sought to turn architecture into a science, he fought to maintain the primacy of its cultural origins. In the 1970s, under the influence of La Tendenza, he embraced the idea of typology, which reflects a Platonic idealism. But more recently, when looking back at the Urumea building, he has suggested a more Aristotelian position:

> The notion of type implies the recognition of common features that allow us to identify those works of architecture that share the same formal structure, leading us, again, to the age-old question of universality. The side one chooses to be on – Plato versus Aristotle – is crucial in defining the concept of type. While for Platonists a type is the eternal representation of the original idea, regardless of specific examples, for Aristotelians it is the common denominator that can be perceived through the careful observation of a series of works that maintain the principle of continuity through which history unfolds. These two approaches lead to clearly differentiated theories in architecture.[2]

Since Moneo's career has spanned the period of postmodernism, it would be possible to see him, as most have seen Venturi, as an architectural postmodernist. But his use of history is not ironic, and this is a crucial difference.[3] In some cases his procedure of borrowing motifs from history may be less than

---

2   Rafael Moneo, *Remarks on 21 Works*, New York: Monacelli Press, 2010, p. 19.
3   For Venturi, irony is a central tenet, just as it is in the philosophy of someone like Richard Rorty.

successful (arguably, the vaults in Seville airport, for example), but their use is entirely serious, and it is a part of Moneo's theory that critical reasoning can be brought to bear on any decision.[4]

Nevertheless, critics have been disturbed by his eclecticism. 'In what sense does Moneo have a consistent style of his own?' wondered William Curtis.[5] Is 'the move from Mérida to Kursaal' merely a reflection of changing fashions? Curtis identifies some formal continuities: the use of 'a perimeter wall with fragments or staccato pieces set off against it'; 'a relatively neutral container with a turbulent interior section'; a fascination with 'geometrical systems' both in the plan and in the façade. But although Curtis recognizes him as 'one of the most cultivated of present day architects' he finds that 'his passion for inclusion clogs the means of expression'. In part this is 'the reflection of a temperament', he concludes, 'but it also embodies some of the dilemmas of a period'.

It is possible perhaps to distinguish two kinds of eclecticism: an ironic postmodern position, represented by the work of Venturi referred to above, and an eclecticism that is consistent with a modern position – albeit one mediated by the sense of history that many architectural modernists foreswore. An analogy with twentieth-century music may be fruitful here. The Viennese composer Arnold Schoenberg, faced with the collapse of tonal musical conventions in the first decade of the twentieth century, felt compelled in the 1920s to invent an entirely new technique for ordering his compositions, and obeyed its rules, with few exceptions, in all his subsequent work. But his contemporary, the Russian émigré Igor Stravinsky, surprised everyone, after his pioneering 1913 *Rite of Spring*, by embracing a neoclassical style, in *Pulcinella* for example (1920, based on themes by Pergolesi), and played with eighteenth-century forms in *Apollon Musagète* and the music of Tchaikovsky in *The Fairy's Kiss* (both 1928). Later, after 1954, he even adopted Schoenberg's twelve-tone technique. Does this make Stravinsky a lesser composer than

---

4   In this respect one might point to the thinking of a philosopher such as Hans-Georg Gadamer, whose hermeneutics sees truth not as an absolute, but based on multiple confrontations with critical reason.

5   William Curtis, 'Pieces of City, Memories of Ruins', *El Croquis 20+64+98*; Fernando Márquez and Richard Levene (eds), *Rafael Moneo 1967–2004: Imperative Anthology*, Madrid: El Croquis Editorial, 2005, pp. 553–81.

Schoenberg? Some, such as Theodor Adorno, have thought so, but most dis-
agree.[6] Literary eclectics would include James Joyce, whose *Ulysses* (first published in its entirety in 1922) is full of parodies and allusions to writing in all
previous periods, yet it would be extraordinary to term it postmodernist.[7] In
the music of Stravinsky or the prose of James Joyce, however, it is always possible to recognize their own voice, and it will be up to individual judgement to
decide whether the same can be said for the numerous and diverse works of
Rafael Moneo.

There is also a suggestion in Curtis' criticism that Moneo has practiced
in a different time – one where a form of eclecticism is a necessity. If the
circumstances, after a period of 'heroic' modernism, do in fact require an eclectic response, then that requirement is not merely a matter of temperamental
leaning, but an ethical duty on the part of architects to educate themselves
in their discipline so that they can make informed choices, rather than being
bound to aspire to the ideal of a Master with a consistent style of their own.
And of course, as a teacher, that ethical duty extends to offering the full scope
of the 'canon' to one's pupils.

So, if architecture, as a discipline, can be understood as a form of thought
about the world as it is or as it might be, it is necessary to interpret Moneo's
career as being one that has consistently pursued a difficult middle course.[8] It
is not easy to summarize the position of someone who has refused to see technology as a liberating tool that allows the architect to engage in formal games,

---

6   Theodor W. Adorno, *Philosophy of New Music*, trans., ed. and with an introduction by Robert Hullot-
     Kentor, Minneapolis: University of Minnesota Press, 2006.

7   For an accessible yet comprehensive account of literary modernism's indebtedness to its pre-modern-
     ist antecedents, see Peter Nichols, *Modernisms: A Literary Guide*, Berkeley and New York: University
     of California Press, 1995. Attitudes to literary precedents varied, of course, between individuals such
     as Pound, Joyce, Eliot or Woolf.

8   It is possibly analogous to those philosophers who are engaged in that perpetual struggle to rec-
     oncile subjective and objective ways of seeing the world. The subjective/objective debate has been
     examined from a variety of perspectives by the American philosopher Thomas Nagel, who writes of
     objectivity, 'It is underrated by those who don't regard it as a method of understanding the world as it
     is in itself. It is overrated by those who believe it can provide a complete view of the world on its own,
     replacing the subjective views from which it has developed. These errors are connected: they both
     stem from an insufficiently robust sense of reality and of its independence of any particular form
     of human understanding.' Thomas Nagel, *The View from Nowhere*, Oxford: Oxford University Press,
     paperback edition, 1989, p. 5.

or, on the other hand, to accept that it is possible to fully engage with the art of architecture without experiencing it in the flesh. Philosophers of a similar cast of mind are equally hard to pin down. Scholars differ, for example in how they describe Spinoza: is he a theist, an atheist, or a pantheist? It is clear that he privileges thinking, but he is equally emphatic that minds cannot exist except within a body, thus distinguishing his position from that of both the philosopher Descartes and the theologian Calvin: contemplation *per se* can never constitute as complete a form of understanding as that which arises out of the combination of embodied experience and critical knowledge. To build seriously is to think about architecture, and a thorough way of thinking about architecture will necessarily involve building. Moneo's rounded career, as thinker, teacher, writer and builder, can be seen in this sense as an ethical necessity: the greatest good consists in a balance between contemplation and action, each being incomplete without the other. And Moneo's respect for the logic of someone like Durand, and at the same time his acknowledgement of poetics as fundamental, not surprisingly mesh with the phenomenon of 'having it both ways' that is characteristic of Pareyson, the philosopher to whom Moneo most frequently refers.

Thus, while Moneo's complex and subtle thinking underpins all his work as a writer, teacher and practitioner, it can be understood fully only by a direct experience of the buildings themselves, together with an engagement with its theoretical foundations. Our hope is that this book will have encouraged its readers to visit his buildings, and will have gone some way towards introducing the ideas that they represent. We believe that both aspects of Moneo's achievement will remain relevant and inspirational for architects who seek to engage responsibly in their vocation, and culturally significant for others who want to understand and appreciate the work of a man who has steered a singular and steadfast course through a period of cultural confusion.

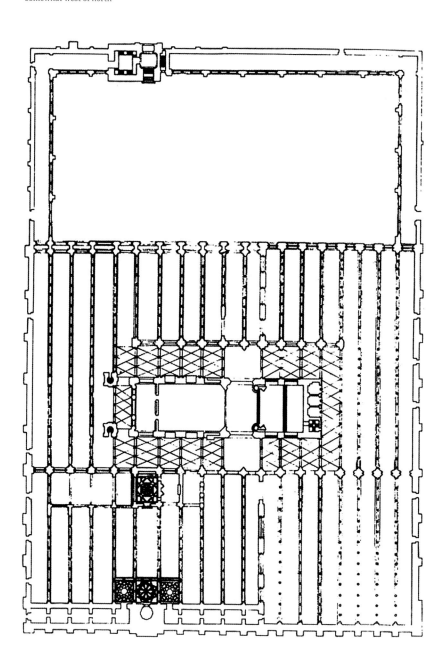

89 Plan of the Mosque at Córdoba, with the transept insertion according to Moneo. The top of the plan is oriented somewhat west of north

This essay by Rafael Moneo was originally a lecture, versions of which were delivered at the Syracuse University School of Architecture on 23 February 1997, at the Harvard University Graduate School of Design on 6 May 1977, and at the Department of Architecture of École Polytechnique Fédérale de Lausanne in June 1979. It was first published in French as 'La Vie de bâtiments: extensions de la Mosquée de Cordoue', in *DA Informations* 62, 1979, pp. 23–45. A Spanish version also circulated in manuscript to ETSAM students in about 1982, and was first published as 'La vida de los edificios' in *Arquitectura* 256, September–October 1985, pp. 26–36. It seems an original unpublished English manuscript was lost in Moneo's archives. This translation of the Spanish version by Adriana Massida and the authors is therefore the first published English version of this text.

Those who write about architecture nowadays pay little attention to the life of buildings. And yet works of architecture are affected by the passage of time in a specific, characteristic and singular way. A work of architecture ages in a very different way to a painting. Time gives more than a patina to buildings, and they frequently accept extensions, incorporate refurbishments and have their spaces altered and architectural elements changed, thus transforming or even losing the image they originally possessed. Change, continuous intervention, is the fate, whether one wants it or not, of architecture. Architects' concern to take into account continuous change, thus ensuring the work of architecture answers adequately to the passage of time, has led to the introduction of the concepts of flexibility and multi-functionality. These concepts are born from the implicit idea that the eternal youth of a building, its resistance to the passage of time, would be achieved through an 'open project', permitting a continuous adaptation to a reality that is necessarily changing. The architect would enable her or his work to withstand the passage of time, provided the project could qualify as 'open'.[1] But experience shows that the life of buildings manifests itself through the permanence over time of a building's most distinctive formal characteristics and, therefore, its life does not reside as much in the project's process as in the autonomy that the building acquires once built.

In other words, the architect realises a building and creates an entity that is perfectly understandable in itself, thanks to the formal principles embedded in its architecture: the work of architecture transcends the architect, going beyond the moment when its construction is completed, and it can, therefore, be contemplated in the changing perspective of history without its identity being lost over the passage of time. The principles of the discipline, established by the architect at the time of the construction of the work, will be kept throughout its history and, if they are robust enough, the building will be able to absorb transformations, changes, distortions, and so on, while never ceasing to be the building it was – respecting, in short, its origins.

I will try to explain some of these ideas by making use of the Mosque of Córdoba, a singular building whose history spans a period of eight centuries. The key to understanding its development resides – or at least this is how I see it – in its formal structure, and in the principles upon which this structure depends. These principles were in fact defined with enough clarity for them to be always present – despite the apparent contradictions – and always respected by the architects working on the mosque, remaining constant, therefore, throughout the continuous interventions undertaken.

The mosque of Córdoba was built by Abd ar-Rahman I.[2] Córdoba had been one of the most notable cities of the Iberian Peninsula, under both Roman and Visigoth domination. It was the last bridge over the river Guadalquivir and its strategic commercial and political importance had always been appreciated. Abd ar-Rahman, an Umayyad prince, fled from his homeland for internal political reasons and made Córdoba the capital city of a new emirate. When, after years of fighting against the Christian kingdoms of the peninsula, Abd ar-Rahman restored peace, he decided to erect a temple to proclaim the stability of his new independent dominion. The site chosen was, almost inevitably, the sacred place of the city *par excellence*, where the Christians had built the church of San Vicente, overlooking the bridge over the Guadalquivir.[3] Initiated in specific historic circumstances, with intentions and purposes that we might nowadays call foundational, the new Mosque of Córdoba was, for its architects, sufficient opportunity to develop an architecture that was able to stand as a model for the future.

As a member of the Umayyad family, Abd ar-Rahman made sure that his architects respected the precedent of the old Mosque of Damascus, which he had known in his youth. Despite using Christian structures and architectonic elements, the Mosque of Damascus had created the typological pattern for most later mosques by establishing, once and for all, the idea of Islamic religious space – a space that reflects a new way of understanding the relationships between man and God.[4] It is evident that the builders of the Mosque of Córdoba bore the Mosque of Damascus in mind and that they were conscious, therefore, of the clear differences that stand between Islamic and Christian theologies – differences that, naturally, were to be reflected in its architecture.

Islam emphasizes the omnipotent presence of God, who is uniquely endowed with the power of creation. Thus, the deliberate absence of images created by man in Islamic culture has to be understood as a sign of respect for God. The extension of these ideas to architecture implied the withdrawal of the unity and the singularity that characterized traditional western architecture and the emergence, as an alternative, of a generic, non-particularised architecture. In the latter the new idea of prayer brought by the Islamic religion could find the atmosphere that it needed: the diffuse presence of God was thus materialized in the infinitude of the artificial space of the mosque. In other words, both the axiality and sequentiality of the first Christian churches and basilicas, as well as their imposing centrality, were removed, to be replaced by a neutral, non-characterized space. The focus of the Christian space – the altar – was absorbed by the whole. The new focus was the *qibla*, a continuous 'prayer wall', with a small niche – the *mihrab* – probably inzspired by Christian apses but without their liturgical significance. The *mihrab*, however, implied the need for symmetry, which once again appears as an unavoidable formal principle, capable of imposing a certain order even under the circumstances of abstraction and indifferentiation inherent in the architecture of the mosque. The Christian church, longitudinal and processional, became a building with a courtyard, in the manner of a sacred city, where a transition to covered space has to be understood as a step forward in the private and individual relationship that the adherent to Islam establishes with God.

The covered space of the Mosque of Damascus was formed by three parallel naves oriented towards the wall of the *qibla*. The central space, located under a dome that reinforced the presence of the *mihrab*, was a significant tribute to centrally planned Christian churches, which were inheritors of the late Roman tradition. A desire to relax the tension of the Christian churches, due, in some cases, to their powerful sensation of directionality, and in other cases to the existence of an absorbing centrality, is perceptible. The small

dome is more an architectonic element than an ideological or ritual imposi-
tion. In the Mosque of Baalbek and, later on, in some Egyptian mosques, this
central space disappeared and the parallel walls became the most important
elements of the building. The mosque is consolidated as a new architectural type, which, judging by these antecedents, can be interpreted as a radical
transformation of late Roman basilical architecture. The introduction of a different syntax, inspired by a different conception of the world, is, ultimately,
responsible for that transformation, and it does not really matter that, both
in Damascus and in Cairo, columns and elements taken directly from Roman
architecture are used: the mosque reveals itself as a very well-defined type,
fully presented, and with it emerges a whole new architecture – the Islamic.

Let me now turn to Córdoba. I have already explained how previously
established types were respected in Abd ar-Rahman's mosque, but at the same
time they underwent such deep changes that this mosque can be considered
a unique and singular architectonic event. The first characteristic that makes
it unique and singular is, no doubt, the change in the orientation of the walls:
perpendicular to the *qibla*, not parallel as is usual. This seems logical in terms
of privileging the visibility of the *qibla*. However, such a change follows a
complex structural decision, which, as will be explained later, was decisive for
the spatial ordering of the mosque.

A simple description of the structure would be to say that that the load-
bearing walls have been perforated by means of arches over columns, but that
would mean reducing the constructive problem of the mosque to a problem
of planar geometry. The reason why we talk about walls when describing the
mosque is perhaps because these are identified, metaphorically, with aqueducts. So we see how, in the Mosque of Córdoba, a system of walls, that drains
rainwater at the same time that it spans over the internal space, becomes an
element of special interest as the walls accept, with naïve literality, their condition as aqueducts.[5] But immediately, once that metaphor is accepted, it is
important to see that this is only a starting point, since the final constructive technique was developed well beyond such an 'image': the availability of
'already-used elements' became the key for the architects who used these elements as the basis for their work. The materials, thus, were given; columns
and capitals were 'already-used elements', taken from Roman buildings as
well as from primitive Christian and Visigoth churches: their complete and

singular condition lent them a certain timeless aura. In fact, these were elements that, in their radical solitude and autonomy, could be reused without paying attention to the stylistic context from which they had been taken.[6]

Relying on these elements, and conceiving the structure as a whole, the architect of the Mosque of Córdoba defined the stereometry of the arches over pillars and the horseshoe arches, while resorting to traditional timber construction supported by load-bearing walls for the design of the roof structure.[7] The construction demanded the introduction of new elements, such as cyma mouldings, to ease the adjustment between the 'already-used elements' and the new geometry that the layout of the mosque required.

A pragmatic interpretation could suggest that the architect, wishing a higher roof and not satisfied with placing it over a wall supported by a series of horseshoe arches over columns, decided to incorporate a new series of semicircular arches – a second order – to reach the height he was aiming for. The increased thickness of the higher arch could be explained by the presence of the gutter that requires a thicker wall. However, if what we seek is an explanation of the formal problems of the mosque, we need to take into account a higher level of complexity in order to understand the thought and reasoning of the architects – thought that led, ultimately, to those formal principles that allowed the construction we now see. Thus, if we accept an explicit wish of greater height as the main aim, we would understand the structure as a series of semicircular arches over slender pillars tied by a hypothetical transverse element – the horseshoe arch – which has been incorporated into the design to guarantee the stability of the structure. Thus, the Mosque of Córdoba would be a system of aqueduct walls that run perpendicular to the *qibla* and ultimately generate the spatial experience: the only perceptible direction would be then this one. However, once we take into account the thickness of those parallel walls, then we can read the semicircular arches defined by them as a series of continuous vaults: a new direction is thus introduced, parallel to the *qibla*.

The formal structure of the mosque depends on the intersection of both systems – an intersection that is of course virtual but is also irreducible. The architectonic definition of the formal structure lies, ultimately, in this intersection: it is because of such a 'virtual intersection' that the architect can proceed to compose the building. This is how both directions can be suppressed in the real space of the mosque and how the insistent and powerful presence of the columns can be understood, as the result of these virtual planes. The space defined by the columns – the abstract grid they form, in which all reference to the past fades away – is a clear expression of the new religious space, neutral and undifferentiated, earlier described. It is also relevant, however, to read the grid in strictly formal terms, those used by the architects to lay the foundations on which to build their works.[8]

In any case, either by starting from the analysis of the roof or by following the chronological order of construction, we will need to take into account other interventions that, although less obvious, cannot be deemed secondary. In some instances they serve to articulate different elements. In other examples, they emphasize effectively and simply the formal structure of the building. But, in either case, such interventions should be understood as a means of providing the architects with the flexibility that they needed when working with pre-existing pieces. This explains the origin of the element that resolves the higher part of the capital, where the pillar, the horseshoe arch and the capital-column converge. The architect defined a new element, as simple as it is effective, that solved the conjunction of them all. In another instance, the transition from the square base to the rectangular section of the pillars was resolved with an element that would acquire especial relevance in Islamic and Mozarabic architecture over time: the *modillón de rollos* as Gómez-Moreno called it.[9]

The colourful voussoirs of the arches are another important feature of the Mosque of Córdoba.[10] It has been frequently stressed that they had already been used in Syrian architecture, as well as in some Roman works, such as the Los Milagros aqueduct in Mérida, which emphasizes the close relationship between Roman examples and the Mosque of Córdoba.[11] However, it is also important to see them as further proof of the presence at Córdoba of the formal mechanism described earlier. Thus, they could be understood as the result of an intimate overlap: the architectonic form in the Mosque of Córdoba results from an interaction between simple elements, each with their own autonomous significance, in very different planes, that merge into a new whole; the result is an integrated form, in which the components that constitute it disappear as such and lose their singular identity, producing a new reading. The horseshoe arch, for example, is a structural element that gives stability

to the slender pillars over the columns; but at the same time it fulfils the delicate formal function of emphasising the spatiality of the direction parallel to
the *qibla*, which, with the help of the arches, trace a never-ending perspective. The colourful voussoirs, in turn, favour such an interpretation by giving
expression to the clash between the horseshoe arches and the pillars.

We have thus reached a point in which it is possible to state that the formal principles of the Mosque of Córdoba were so clearly established from the
beginning and were, in addition, so decisive, that the later extensions of the
building did not lead to its radical transformations. The future life of a building is implied in the formal principles that are present in its origin, and this
is why understanding these gives us clues for understanding the building's
history. This is what we will do now by examining how such principles are
present in the long life of the mosque.

When Abd ar-Rahman II wanted to extend the mosque, the issue was
clear: the mosque would grow southwards. The wall of the *qibla* was partially
demolished to allow a way through, and eight new arcades were built. The
remains of the old *qibla* were retained because suppressing them would have
been structurally risky, since it was necessary to counteract the horizontal
load of the series of arches. But the spatial sensation was not altered, and
the new intervention was absorbed by the existing space without leading to
fundamental changes: the remnants of the old wall of the *qibla* would be, in
the future, only an accident in the continuous space of the mosque. Curiously,
an important modification took place in the *modillones de rollos* – their
mouldings were simplified – which demonstrates that the builder was conscious of the inherent formal problems.[12]

Muhammad I, son of Abd ar-Rahman II, finished the work started by his
father by erecting the west wall.[13] It is believed that he built the Puerta de
San Esteban too, where, once again, the mechanism of overlapping is what
enables us to understand the complex geometrical system that determines
the construction. It would be very difficult to explain such intricate ornamentation without resorting to the idea of overlapping as a basic formal mechanism. Only in this way is it possible to understand how the plane of the wall
is treated as a geometrical surface: various virtual planes intertwine in it, defining a whole series of geometrical conventions that make the architectural
construction possible.[14]

Under Abd ar-Rahman III, in the zenith of the emirate, minor alterations were undertaken. The works continued and a second façade was erected, duplicating the existing one and repeating the theme of the columns tied to pillars.[15] Later on, in subsequent extensions, this solution of the double wall would be repeated, transforming what had been a specific and singular design dictated by necessity into a reproducible model.

The extension of Al-Hakam II was no doubt the most important one: it completely transformed the dimensions of the mosque and introduced a new spatial order. The scale of this intervention led to a new interpretation of the whole mosque: through the work of Al-Hakam's architect, the mosque became a new building in which daring inventions coexisted with the formal principles previously established.[16]

The first mosque – that of Abd ar-Rahman I – made a wide precinct where all reference to the processional directionality that characterized the Christian churches had been abandoned. The memory of the Mosque of Damascus, as has already been noted, had been maintained by privileging the direction parallel to the *qibla*, despite the new orientation of the naves. The extension of Abd ar-Rahman II neutralized the space, leaving it virtually square. The original mosque, that of Abd ar-Rahman I, became in fact a precinct that gave access to the extension, which could thus be conceived, in a way, as an independent, autonomous space. But even so it is important to stress that the scale of the intervention, carefully established, made it possible for its original space to remain unaltered.

The later extension by Al-Hakam clearly introduced a sense of depth – in opposition to the frontal, flat condition of the first mosque – completely transforming the existing construction through the use of new elements and the incorporation of new formal mechanisms. The mosque, though, was transformed without losing the continuity with the existing fabric. The mosques of Abd ar-Rahman I and Abd ar-Rahman II became a real threshold and an authentic sanctuary in the inevitable transition towards the new mosque.[17] The new precinct, the extension of Al-Hakam, had approximately the same dimensions as the first mosque in plan, but it is difficult to compare them because their differences are pronounced. The wall of the *qibla* was perforated with extreme care, introducing once again additional columns that, standing on the nave, narrowed it down, making clear that this was the entrance to a new precinct. It was in this entrance that the most important change was introduced, since sophisticated skylights were built with the help of high-level domes of ribbed construction. These would have a decisive influence both on the plan and on the appearance of the interior spaces, since they transformed the lighting conditions. In addition, domes and skylights facilitated the way to the *mihrab* and created independent autonomous spaces capable of being appreciated in their own right despite sitting over the general grid of columns of the mosque.

The first of these spaces, the present Capilla de Villaviciosa, was a virtual precinct situated on the axis that led to the *mihrab*, over the threshold of the entrance to the area built by Al-Hakam. It took up three bays of the axial nave and was defined by a pair of columns standing in the central opening, forming the angles of the virtual rectangle, reinforced by three independent columns. This structure, with a simple plan, sustained quite a complex volume: the planes that contained the arches had to be substantially modified given the necessity for higher walls that could support the dome.

The mosque was thus heightened and it was necessary to modify the previous structure, which was too fragile. The architect of the extension found a subtle solution to this problem by building a pseudo-wall with interwoven arches, resorting to the same complex geometry used in other elements of the mosque. The mechanism of overlapping described before once again took on a definitive importance for the perforated walls, converted now into complex three-dimensional structures: the key to understanding this geometry is to always read the planes as such and imagine that over each of them others can be superimposed and related to each other through their intertwining.[18]

This method of conceiving the architectural construction reached its higher expression, both in complexity and beauty, in the domes of the Mosque of Córdoba, where, more than a century before the emergence of the ribbed vault in France, ribs were used for vaulting a space, giving rise to a work of architecture in which technological invention and delicate geometry were fused.[19] The arches keep their integrity but, at the same time, there is a three-dimensional awareness that converts the domes into independent autonomous elements. Architecture has often been bound to geometry, but the intimate relationship between them has very seldom achieved that zenith of perfection reached in the Mosque of Córdoba, where the stereometry was produced with outstanding accuracy.

The new Capilla de Villaviciosa played the role of articulation – a virtual door between the old and the new mosques – and so became the authentic threshold of the way that led to the *qibla*. This virtual function was reinforced by lighting, which, cast from above, invested this entrance, which was the only access to the most sacred of the precincts, with notable importance. Thus, this space, which would later be called the 'sky-lit chapel', defined the way to the *qibla* and anticipated the presence of the most sacred place, the *mihrab*, which could be perceived in the background by means of natural light that drew fantastic patterns as it slid through the geometry of the three precincts built around it. [20]

The autonomy of the spaces was emphasized once again by the presence of columns in the free space of the nave. It is important to point out that, in the dimness of the mosque, this wall, taller, illuminated by the windows of the dome, brought about a strange sensation of clarity with the light falling through the voids traced by the interwoven arches. The spatial neutrality of the first mosque gave way to a complex space in which lighting played a key role. And this is perhaps the adequate occasion to note that, produced as they were in the context of Islamic architecture, with its characteristic absence of spatial sequence, the punctual interventions became more evident. The result was an architectonic experience whose formal mechanisms were not despotically imposed, and which only careful investigative study could uncover.[21]

The next extension of the mosque was carried out under the direction of Almanzor, who managed to get control of the Córdoba empire after the death of Al-Hakam. The new extension of the mosque was neither justified by the development of the building itself – its internal logic – nor by the need of a larger sacred space, and made sense only from the political point of view, as a monumental public work, as a demonstration of power.

Almanzor's extension was undertaken sideways, completely ignoring the axis of the entrance, and did not bring about any innovations. The wall of the *qibla* had been recently erected and was fortunately not altered. The only formal reasons that could help to explain this new extension are the ones related to the desire of achieving a more even, squarer space, able to neutralize the axiality of the mosque of Al-Hakam. However, despite the unfavourable comments made by historians and critics, this extension deserves, in our opinion, some attention.

Thus, the fact that the architects appreciated the necessity of dividing the large built area is a clear sign their sensitivity. With this aim they extended the *qibla* of Abd ar-Rahman II. The intersection formed by the east wall and the *qibla* became one of the most important elements of the mosque. This introduced a new feature, a solid structure in the void between columns, which would generate a new orientation: among the forest of columns, the two thick perpendicular walls built by Almanzor imposed a new reading of the mosque. Once the directionality of the mosque of Al-Hakam was diluted, an undifferentiated space became once again the most significant characteristic of the building.

Furthermore, the ability of the architects – probably still under the influence of the builders of Al-Hakam – can be also found in the solutions given to specific problems, such as the skill with which the openings communicating both mosques were carved: the buttresses of the east wall were removed and the thickness of the wall was distorted by means of large horseshoe arches supported by pairs of columns.[22]

However, the columns lost their refined profile and the capitals were not carved with the exquisite gentleness that had been characteristic of the period of Al-Hakam. In fact, the sculptural elements of the extension of Almanzor lacked the elegance that distinguished their predecessors, even though the abstract synthesis of the capitals displays a talent that deserves our admiration and respect.

During the two following centuries the Mosque of Córdoba remained as Almanzor had left it. But at the beginning of the thirteenth century the city fell into Christian hands and the mosque once again became the subject of changes and alterations.

It seems that the transformation of the mosque into a Christian church was undertaken without affecting its architectonic structure. Fernando III El Santo discreetly occupied one of the corners of Almanzor's extension in order to allow the conquerors to conduct their worship. Some years later, the entrance to the mosque of Al-Hakam – the first of the domes of ribbed arches and wonderful skylights – became the main chapel and was named 'Capilla de Villaviciosa'. The Christian focus of the mosque was thus established there, while the rest remained virtually unaltered.

When Alfonso X El Sabio decided to build his burial chapel, he chose to do so close to the Capilla de Villaviciosa.[23] It is interesting to note here that the Capilla Real (Royal Chapel) was built in the same way as the mosque, and indeed that it was executed by Islamic labour, without giving way to the gothic style of the conquerors. This shows some tolerance by the Christian builders of the culture and religion of those they had defeated. The Capilla Real repeated the structural scheme of the existing domes, adding only a more abundant and less taut decoration.

The mosque remained, therefore, almost unaltered from the times of Almanzor until the late-fifteenth century. It was then, in 1489, when the bishop Manrique, influenced no doubt by the re-emergence of war – Granada, the last of the Moorish kingdoms, would fall a few years later – decided to transform the mosque into a proper Christian church.

The lack of spatial articulation of the mosque was inadequate for Christian worshippers, who had been used to the axiality of basilicas and cathedrals for many centuries. Thus, the first step towards a Christian church was to open a longitudinal nave, which was possible by replacing three arches by only a single lancet arch. This was the start of a new time in the life of the Mosque of Córdoba. It is necessary, however, to stress that the Christian builders operated with a deep knowledge of the mosque and its significance. This understanding is especially evident in the change of the orientation. The Christian builders understood the importance of the orientation and, since they wanted to avoid the use of the Islamic mosque, they completely changed it. In addition, the axis of the old mosque of Al-Hakam was interrupted by the longitudinal church set into it. Such insertion was undertaken with great accuracy: the Christian builders chose to place it on the boundary between the mosques of Abd ar-Rahman II and Al-Hakam and, by doing this, distorted the order of the mosque, cleverly managing its architecture. Thus, employing Moorish labour, they set the chevet of the new church in the so-called Capilla de Villaviciosa. The former articulation between the mosques of Abd ar-Rahman II and Al-Hakam, the key point in the ensemble, thus became a virtual transept in the new Christian church.

In addition, from a pragmatic point of view, the new church would be intelligently located: the Christian builders used one of the old *qiblas* to support the horizontal loads of the arches of the new church, therefore needing buttresses on only one side. The first Christian intervention in the mosque was then characterised by both its economy and its efficacy.

The second intervention requires a more careful analysis: it is not as clear as the first, and the same uncertainty that accompanied its construction has always remained present in the criticisms made about it.[24]

The Mosque of Córdoba, which had survived for 200 years in Christian hands without major changes, was faced with a major threat when at the end of the war, with the fall of Granada in 1492, and not satisfied with merely having set Christian worship in it, people argued for its complete transformation into a Christian cathedral. The campaign gave rise to heated debates, including royal interventions and popular outcry, which only ended when, in 1523, Carlos I approved Cabildo's project. Christians were unsettled by the perceptibly Muslim sacred quality of the space of the mosque and saw the construction of the new cathedral as its necessary purification. Nobody discussed the project in terms of an extension to the structure. The discussion was rather centred on how to build in the interior of the old mosque: inclusion rather than expansion.

The work was entrusted to an experienced Castilian architect, Hernán Ruiz El Viejo, who worked in the prosperous area of Andalucía in the sixteenth century, where he was highly respected as the master builder for the cathedral of Seville.[25] It is worth recognizing that, despite the severe and repeated criticism levelled at the cathedral, the work of Hernán Ruiz was undertaken with skill and talent. It was a difficult job and was resolved with extreme wisdom: nobody will deny that, in order to insert a late gothic cathedral within the continuous – and fragile – structure of a mosque, a clear knowledge of both architectures was needed. Hernán Ruiz knew both of them well and was capable of carrying out such adaptation without causing any considerable damage to the old structure, which naturally imposed limitations on the new one.

The choice of location within the mosque was made with a full awareness of the problems that this implied, and those problems were resolved with masterly talent. As for the construction of the first Christian church, the analysis of the existing elements was carried out thoroughly and its reutilization in the new building contributed to the success of the operation. Thus, the wall of the *qibla* built by Abd ar-Rahman I – which had been perforated by Abd ar-Rahman II and later extended by Almanzor – was rightly considered one of the most solid elements of the mosque and used as basis for a series of buttresses. The resulting symmetric system absorbed two of the columns, ensuring maximum respect for the existing structure by avoiding their destruction.

Such respect for the grid of columns, continuous and rectangular, can be appreciated in the plan of the gothic precinct, aligned to the oldest qibla, which implies the emergence, in inevitable symmetry, of a new wall, without any additional substantive structural element apart from the grid of slender columns of the mosque.

The transept ran beside the east wall, the one perforated in Almanzor's extension, and its horizontal loads were absorbed by a system of cross-buttresses and a new structural element settled over the grid of columns. The horizontal loads of the door and the access to the nave were absorbed by a series of small rear chapels and by a pre-portico that defined an entrance hall.

The new cathedral demanded a new reading of the building: the continuity of the space had been broken, and a new architecture emerged, miraculously, in the space that was now fragmented, and whose stylistic characterization would be difficult. The axis that used to lead to the *mihrab* was used as the way to the entrance to the cathedral, and the pre-portico was set over it. But the axis of the mosque was interrupted by the two churches, and thus Al-Hakam's route to the *mihrab* was definitely lost. Despite the apparent regularity of the perimeter wall, the mosque has remained ever since a fragmented building that is difficult to apprehend.[26]

The insertion of the cathedral was carried out with such accuracy that its presence in the interior of the mosque still constitutes a continuous surprise for those fond of observing the problems faced by architects. It is not possible to appreciate in plan the clever way in which the void of the cathedral violently negates the moderate height of the mosque, capitalizing in this way on the intensity that can be achieved when two such different architectures collide. Paradoxically, the cathedral actually enhanced the unity of the mosque. Even Almanzor's extensions, which had so far not made sense, acquired coherence when wrapping up the body of the Christian church. The presence of the former mosques, from Abd ar-Rahman I to Almanzor, emphasized by the different *qiblas*, was dissolved through this operation, and only one mosque survived: the complex and elusive Mosque of Córdoba. Critics and historians have frequently regretted what happened and have even proposed cleaning up the mosque by eliminating the most recent intervention, the one that led to the construction of the Christian cathedral. Carlos I's statement when visiting Córdoba has been repeatedly quoted, since it is known that he was fascinated by the mosque; faced by advisors who recommended that he insist on the construction of the cathedral, he complained that, by doing 'what can be done elsewhere', they would destroy 'what was unique in the world'.[27] I do not believe, however, that all these refurbishments have destroyed the mosque. I rather think that the fact that the mosque is still itself after all the interventions undertaken constitutes a homage to its own integrity. Its general physical features, its architecture, have remained, despite the vicissitudes here described. The fact that the future life of a building is implied in its architecture does not mean that history will flow through it, converting it automatically in a reflection of time. The life of a building is a complete course through time – a course supported by its architecture, by its characteristic formal features. This means that, from the moment at which the building emerges as the reality desired for the project, such reality will stand only by virtue of its architecture, which will undergo its own unique development over time.

It is usually thought that the life of buildings concludes with their construction and that the integrity of a building consists of keeping it exactly as its builders left it. This would reduce its life to a single, condensed instant. In some cases it is relevant to insist on the strict conservation of a building; however, that means, in a way, that the building has died; perhaps for fair and understandable reasons, it has been violently interrupted. I agree with the comments made by Ruskin in the 'Lamp of Memory', when he explains his ideas about restoration and the problems involved.[28] He says that a building without life stops being a building and becomes another type of object. A museum of architecture is impossible, and the attempts that have been made to create one have demonstrated that it is possible to collect fragments of architecture, which perhaps illustrate it, but that they are not capable of recreating the experience that, as a singular phenomenon, any architecture implies.

If the architecture is firmly established, it will stay open to new interventions and these will extend indefinitely the life of the building. The Mosque of Córdoba is perhaps an exceptional example: its characteristics, the formal mechanisms of its composition were so strong that, once they were defined, they set forevermore both the image and the structure of the building, which lasted without being substantially altered by the interventions carried out over time. This way of understanding the life of buildings is far from the concepts of flexibility and multi-functionality proposed by architectural theory some years ago as a solution to the problems that stem from the unavoidable temporality of architecture. At the same time, the idea of 'life' that I am proposing here should not be mistaken for a biological metaphor: I am referring to a real historic life and not to an analogical one. The life of buildings is supported by their architecture and by the permanence of their most distinctive formal features, and, although it may seem a paradox, it is this degree of permanence that makes it possible to appreciate the changes. The respect for the architectonic identity of a building is what makes change possible – it is this that guarantees its life.

R.M.

NOTES

1   In the 1960s, 'openness' was a synonym for modernity. The title of Umberto Eco's book *Opera aperta* can be seen as a clear testimony of this attitude.

2   For a general account of the Mosque of Córdoba, see Fernando Chueca Goitia, *Historia de la arquitectura española*, Madrid, 1965; Manuel Gómez-Moreno, *El arte árabe español hasta los almohades*, Madrid, 1951; Leopoldo Torres-Balbás, *La mezquita de Córdoba y las ruinas de Madinat al-Zahra*, Madrid, 1952. Specific studies about the successive extensions can be found in Élie Lambert, *Las tres primeras etapas constructivas de la mezquita de Córdoba*, Al-Andalus, III, Madrid, 1935, pp. 391–2, and Élie Lambert, *Études sur la grande mosquée de Cordoue*, Études Médiévales, Toulouse, 1956. See also the studies of Keppald Creswell, *A Short Account of Early Muslim Architecture*, London, 1958; and Georges Marçais, *L'architecture musulmane d'Occident*, Paris, 1954. In regard to hispano-islamic culture see Henri Terrasse, *L'Islam d'Espagne*, París, 1958 and François de Montêquin, *Compendium of Hispano-Islamic Architecture*, Saint Paul Minn., 1976.

3   See Gómez-Moreno, *El arte árabe español hasta los almohades*, pp. 19–20, and later on, pp. 24–30. The old church of San Vicente was shared by both religions, Christian and Muslim, after the Arabic conquest. The Christian half was completed in AD786. It is likely that San Vicente was an important church, although exactly how it looked is unknown; however, Gómez-Moreno suggests that 'there is no doubt about the materials used, and it was probably built at large scale'. For San Vicente, see also M. Ocaña Jiménez, *La basílica de San Vicente en la gran mezquita de Córdoba*, Al-Andalus, VI, Madrid, pp. 347–66.

4   Other writings about the mosque have also insisted on this strong relation between architecture and theological thought; see Gómez-Moreno, *El arte árabe español hasta los almohades*, p. 30, and Torres-Balbás, *La mezquita de Córdoba y las ruinas de Madinat al-Zahra*, pp. 11–12. But it was Fernando Chueca in particular, their disciple, who examined this topic in his book *Invariantes castizos de la arquitectura española*, Madrid, 1947. Here he explains brilliantly, at the start of the second

chapter, the links between architecture and theology: he explains the spatial discontinuity and the lack of formal resolution in Islamic architecture from the point of view of the Muslim conception of the world. This is why in the Mosque of Córdoba there is not a single viewpoint as in the continuous perspective space of the traditional Western architecture.

5   Gómez-Moreno, Torres-Balbás and Chueca see in the Los Milagros aqueduct at Mérida an antecedent of the Mosque of Córdoba. Torres-Balbás has often stressed how much Islamic architects owed to Roman: there is no doubt that the Arabs were knowledgeable about Roman architecture from the time they passed through the North of Africa on their way to Spain.

6   Bases, columns, capitals and voussoirs were taken from buildings all over the country. The architect used them to define a horizontal structure over which to erect the system of arches and walls. Very often, when levelling the ground, some bases were buried.

7   A complete analysis of the horseshoe arch can be found in Emilio Camps Cazorla, *Módulo, proporciones y composición en la arquitectura califal cordobesa*, Madrid, 1953. Once again, Torres-Balbás insists on their Roman origin; Torres-Balbás, *La mezquita de Córdoba y las ruinas de Madinat al-Zahra*, p. 30.

8   If we start from the roof, the Mosque of Córdoba could be clearly read as a system of columns and arches that define a wall. These columns have been trimmed and laid on a sophisticated series of arches and columns that support them with a stunning equilibrium: in this interpretation the horseshoe arches act as ties between the columns, guaranteeing stability. However, if we start from the ground, the fragile system of columns and arches grows up in thickness, defining a continuous series of semicircular arches that allow for a horizontal roof. It is evident that the *raison d'être* of the complex mechanism of connection between wall and column distinctive of the Mosque of Córdoba is not just the desire to raise the roof. And in this subtle contest between the horseshoe and the semicircular arches, 'the architect of the Mosque of Córdoba preferred the horseshoe to the semicircular, following the Visigoth tradition, for aesthetic reasons – given that it is difficult to find any other explanation', Gómez-Moreno, *El arte árabe español hasta los almohades*, p. 36.

9   It seems that this point was key to the whole construction of the Mosque of Córdoba. The skill of the architect becomes clear when entrusting a new element, the 'modillón de rollos', with the transition from the pillar to the spring. The book *Iglesias mozárabes españolas: arte español de los siglos IX al XI*, by Gómez-Moreno, identifies a series of Mozarabic churches in which one of the characteristic features, used to describe a particular style, is the use of such elements.

10   Later on, Torres-Balbás published an article, *Los modillones de lóbulos: Ensayo de análisis de la evolución de una forma arquitectónica a través de dieciseis siglos*, Madrid: Archivo Español de Arte y Arqueología, 34 and 35, 1936, which contains an extremely precise study of the evolution of the element. See also Manuel Gómez-Moreno, *La Mezquita mayor de Tudela*, Príncipe de Viana, Pamplona, 1945.

11   Voussoirs alternating marble and basalt had been already used in the Mosque of Damascus, which may have influenced the architects of the Mosque of Córdoba. However, most historians (Gómez-Moreno, Torres-Balbás, Chueca) prefer to trace a closer relation to some late Roman works, especially with the Los Milagros aqueduct mentioned earlier. Gómez-Moreno has advanced an explanation that underlines the necessity of flexibility during construction; Gómez-Moreno, *El arte árabe español hasta los almohades*, p. 36.

12   See Leopoldo Torres-Balbás, *Los modillones de lóbulos*, Archivo de Arte y Arqueología, XII, 1936, p. 44; and also Gómez-Moreno, *El arte árabe español hasta los almohades*, pp. 47–51.

13   Élie Lambert has suggested that Muhammad's contribution was greater than it is generally believed. Lambert states that the two aisles were modified during Muhammad 's reign; he supports his argument by means of documents uncovered by Levi-Provençal and on an analysis of the *modillones* of the aisles. See Lambert, '*Études sur la grande mosquée de Cordoue*. Torres-Balbás indicates his disagreement in *Los modillones de lóbulos*, Archivo Español de Arte y Arqueología, 1936.

14   See the drawings of the book of Camps Cazorla, *Módulo, proporciones y composición en la arqui-tectura califal cordobesa*. Camps stresses the abstract character of such a geometrical system and offers a very interesting group of drawings exploring the mechanisms of the composition.

15   Later on, in the early seventeenth century, the tower would be absorbed by a newer tower. The second façade was probably constructed for aesthetic reasons: the horizontal load of the horseshoe arches had already been taken by the original façade.

16   Gómez-Moreno gives the name of C'haafar, 'the slave', as architect of the Mosque of Córdoba. See Gómez-Moreno, *El arte árabe español hasta los almohades*, p. 91.

17   Chueca has drawn the hypothetical plan of the new mosque, treating it as an independent and autonomous building. Fernando Chueca, *Historia de la arquitectura española*, Madrid, 1965, p. 99.

18   Camps Cazorla, *Módulo, proporciones y composición en la arquitectura califal cordobesa*, pp. 74–83, incl. figures.

19   See Manuel Gómez-Moreno, *El cruzamiento de los arcos*, Paris: Congreso de la Historia del Arte, 1921, and also Élie Lambert, *Les voûtes nervurées hispano-musulmanes*, Hesperis, VI, Rabat, 1928, re-printed later in Lambert, *Études sur la grande mosquée de Cordoue*.

20   A precise and complete description that takes into account these two texts can be found in Leopoldo Torres-Balbás, *Las bóvedas nervadas andaluzas y los orígenes de la ojiva*, Al-Andalus, III, Madrid, Granada, 1935.

21   There is a complete study in Gómez-Moreno, *El arte árabe español hasta los almohades*, pp. 110–49. The explanation of the geometrical system proposed by E. Camps Cazorla is also interesting. See Camps Cazorla, *Módulo, proporciones y composición en la arquitectura califal cordobesa*, pp. 111–14 and figures 85–9.

22   See Gómez-Moreno, *El arte árabe español hasta los almohades*, p. 163, and Leopoldo Torres-Balbás, *La mezquita de Córdoba y las ruinas de Madinat al-Zahra*, Madrid, 1952, pp. 88–94.

23   See Torres-Balbás, *La mezquita de Córdoba y las ruinas de Madinat al-Zahra*, pp. 100–105.

24   In general, the construction of the cathedral within the Mosque of Córdoba has been subjected to severe criticism, and cleaning up the mosque by demolishing the cathedral has been often pro-posed. The last such attempt, in the early 1970s, was abandoned after the difficulties of the task were established. Even someone like Fernando Chueca wondered about the convenience of demol-ishing the cathedral; see Fernando Chueca, *Historia de la arquitectura española*, Madrid, 1956, p. 106. Torres-Balbás accepts the presence of the cathedral as a necessary tribute to the conservation of the rest: Torres-Balbás, *La mezquita de Córdoba y las ruinas de Madinat al-Zahra*, p. 116.

25   Hernán Ruiz El Viejo was head of a family of Castilian architects who worked in Andalucía through-out the sixteenth century. He died in Córdoba in 1547 and was succeeded by his son Hernán Ruiz El Joven, who continued his father's work until his death in 1569. The last vaults were finished in 1607 under the direction of Juan de Oliva.

26   See Fernando Chueca, *Arquitectura del siglo XVI*, Ars Hispaniae, Madrid, 1953, pp. 199–201; Martin Soria and George Kubler, *Art and Architecture in Spain and Portugal*, London: Pelican History of Art, 1958; A. de la Banda, *Hernán Ruiz II*, Seville, 1975. The theoretical works of Hernán Ruiz El Joven have been published by Pedro de Navascués in *El libro de la arquitectura de Hernán Ruiz, el Joven*, Publicaciones de la ETSAM, Madrid, 1971.

27   The new cathedral was built after a dispute between the Church and the Council. Eventually, Carlos I found in favour of the bishop. Nevertheless, on his first visit to Córdoba, he said: 'I was not aware of what this was, because otherwise I would not have allowed them to reach the old [structure]; because you have done what can be done elsewhere and have destroyed what is unique in the world.' Quoted by Antonio Ponz in *Viaje a España*, XVII, Madrid, 1792, p. 2.

28   John Ruskin, *The Stones of Venice*, London, 1858.

H Muebles, 1960. Furniture competition entry, first prize.

'Muebles Populares' for the Ministry of Housing, 1961.

School centre in Soria, 1961. Competition entry (with José María Castro Martínez, Julio Enrique Simonet Barrio and Antonio Sánchez Martínez-Conde).

Restoration centre for the University of Madrid, 1961. National Prize of Architecture (with Fernando Higueras).

Housing Peláez, Tudela, 1961–2.

Proposal for a building at the Obradoiro Square, Santiago de Compostela, 1962. Competition for a scholarship to stay at the Spanish Royal Academy in Rome, Prix de Rome, 1962.

Market in Caceres, 1962. Competition entry, second prize.

Asúa Valley urban plan, Bilbao, 1962. Competition entry.

Montbau church, Barcelona, 1963. Competition entry.

Madrid Opera, 1964. Competition entry.

Spanish Pavilion at the New York 1964 International Exposition, 1964. Competition entry.

Vizcaya Bank, 1964. Competition entry.

Hostel at San Miguel de Aralar, Navarra, 1965. Competition entry.

Diestre Transformer Factory, Zaragoza, 1965–7.

Housing building in Tudela, Navarra, 1965–7.

Confecciones Gallego shops in Tudela, Calatayud and San Sebastián, 1966–72.

Pamplona Bullring Extension, 1966–7. From a first prize-awarded competition entry.

Burgos Bullring, 1966. Competition entry.

Schools in Tudela, 1966. Competition entry, second prize.

Gómez-Acebo House, La Moraleja, Madrid, 1966–9.

Proposal for housing at Paseo de la Habana, Madrid, 1966–7.

Houses for Quimicas Ebro in Cortes, Navarra, 1967–8.

Irati housing, Pamplona, 1967–70.

Amsterdam town hall, 1967–8. Competition entry, shortlisted.

Urban plan for Sector 8 at Vitoria, 1968 (with Carlos Ferrán and Eduardo Mangada).

Autonomous University of Bilbao, 1969. Competition entry (with Francisco Javier Sáenz de Oíza).

Zaragoza historical centre refurbishment, 1969–70. Competition entry, second prize (with Manuel de Solà-Morales).

Urumea Housing Building, San Sebastián, 1969–73 (with Javier Marquet, Javier Unzurrunzaga and Luis Zulaica).

Elvira España School, Tudela, 1969–71 (based on a modified design of the Schools of Tudela competition entry, submitted in 1966).

Plaza de los Fueros in Pamplona, 1970–75 (with Estanislao de la Cuadra-Salcedo).

Mery López Huici House, Santo Domingo, Madrid, 1970–72.

INI Pavilion for the Barcelona Trade Fair, 1971.

Royal House of Mercy, Tudela, Navarra, 1972–83.

Telefónica headquarters, San Sebastián de los Reyes, Madrid, 1972–3.

Bankinter headquarters, Madrid, 1972–6 (with Ramón Bescós) .

Theo Gallery, Barcelona, 1973 (with Elias Torres).

Madrid Stock Exchange Building, 1973. Competition entry.

Éibar city centre refurbishment, 1972–3. Competition entry, first prize.

Lirón de Robles House, Somosaguas, Madrid, 1973–6.

Masaveu Gallery, Madrid, 1973–7.

Housing in Paseo de La Habana, Madrid, 1973–7 (with Ramón Bescós).

Fénix Mutuo headquarters, Madrid, 1973–6.

Logroño town hall, 1973–81.

Huesca Provincial Government headquarters, 1974. Competition entry, third prize (with Ramón Bescós).

Altos Hornos de Vizcaya Madrid headquarters, Aravaca, 1974. Competition entry.

    Studio Dos Bookshop, Madrid, 1974.

Añón House, Tudela, 1974–6.

Puy House, La Moraleja, Madrid, 1975–6 (with Juan Antonio Cortés).

Residential District Actur de Lakua, Vitoria, 1976–80. Competition entry, first Prize (with Manuel de Solà-Morales).

San Martín House, La Moraleja, Madrid, 1976–7.

Refurbishment of a house in Almuradiel, Ciudad Real, 1978–9.

Housing proposal in Cannaregio, Venice, 1978–9. Proposal for a seminar.

Bank of Spain in Madrid. 1978–9. Competition entry, first prize.

Aranjuez Especial Urban Plan, 1979–82 (with Manuel de Solà-Morales).

Housing in Rua Vieja, Logroño, 1979–82.

Bankinter headquarters extension, Valencia, 1979–90 (with Ramón Bescós).

Bank of Spain in Jaén, 1980–88.

National Museum of Roman Art, Mérida, 1980–86.

Mora de Ebro Hospital, Tarragona, 1981. Competition entry.

Nuevo Riaño, Leon, 1981. Competition entry.

Previsión Española headquarters, Seville, 1982–8.

Cerdá House, Pozuelo de Alarcón, 1982–5.

Urbanization of *Polígono 01–2*, Tudela, 1982–92.

Montjuic Olympic Stadium, Barcelona, 1983. Competition entry (with Francisco Javier Sáenz de Oíza).

Prinz-Albrecht-Palais, Berlin, 1983. Competition entry.

Tarragona Institute of Architects, 1983–92.

Santander Palace of Festivals, 1984. Competition entry.

Bankinter headquarters refurbishment, Seville, 1984–6.

Atocha Railway Station, Madrid, 1984–92. From a first prize-awarded competition entry.

Bicocca Competition, Milan, 1985. Competition entry.

IACP Competition Entry for Il Campo di Marte, Venice, 1985. Competition entry, first prize *ex aequo*.

Seville Expo 92, 1986. Competition entry.

Museumsquartier Messepalast, Vienna, 1986. Competition entry.

Saint Scholastic Priory, Cambridge, Mass., 1987. Competition entry.

L'Auditori, Barcelona, 1987–99.

San Pablo Airport, Seville, 1987–92.

Joan and Pilar Miró Foundation, Palma de Mallorca, 1987–92.

L'Illa Diagonal building, Barcelona, 1987–93. From a first prize-awarded competition entry (with Manuel de Solà-Morales).

Villahermosa Palace refurbishment, Thyssen-Bornemisza Museum, Madrid, 1989-92.

Concert hall and cultural centre in Lucerne, 1990. Competition entry, second prize.

Principality of Asturias Auditorium, 1990. Competition entry.

Palazzo del Cinema, Lido, 1990. Competition entry, first prize.

Davis Museum, Wellesley College, Massachusetts, 1990–93.

Kursaal Auditorium and Congress Centre, San Sebastián, 1990–99. From a first prize-awarded competition entry.

Museum of Modern Art and Architecture, Stockholm, 1991–8. From a first prize-awarded competition entry.

Murcia town hall extension, 1991–9.

Monastery of Guadalupe refectory, Cáceres, 1991–4.

Cultural centre in Don Benito, Badajoz, 1991–7.

Cranbrook Academy of Arts Extension, Bloomfield Hills, 1991–2002 (with Moneo-Brock).

Guadiana Hydrographical Confederation headquarters, Mérida, 1991–2007.

Baluard de Sant Pere, Palma de Mallorca, 1991. Competition entry.

Magaña Winery, Tudela, 1991–2.

Chivite Winery, Arinzano, 1991–2002.

Red Eléctrica headquarters, San Sebastián de los Reyes, Madrid, 1992–7.

Audrey Jones Beck Building Museum of Fine Arts, Houston, 1992–2002.

Potsdamer Platz urban proposal, Berlin, 1992. Competition entry.

Amiens University library, 1993. Competition entry, finalist.

Grand Hyatt Hotel and Office Building and Office Building at Potsdamer Platz, Berlin, 1993–8.

Santa Teresa Square refurbishment, Ávila, 1993–2004.

Zaragoza Museum of Modern Art, 1993. Competition entry.

OPCW Building, The Hague, 1994. Competition entry (by invitation).

Cardiff Opera House, 1994. Competition entry.

Tate Gallery Bankside, London, 1994–5. Competition entry (by invitation).

Roofing system for the Helsinki Railway Station, 1994. Competition entry, second prize.

General and Royal Archives of Navarra, Pamplona, 1995–2003.

ODA Gallery, Barcelona, 1995 (one page).

Bibliotheca Hertziana, Rome, 1995. Competition entry (by invitation).

Ambassador's residence in Washington, 1995–2002.

National Gallery of Scottish Art, Glasgow, 1996. Competition entry (by invitation).

Cathedral of Our Lady of Angels, Los Angeles, 1996–2002. From a first prize awarded competition entry.

Pollalis House, Belmont, Mass., 1996–2005.

Beirut Souks, 1996–2009.

Multi-purpose sports ring, Cáceres, 1997. Competition entry.

Steinenberg Theatre, Basel, 1997. Competition entry.

Administrative building for Seville Municipality, 1997–9 (unbuilt).

Housing in a former military barracks area, Logroño, 1997–9.

Arenberg Campus Library, Leuven, 1997–2002.

Bridge over Pisuerga River, Valladolid, 1997–2004 (with engineer Julio Martínez Calzón).

Gregorio Marañón Maternal and Paediatric Hospital, Madrid, 1997–2003 (with José María de la Mata).

Office building in Salvi Gardens, Vicenza, 1998 (unbuilt).

Prado Museum Extension, Madrid, 1998–2007. From a first prize-awarded competition entry.

Office and workshops for Camper, Son Fortaleza, Alaró, Mallorca, 1998–2003 (with Antonio Esteva).

BSCH Campus, Boadilla del Monte, Madrid, 1999. Competition entry (by invitation).

Business School, University of Chicago, 1999. Competition entry (by invitation).

Beulas Foundation, Huesca, 1999–2004.

Housing in Rabbijn Maarssenplein, The Hague, 1999–2004.

Hotels for Panticosa Resort, 2000–08.

Housing at Tres Creus, Sabadell, 2000–05 (with José Antonio Martínez Lapeña and Elias Torres).

LISE, Harvard University, Cambridge, Mass., 2000–07.

Museum and Cornisa Park of the Roman Theatre Museum in Cartagena, 2000–08.

Chase Centre for the RISD, Providence, 2000–08.

Aragonia building, Zaragoza, 2000–10.

Convention Centre 'El Miradero', Toledo, 2000–12.

Sydney Museum of Contemporary Art, 2000. Competition entry (by invitation).

Córdoba Congress Centre, 2001. Competition entry (by invitation).

New headquarters for the Government of Cantabria, Santander, 2001. Competition entry, first prize.

Bank of Spain Extension, Madrid, 2001–6 (modified design of the Bank of Spain competition
    entry submitted in 1979).
University of Deusto Library, Bilbao, 2001–9.
Iesu Church, San Sebastián, 2001–11.
Danish Radio Concert Hall, Ørestad, 2002. Competition entry (by invitation).
Sammlung Brandhorst, Munich, 2002. Competition entry (by invitation).
Avery Fisher Hall, Lincoln Center, New York, 2002. Competition entry.
Constanza Hotel, Barcelona, 2002–7 (with Manuel de Solà-Morales and Lucho Marcial).
Government of Cantabria headquarters, Santander, 2002–8. Competition entry, first prize.
One New Change, London, 2003. Competition entry (by invitation).
Cultural Centre in San Francisco Monastery, Tudela, 2003–2010.
Opera house, office building, housing and 'Kolizej' shopping centre, Ljubljana, 2004. Competition
    entry (by invitation).
Palazzo del Cinema, Lido, 2004–6. Competition entry (by invitation).
City-port urban redevelopment, Las Palmas de Gran Canaria, 2004. Competition entry (by
    invitation).
Office building for L-Bank, Karlsruhe, 2004. Competition entry (by invitation).
Ascona Conference Centre, 2005. Competition entry (by invitation).
Hotel and conference centre in Mallorca, 2005. Competition entry (by invitation).
Zürichforum, Zurich, 2005. Competition entry, first prize.
Hoyo de Esparteros redevelopment, Malaga, 2005– (in progress).
Laboratory for Novartis, Basel, 2005–8.
Northwest Science Building at the University of Columbia, New York, 2005–10 (with
    Moneo-Brock).
Mercer Hotel, Barcelona, 2005–12 (with Lucho Marcial).
Refurbishment of the Ávila Institute of Architects, Avila, 2006.
Domplatz Bebauung, Hamburg, 2006. Competition entry (by invitation).
Unicabebauung, Vienna, 2006. Competition entry (by invitation).
Philadelphia Museum of Fine Arts extension, 2006. Competition entry (by invitation).
Cultural centre in Estepona, 2006 (unbuilt).
Baltasar Lobo Museum in the Zamora Castle, 2006–9.
Peek & Cloppenburg department store, Vienna, 2007. Competition entry (by invitation).
Hotel in St Moritz, 2007. Competition entry (by invitation).
Barnes Foundation, Philadelphia, 2007. Competition entry (by invitation).
Marshall Site, Jesus College, Cambridge, 2007. Competition entry (by invitation).
Auditorium in Pollença, 2007 (unbuilt).
Packard Hotel, Havana, 2007–10 (unbuilt).
Atocha Station Extension, Madrid, 2007–12 (with Pedro Elcuaz).
Commonwealth Institute, Kensington & Chelsea, London, 2008. Competition entry (by
    invitation).
Abrizzi-Franchetti Conference Centre, Treviso, 2008 (unbuilt).
New town hall building and surrounding areas, Vigo, 2009–10 (unbuilt).
European Embankment, St Petersburg, 2009. Competition entry (by invitation).
Erweiterung Stadthalle, Heidelberg, 2009. Competition entry (by invitation).
Kunstmuseum, Basel, 2009. Competition entry (by invitation).
Kulturzentrum 'Les Arts Gstaad', Gstaad, 2010. Competition entry (by invitation).
Housing and shopping area in Udine city centre, 2010– (in progress).
Office building for EADS, Toulouse Airport, 2012 (unbuilt)
Contemporary Art Museum of the University of Navarra, Pamplona, 2011–14.
Puig Tower, Hospitalet de Llobregat, 2012–14 (with Lucho Marcial and GCA).
Santiago Bernabeu Stadium Extension, Madrid, 2013–14. Competition entry (by invitation; with
    Herzog and de Meuron).

INTERVIEWS AND CONVERSATIONS WITH THE AUTHORS

González de Canales, Francisco, personal conversation with Luis Moreno Mansilla, Cambridge, Mass., Cafe Pamplona, February 2006

—, personal conversation with Antón Capitel, London, Soho, June 2011

—, personal conversation with Rafael Manzano, Seville, Santa Justa Station, 6 March 6 2012

—, interview with Rafael Moneo, Madrid, Cinca 5 and Atocha Station, 5 December 2012

—, personal conversation with Emilio Tuñón, March 2014

Ray, Nicholas, interview with Enrique de Teresa, Madrid, Círculo de Bellas Artes, 4 April 2012

Ray, Nicholas, and Fernando Pérez Oyarzun, personal conversation with Rafael Moneo, March 2008

ARTICLES

"Premios de Roma 1962', *Arquitectura* 50, 1963, pp. 18–26

'El Ayuntamiento de Logroño', *Arquitectura* 236, May–June 1982, pp. 19–33

'Rafael Moneo: Interview', *Progressive Architecture* 6, June 1986, pp. 78–85

Mansilla+Tuñón: Recent Work', *2G* 27, 2003 (with texts by Luis Díaz Mauriño, Carles Muro, Luis Rojo and Rafael Moneo)

Area 67, March–April 2003 (special issue on Rafael Moneo)

Arkinka 94, August 2003 (*Rafael Moneo: Obras Recientes*)

Arquitectura Bis 23–4, July–September 1978 (special issue on the School of Madrid)

A+U 227, August 1989 (special issue on Rafael Moneo)

A&V Monografías de Arquitectura y Vivienda 36, July–August 1992 (*Rafael Moneo 1986–1992*; English edition, trans. Gina Cariño and ed. David Cohn)

Casabella 498–9, February 1984 (*Archittectura come modificazione*)

Casabella 765, April 2008 (*Madrid*, pp. 56–104)

Documentos de Arquitectura 34, 1996 (*Fundación Pilar y Joan Miró*)

El Croquis 20, April 1985 (*Rafael Moneo*); *El Croquis* 43, June 1990 (*Seis Propuestas Para San Sebastián: Moneo, Navarro Baldeweg, Peña/Corrales, Botta, Foster, Isozaki*); *El Croquis*, 64, February 1994 (*Rafael Moneo 1990–1994*); *El Croquis*, 98, March 2000 (Fernando Márquez and Richard Levene (eds), *Rafael Moneo 1967–2004: Imperative Anthology*, Madrid: El Croquis Editorial, October 2004

Hogar y Arquitectura 76, May–June 1968 (*Obras de Rafael Moneo*).

Scalae: Documentos Periódicos de Arquitectura 1, 2003 ('Rafael Moneo: Autor de Arquitectura')

Nueva Forma 108, 1975 (*La Obra Arquitectónica de Rafael Moneo 1962–1974*)

Tectónica 12, October 2000 (*Kursaal*)

Angelillo, Antonio, 'Conversazione con Rafael Moneo', *Casabella* 621, March 1995, pp. 4–19

Argan, Giulio Carlo, 'On the Typology of Architecture', *Architectural Design* 33: 12, 1963, pp. 564–5 (reprinted in Kate Nesbitt (ed.), *Theorizing a New Agenda for Architecture*, New York: Princeton Architectural Press, 1996, pp. 242–6

Baldellou, Miguel Angel, 'Lo cóncavo', *Arquitectura* 319, 1999, pp. 8–13

Banham, Reyner, 'Neo-Liberty: The Italian Retreat from Modern Architecture', *Architectural Review* 125/747, April 1959, pp. 231–5

Bohigas, Oriol, 'Notas sobre el concurso Bicocca', *Arquitectura* 260, May–June 1986, pp. 9–13

Buchanan, Peter, 'Moneo Romana Mérida: Museum, Mérida, Spain', *Architectural Review* 178: 1065, November 1985, pp. 38–47

Capitel, Antón G., 'Apuntes sobre la Obra de Rafael Moneo', *Arquitectura* 236, 1982, pp. 9–17

—, 'En torno a la figura de Rafael Moneo', *Tectónica* 12, 2000, pp. 4–19

—, 'Compacidad y luz cenital: la culminación de un método en el Museo de Houston', *Arquitectura* 332, June 2003, pp. 11–18

Cohen, Preston Scott, 'Intersection in the Architecture of Rafael Moneo', *Prototypo* 9, May–June 2004, s.n.

Colquhoun, Alan, 'Typology and Design Method', *Perspecta* 12, 1969, pp. 71–4 (first published in *Arena* 33, June 1967, reprinted in *Essays in Architectural Criticism*, Cambridge, Mass.: MIT Press, 1981, pp. 43–50

—, 'Between Type and Context: Forms and Elements of a Unique Architecture', *A&V* 36, 1992, pp. 8–11

Dal Co, Francesco, 'Roman Brickwork: The Museum of Roman Art of Mérida by Rafael Moneo', *Lotus International*, 46: 2, June 1985, pp. 22–35

—, 'Per una teoria dell'architettura: Rafael Moneo e Giorgio Grassi', *Casabella* 666, April 1999, pp. 30–33

—, 'La Cattedrale di Nostra Signora degli Angeli', *Casabella* 712, June 2003, pp. 68–87

De Teresa, Enrique, 'La analogía Romana', *Anales de Arquitectura* 1, 1989, pp. 73–80

Díaz Medina, Carmen, 'El Lucernario hecho museo. Rafael Moneo, ¿a la busqueda de un nuevo tipo?', *Anales de Arquitectura* 7, 1996, pp. 72–85

Feduchi, Luis, and Francesco Dal Co, 'Rafael Moneo a Helsinki e Madrid: Moneo e i concorsi', *Casabella* 646, June 1997, pp. 2–14

Fernández-Galiano, Luis, 'Professor Moneo', *Arquitectura Viva* 63–4, 1997, pp. 194–9

—, 'El Prado, suma y sigue', *Arquitectura Viva* 63, November–December 1998, pp. 67–9

—, 'K de Kursaal. Dados en la arena: de la necesidad y el azar', *Arquitectura Viva* 69, November–December 1999, pp. 88–9

—, 'Se construye con ideas. Rafael Moneo, una conversación', *Arquitectura Viva* 77, March–April 2001, pp. 71–3

Fullaondo, Juan Daniel, 'Notas de Sociedad', *Nueva Forma* 108, 1975, pp. 2–13

González Serna, Antonio, 'Un retablo abstracto', *Arquitectura Viva* 62, September–October 1998, pp. 74–5

Granell Trias, Enrique, 'Uno strano progetto: Il nuevo Museo del Prado', *Casabella* 646, June 1997, pp. 20–21

Gregotti, Vittorio, 'The Form of the Territory', trans. Walter van der Star, *OASE* 80: *On Territories*, Spring 2010, pp. 7–22

Hernández de León, Juan Miguel, 'The Impossibility of the School of Madrid', *UIA International Architect* 2, 1983, p. 10

Jiménez, Carlos, 'The Cathedral by Moneo in Los Angeles', *AV Monografías* 95, May–June 2002, pp. 108–21

Kipnis, Jeffrey, 'On Moneo's Anxiety', *Harvard Design Magazine*, Fall 2005–Winter 2006, pp. 97–104

Mangada, Eduardo, 'Dibujar después de construir: reflexión personal sobre la arquitectura, a propósito de la obra de Rafael Moneo', *Arquitectura* 252, February 1985, p. 16

Muro, Carles, 'Hacia una arquitectura potencial', *Circo* 97, 2002

Poisay, Charles, 'Entretien. Rafael Moneo. Museo de Arte Romano de Mérida', *Le Moniteur A.M.C.* 8, June 1985

Roberts, Nicholas W., 'Design as Materials Research: Building a Cathedral to Last 500 Years', *arq* 7: 3/4 pp. 333–51

Rogers, Ernesto Nathan, 'L'evoluzione dell'architettura: risposta al custode dei frigidaires', *Casabella–continuità* 228, pp. 2–4 (English edition, 'The Evolution of Architecture: Reply to the Custodian of Frigidaires', in Joan Ockman (ed.), *Architecture Culture 1943–1968: A Documentary Anthology*, New York: Rizzoli, 1993)

Rowe, Colin, 'The Mathematics of the Ideal Villa: Palladio and Le Corbusier Compared', *Architectural Review* 101, March 1947, pp. 101–4; reprinted in *The Mathematics of the Ideal Villa and Other Essays*, Cambridge, Mass.: MIT Press, 1976

Ruiz Cabrero, Gabriel, 'Todo son tentaciones para Rafael Moneo', *Arte y Parte* 3, June–July 1996, pp. 8–20

Sloterdijk, Peter, 'Rules for the Human Zoo: A Response to the Letter on Humanism', *Environment and Planning D: Society and Space* 27, 2009, p. 12, trans. Mary V. Rorty (original edition, *Regeln für den Menschenpark: ein Antwortschreiben zu Heideggers Brief über den Humanismus,* Frankfurt: Suhrkamp, 1999, transcription of a lecture given in Basel, 15 June 1997)

Solà-Morales, Ignasi de, 'From Contrast to Analogy', *Lotus International* 46: 2, June 1985, pp. 34–46

—, 'La recherche patiente', *Arquitectura* 271–2, March–July 1988, p. 24

Tuomey, John, 'Rafael Moneo and the Responsibility for Form', *Journal of the Royal Institute of Architects of Ireland* 162, November/December, 2000

Vitale, Daniele, 'Rafael Moneo, Architect: Designs and Works', *Lotus International* 33: 4, 1981, pp. 67–70

BOOKS

Abrantes, Vitor, and Barbara Rangel, *Columbia University Northwest Science Building: Design, Construction, Technologies,* Porto: Gequaltec, 2011

Adorno, Theodor W., *Philosophy of New Music,* trans., ed., and with an introduction by Robert Hullot-Kentor, Minneapolis: University of Minnesota Press, 2006

Alberti, Leon Battista, *De Re Aedificatoria: On the Art of Building in Ten Books,* trans. Joseph Rykwert, Robert Tavernor and Neil Leach, Cambridge, Mass.: MIT Press, 1988

Banham, Reyner, *Theory and Design in the First Machine Age,* London: Architectural Press, 1960

Bloom, Harold, *The Western Canon,* New York: Riverhead Books, 1994

Capella, Juli, *Rafael Moneo Diseñador,* Barcelona: Santa & Cole, ETSAB, 2003

Casamonti, Marco, *Rafael Moneo,* Milan: Motta architettura, 2008

Charlottesville Tapes: Transcripts of the Conference Held at the University of Virginia School of Architecture, Charlottesville, Virginia, November 12 and 13, 1982, Random House Incorporated, 1985

Cortés, Juan Antonio, and Duccio Malagamba, *Rafael Moneo International Portfolio 1985–2012,* Fellbach: Edition Axel Menges, 2013

Coverdale, John F., *The Political Transformation of Spain after Franco,* New York: Praeger, 1977

Dal Co, Francesco (ed.), *10 immagini per Venezia: Raimund Abraham – Carlo Aymonino – Peter Eisenman – John Hejduk – Bernhard Hoesli – Rafael Moneo – Valeriano Pastor – Gianugo Polesello – Aldo Rossi – Luciano Semerani: mostra dei progetti per Cannaregio ovest; Venezia, 1 aprile–30 aprile 1980,* Venice: Officina Edizioni, 1980

Davison, Cynthia (ed.), *Eisenman-Krier: Two Ideologies: A Conference at Yale University School of Architecture,* New York: Monacelli Press, 2004

Deleuze, Gilles, *Expressionism in Philosophy: Spinoza,* trans. Martin Joughin, New York: Zone Books, 1990 (first published in French in 1968)

—, *Spinoza: Practical Philosophy,* trans. Robert Hurley, San Francisco: City Lights, 1988 (first published in French in 1970, revised and expanded 1981)

—, *En Medio de Spinoza,* trans. Equipo Editorial Cactus, Buenos Aires: Editorial Cactus, 2008 (a compilation of Gilles Deleuze's lectures on Spinoza, given at the University of Vincennes, 1980–81, trans. from a recording at the National Library of France)

—, *The Fold: Leibniz and the Baroque,* trans. Tom Conley, Minneapolis: University of Minnesota Press, 1993 (originally published in French in 1988)

Descombes, Vincent, *Modern French Philosophy,* trans. Lorna Scott-Fox and J. M. Harding, Paris: Minuit, 1980, pp. 77–109 (originally published in French in 1979)

Diéguez Patao, Sofía, *La generación del 25: Primera arquitectura moderna en Madrid,* Madrid: Cátedra, 1997

Durand, Jean-Nicolas-Louis, *Précis de leçons d'architecture données à l'École Royale Polytechnique* (1802–5), facsimile edition, Paris: L'École Royale Polytechnique, 1819 (English edition, *Précis of the Lectures on Architecture, with Graphic Portion of the Lectures on Architecture,* trans. David Britt, Los Angeles: Getty Research Institute, 2000)

Esteban Maluenda, Ana, 'Sustrato y sedimento. Los viajes en la formación y evolución del arquitecto: el caso de Rafael Moneo', in *Viajes en la transición de la arquitectura española hacia la modernidad*, Pamplona: Universidad de Navarra, 2010

Etxepare Zugasti, Carlos (ed.), *Rafael Moneo: museos, auditorios, bibliotecas*, San Sebastián: Kutxa Fundazioa, 2005

Feduchi, Luis M., *La casa por dentro*, Madrid: Afrodisio Aguado, 1948

—, *Interiores de hoy*, Madrid: Afrodisio Aguado, 1955

—, *Historia del mueble*, Madrid: Abantos, 1966

—, *Estilos del mueble español*, Madrid: Abantos, 1969

—, *Itinerarios de arquitectura popular española*, Barcelona: Blume, 1974–84 (5 vols)

Flores Caballero, Manuel (ed.), *Rafael Moneo: Writings and Conversations in Peru*, Lima: Pontificia Universidad Católica del Perú, Facultad de Arquitectura y Urbanismo, 2009

Frampton, Kenneth, *Studies in Tectonic Architecture, The Poetics of Construction in Nineteenth- and Twentieth-Century Architecture*, Cambridge, Mass.: MIT Press, 1995

—, 'Moneo's Paseo: The Bankinter', in *Labor, Work and Architecture: Collected Essays on Architecture and Design*, London: Phaidon Press, 2002, pp. 278–87

Giedion, Sigfried, *Space, Time and Architecture*, Cambridge, Mass.: Harvard University Press, 1982 (first edition 1941)

Gombrich, Ernst, *Norm and Form: Studies in the Art of the Renaissance*, London: Phaidon, 1966

González Capitel, Antón, 'Apuntes para un ensayo sobre la obra del arquitecto Rafael Moneo', in *Oteiza – Moneo: Pabellón de Navarra: Exposición Universal de Sevilla*, Pamplona: Caja Municipal, 1992, pp. 61–88

González de Canales, Francisco (ed.), *Rafael Moneo: Una Reflexión Teórica desde la Profesión. Materiales de Archivo (1961–2013)*, La Coruña: Fundación Barrié de la Maza, 2013

Gregotti, Vittorio, *Il Territorio dell'Architettura*, Milan: Feltrinelli, 1966

—, 'Architecture, Environment, Nature', in Joan Ockman (ed.), *Architecture Culture 1943–1968: A Documentary Anthology*, New York: Rizzoli, 1993, pp. 399–401

—, 'Territory and Architecture', in Kate Nesbitt (ed.), *Theorizing a New Agenda for Architecture*, New York: Princeton Architectural Press, 1996, pp. 338–44

—, 'On Modification', in *Inside Architecture*, trans. Peter Wong and Francesca Zaccheo, Chicago and Cambridge, Mass.: Graham Foundation and MIT Press, 1996, pp. 67–73 (originally published in Italian in 1991)

Hawkes, Dean, *The Environmental Imagination – Technics and Poetics of the Architectural Environment*, London: Taylor & Francis, 2008

Heidegger, Martin, 'Letter on Humanism', trans. Frank A. Capuzzi, in *Basic Writings: Martin Heidegger*, London: Routledge, 1977 (originally published in German in 1949)

IUAV, *Aspetti e problemi della tipologia edilizia*, Venice: Cluva, 1964

IUAV, *Rapporti tra la morfologia urbana e la tipologia edilizia*, Venice: Cluva, 1966

Kaufmann, Emil, *Architecture in the Age of Reason: Baroque and Post-Baroque in England, Italy and France*, Cambridge, Mass.: Harvard University Press, 1955

Kipnis, Jeffrey, 'Cincinnati Impressions', *Morphosis IV*, New York: Rizzoli, 2006, pp. 14–19

Lévi-Strauss, Claude, *Structural Anthropology*, London: Penguin, 1968

Levine, Neil, 'The Book and the Building: Hugo's Theory of Architecture and Labrouste's Bibliothèque Ste-Genevieve', in Robin Middleton (ed.), *The Beaux-Arts and Nineteenth-Century French Architecture*, London: Thames and Hudson, paperback edition, 1984, pp. 138–73

Márquez, Fernando, and Richard Levene (eds), *Rafael Moneo 1967–2004: Imperative Anthology*, Madrid: El Croquis Editorial, 2005

Martín Casas, Julio, and Pedro Carvajal Urquijo, *El exilio Español, 1936–1978*, Barcelona: Planeta, 2002

Muriel, Emmanuel, *Contemporary Architects*, New York: St. Martin's Press, 1980, pp. 551–2

Nagel, Thomas, *The View from Nowhere*, Oxford: Oxford University Press, paperback edition, 1989

Negri, Antonio, *Subversive Spinoza: (Un)Contemporary Variations*, trans. Timothy S. Murphy, Manchester: Manchester University Press, 2004

Nichols, Peter, *Modernisms: A Literary Guide*, Berkeley: University of California Press, 1995

Norberg-Schulz, Christian, *Genius Loci: Towards a Phenomenology of Architecture*, New York: Rizzoli, 1980

—, *Louis I. Kahn: Idea e Imagine*. Roma: Officina Ed., 1980

Ortega y Gasset, José: *Meditations on Quixote*, trans. Evelyn Rugg and Diego Marín, and introduction by Julián Marías, Chicago and Urbana: The University of Illinois Press, 2000, p. 45 (originally published in Spanish in 1914)

—, *Invertebrate Spain*, trans. Mildred Adams, New York: Howard Fertig, 1974 (originally published in Spanish in 1921)

—, *El tema de nuestro tiempo*, Madrid: Revista de Occidente, 1981 (first published 1923)

—, *Mission of the University*. Princeton, N.J.: Princeton University Press, 1944

—, *History as System*, trans. Helene Weyl, E. Clark and W. Atkinson, San Diego: Academic Press, 1962

Pareyson, Luigi, *Existence, Interpretation, Freedom: Selected Writings*, ed. with an introduction and notes Paolo Diego Bubbio, trans. Anna Mattei, Auroro, Colo.: The Davies Group, 2009

Pérez-Gómez, Alberto: *Architecture and the Crisis of Modern Science*, Cambridge, Mass.: MIT Press, 1983

Pizza, Antonio (ed.), *J. Ll. Sert and Mediterranean Culture*, Barcelona: COAC, 1996

Robbins, Edward, 'Interview with Rafael Moneo' in *Why Architects Draw*, Cambridge, Mass.: MIT Press, 1994, pp. 247–69

Rogers, Ernesto Nathan, *Esperienza dell'architettura*. Turin: Einaudi, 1958 (also consulted in its Spanish version: *Experiencia de la Arquitectura*, Buenos Aires: Nueva Visión, 1965)

Rossi, Aldo, *The Architecture of the City*, Cambridge, Mass.: MIT Press, 1982 (originally published in Italian in 1966)

—, *A Scientific Autobiography*, Cambridge, Mass.: MIT Press, 1984

—, *Contributo al problema dei rapporti tra tipologia edilizia e morfologia urbana*, Milan: ILSES, 1964 (reprinted in Aldo Rossi, *Scritti scelti sull'architettura e la città*, Milan, CLUP, 1975, pp. 253–60)

Rowe, Colin, 'Introduction' in *Five Architects*, New York: Wittenborn, 1972

—, and Fred Koetter, *Collage City*, Cambridge, Mass.: MIT Press, 1978

Ruiz Cabrero, Gabriel, *The Modern in Spain: Architecture after 1948*. Cambridge, Mass.: MIT Press, 2001

Rykwert, Joseph, *The First Moderns – The Architects of the Eighteenth Century*, Cambridge, Mass.: MIT Press, 1980

Sáenz Guerra, Francisco Javier, *Francisco Javier Sáenz de Oíza, José Luis Romany, Jorge Oteiza: A Chapel on St. James Way*, 1954, Madrid: Rueda, 2004

Santinello, Giovanni, 'Nicolo Cusano e Leon Battista Alberti, Pensieri sul bello e su L'arte', in *Nicoló da Cusa, Relazioni tenute al Convegno Internazionale di Bressanone nel 1960*, Florence: Sansoni Editore, 1962, pp. 147–83

Sartre, Jean-Paul, 'Existentialism is a Humanism', trans. Philip Mairet, in *Existentialism from Dostoyevsky to Sartre*, ed. Walter Kaufman, New York: World Publishing Company, 1956 (from a lecture originally published in French in 1946)

Somol, Robert, '12 Reasons to Get Back in Shape' in *Content*, ed. Office of Metropolitan Architecture and Rem Koolhaas, Cologne: Taschen, 2004, pp. 86–7

Steele, Brett, and Francisco González de Canales, *First Works: Emerging Architectural Experimentation of the 1960s & 1970s*, London: Architectural Association, 2009

Tafuri, Manfredo, 'Design and Techno Utopia' in Emilio Ambasz, *Italy, The New Domestic Landscape*, New York: MoMA, 1972

—, *Architecture and Utopia, Design and Capitalist Development*, trans. Barbara Luigi La Penta, Cambridge, Mass.: MIT Press, 1976 (originally published in Italian in 1973)

Thorne, Martha, *Rafael Moneo: Audrey Jones Beck Building, The Museum of Fine Arts, Houston*, Fellbach: Edition Axel Menges, 2000

Tigerman, Stanley, and the University of Illinois at Chicago, *The Chicago Tapes: Transcript of the Conference at the University of Illinois at Chicago, November 7 and 8, 1986*, New York: Rizzoli, 1987

Tusquest Blanca, Oscar, *Todo es comparable*, Barcelona: Anagrama, 1998

Unamuno, Miguel de, *The Tragic Sense of Life*, trans. J. E. Crawford Flitch, New York: Dover Publications, 1954 (originally published in Spanish in 1913)

Unger, Roberto Mangabeira, *The Critical Legal Studies Movement*, Cambridge, Mass.: Harvard University Press, 1983

Van Schaik, Leon, 'Failing to Elevate Innovations into a Metropolitan Discourse – Rafael Moneo', in *Mastering Architecture: Becoming a Creative Innovator in Practice*, London: Wiley Academy, 2005, pp. 178–81

Venturi, Robert, *Complexity and Contradiction in Architecture*, New York: Museum of Modern Art, 1966

Vescovini, Graziella Federici, 'Nicholas of Cusa, Alberti and the Architectonics of the Mind', in *Nexus II: Architecture and Mathematics*, Fucecchio: Edizioni Dell'erba, 1998, pp. 159–71

Vidler, Anthony, *Histories of the Immediate Present: Inventing Architectural Modernism*, Cambridge, Mass.: MIT Press, 2008

VV.AA., *Arquitecturas Desplazadas*, Madrid: Ministerio de Asuntos Exteriores, 2007

Weston, Richard, *Utzon: Inspiration, Vision, Architecture*, Hellerup: Blodal, 2002

Wittkower, Rudolf, *Architectural Principles in the Age of Humanism*, London: Warburg Institute, University of London, 1949

Zevi, Bruno, *Arquitectura in Nuce: Una definición de arquitectura*, Madrid: Aguilar, 1969 (trans. from the Italian by Rafael Moneo)

WEBSITES

Bray, Xavier, 'Giving the Prado Space to Breathe', *Apollo magazine*, 7 January 2008: www.apollo-magazine.com/features/434546/giving-the-prado-space-to-breathe.html

Capitel, Anton, 'Mis Memorias en la Escuela', 2009: http://acapitel.blogspot.com.es/2009/05/mis-memorias-de-la-escuela-de.html

Eisenman, Peter, and Mark Wigley, moderated by Enrique Walker, 'The Cat Has Nine Lives' (fourth lecture of the Wobble series), Columbia GSAPP, 12 September 2012: www.youtube.com/watch?v=Gu4-ErX6hDA&playnext=1&list=PLhRIxbhj2G OO-eSO6aEVL_XAuRKwtPeXQ&feature=results_video

Gedin, Andreas, ‚Moneo on Moderna Museet in Stockholm: To Locate a Large Building on Skeppsholmen', 1998: www.artnode.se/artorbit/issue1/i_moneo/i_moneo.html

Louis I. Kahn, Graduate Master Class at the University of Pennsylvania, 1971: www.youtube.com/watch?feature=player_embedded&v=2CYRSg-cjs4

Netherlands Architecture Institute, ‚Amsterdam Town Hall Competition', summer 2005: http://static.nai.nl/stopera/

DISSERTATIONS

Koukoutsi-Mazarakis, Valeria, 'José Rafael Moneo Vallés, 1965–1985', PhD dissertation, MIT, Cambridge, Mass., 2001

Smith, Stephen, 'Rafael Moneo', third-year dissertation, retained in the library of the University of Cambridge, Department of Architecture, 2002

TEXTS BY RAFAEL MONEO

Articles and essays (chronological)

'El poblado dirigido de Entrevías', *Hogar y Arquitectura* 34, May–June, 1961, pp. 3–28

'Sobre un intento de reforma didáctica (En la facultad de Arquitectura en Roma)', *Arquitectura* 61, January 1964, pp. 43–6

'Una obra de Ignazio Gardella, Casa en *La Zattere*, Venecia', *Arquitectura* 71, 1964, pp. 43–50

'Una visita a Poissy (Villa Saboya, Francia)', *Arquitectura* 74, 1965, pp. 35–6

'Notas sobre la arquitectura griega', *Hogar y Arquitectura* 59, July–August 1965, pp. 67–82

'Sobre Gaudí', *Arquitectura* 75, 1965, pp. 9–14

'A vueltas con la Metodología', *Arquitectura* 82, October 1965, pp. 9–14

'A la Conquista de lo Irracional', *Arquitectura* 87, March 1966, pp. 1–6

'Un Arquitecto del Setecientos: Bernardo Vittone', *Nueva Forma* 13, February 1967, pp. 38–43

'Edificio Girasol, Madrid (José Antonio Coderch Sentmenat)', *Arquitectura* 107, November 1967, pp. 18–38

'El Hombre y El Paisaje', in *IX Congreso Mundial de la U.I.A, Praga, Julio 1967: Memorias de su desarrollo (La arquitectura y el ambiente de la vida del hombre)*, Madrid: Consejo Superior de los Colegios de Arquitectos de España, 1968, pp. 81–9

'Sobre el escándalo de Sydney', *Arquitectura* 109, 1968, pp. 52–4

'La llamada Escuela de Barcelona', *Arquitectura* 121, 1969, pp. 1–7

'Vitrubio y El Buen Salvaje', *Arquitecturas Bis* 2, July 1974, pp. 12–14 (review of Joseph Rykwert, *La casa d'Adamo in Paradiso*, Milan: Adelphi, 1972)

'Gregotti y Rossi', *Arquitecturas Bis* 4, November 1974, pp. 1–4

'Prólogo a la edición Española', in Emil Kaufmann: *La Arquitectura de la Ilustración: Barroco y pos-barroco en Inglaterra, Italia y Francia,* Barcelona: Gustavo Gili, 1974, pp. vii–xxv

'Si te dicen que caí [Sobre las últimas obras de J. Ll. Sert en Barcelona]', *Arquitecturas Bis* 6, 1975, pp. 10–11

'Arquitecturas en las márgenes', *Arquitecturas Bis* 12, March 1976, pp. 2–5 (on Alvaro Siza and J. M. Jujol)

'Aldo Rossi: The Idea of Architecture and the Modena Cemetery', *Oppositions* 5, 1976, pp. 1–30

'Rey muerto, sin rey puesto', *Arquitecturas Bis* 13–14, May–June 1976, p. 48 (on Alvar Aalto)

'On James Stirling: Buildings and Projects 1950–1974', *Oppositions* 7. Winter 1976–7, pp. 90–92

'Entrados ya en el último cuarto de siglo', *Arquitecturas Bis* 22, May 1978, pp. 2–5

'On Typology', *Oppositions* 13, 1978, pp. 23–44; reprinted in Márques and Levene (eds), *Rafael Moneo 1967–2004: Imperative Anthology*

'Madrid 78: 28 arquitectos no numerarios', *Arquitecturas Bis* 23–4, 1978, pp. 22–54

'La Vie de bâtiments: extensions de la Mosquée de Cordoue', *DA Informations* 62, 1979, pp. 23–45

'Designing and Teaching: The Reorganization of the School of Architecture in Barcelona', *Lotus International* 23, 1979, pp. 71–4

'La obra reciente de Aldo Rossi: dos reflexiones', *2C Construcción de la Ciudad* 14, December 1979, pp. 38–41

'A mi entender', *Arquitectura* 228, 1981, pp. 54–6

'The Work of John Hejduk or the Passion to Teach', *Lotus International* 27, 1980, pp. 64–85

'Expansion of the Bank of Spain: The Replica of the Corner', *Lotus International* 32: 3, 1981, pp. 30–34

'Sobre Modern Architecture de K. Frampton', *Arquitecturas Bis* 36–7, 1981, p. 60

'4 citas/ 4 notas (Museo Soane, 12–14 Lincoln's Inn Fields, Londres)', *Arquitecturas Bis* 38–9, 1981, pp. 44–8

'La Propuesta Pedagógica de Jean-Nicolas-Louis Durand', in *J. N. L. Durand, Compendio de Lecciones de Arquitectura (1802–1805)*, Madrid: Pronaos, 1981, pp. i–xxv

'Madrid: los últimos veinticinco años', in *Madrid, Cuarenta Años de Desarrollo Urbano: 1940–1980*, Madrid: Ayuntamiento de Madrid, 1981, pp. 81–99

'Padre común', *Arquitecturas Bis* 41–2, 1982, pp. 48–50 (on Louis Kahn)

'Arquitectura e Historia', in *CA* 36, 1983, pp. 28–9

'The Solitude of Buildings', *A+U*, August 1989, pp. 32–40 (Kenzo Tange Lecture, Harvard University Graduate School of Design, 9 March 1985)

'Prólogo a la edición castellana' in Joseph Rykwert: *La Idea de Ciudad: Antropología de la Forma Urbana en el Mundo Antiguo*, Madrid: Editorial Herman Blume, 1985, pp. vii–x

'Postscript', in Aldo Rossi, *Aldo Rossi: Works and Projects*, New York: Rizzoli, 1985, pp. 310–17

'Ciphered Messages', *Bovisa: On John Hejduk's Bovisa Drawings*, Cambridge, Mass., and New York: Harvard University GSD and Rizzoli International, 1987

'The Idea of Lasting: A Conversation with Rafael Moneo', *Perspecta* 24, 1988, pp. 147–57

'Perfil de Oíza Joven', *El Croquis* 32–3, 1988, pp. 176–81

'Comments on Siza's Architecture', in *Figures and Configurations: Buildings and Projects 1986–1988*, Cambridge, Mass. and New York: Harvard University GSD and Rizzoli International, 1988, pp. 8–9

'Concerning the Hancock Tower by I. M. Pei and Partners', *Harvard Arquitectural Review* 7, February 1989, pp. 176–81

'Unexpected Coincidences', in *Wexner Center for The Visual Arts, Ohio State University: A Building Designed By Eisenman/Trott Architects*, New York: Rizzoli, 1989; reprinted in *El Croquis* 41, *Peter Eisenman*, 1989, pp. 52–61

'Unexpected Coincidences', in *Wexner Center for The Visual Arts, Ohio State University: A Building Designed By Eisenman/Trott Architects*, New York: Rizzoli, 1989, pp. 52–61

'Permanencia de lo efímero: La construccion como arte trascendente', *A&V* 25, 'Frank Gehry 1985–1990', 1990, pp. 9–12

'Reflecting on Two Concert Halls: Gehry versus Venturi', *El Croquis* 64, 'Rafael Moneo 1990/1994', February 1994, pp. 156–75 (Walter Gropius Lecture, Harvard University Graduate School of Design, 25 April 1990)

'The Rigor of Herzog & De Meuron', in Wilfried Wang (ed.), *Herzog & De Meuron Projects and Buildings 1982–1990*, Cambridge, Mass. and New York: Harvard GSD and Rizzoli, 1990, pp. 1–5

'The Murmur of the Site', in Cynthia C. Davison (ed.), *Anywhere*, New York: Rizzoli, 1992; reprinted in Márques and Levene (eds), *Rafael Moneo 1967–2004: Imperative Anthology*, pp. 634–41

'Un Lenguaje sin alardes', *AV Monografías* 40, 'Alvaro Siza, 1988–1993', March–April 1993, pp. 3–4

'Geometry as Unique Abode', *AV Monografías* 44, 'Louis I. Kahn', November–December 1993, pp. 2–3

'The Indifference of Anyway', Cynthia C. Davison (ed.), *Anyway*, New York: Rizzoli, 1993, pp. 176–83; reprinted in Márques and Levene (eds), *Rafael Moneo 1967–2004: Imperative Anthology*, 2004

'Recent Architectural Paradigms and a Personal Alternative', *Harvard Design Magazine*, Summer 1998, pp. 71–5; reprinted in Márques and Levene (eds), *Rafael Moneo 1967–2004: Imperative Anthology*, pp. 651–9

'Sul mestiere dell'architetto', in *Archi* 1, March 1998, pp. 11–13

'Sul concetto di arbitrarietà in architettura', *Casabella* 735, July–August 2005, pp. 22–33; reprinted in English in Flores Caballero, *Rafael Moneo: Writings and Conversations in Peru*, pp. 53–131

'La geometría de la Ópera de Sydney', in Paloma Alarcó Canosa, Xavier Antich, Javier Arnaldo: *Estudios de Historia del Arte en honor de Tomas Llorens*, Madrid: Machado libros, 2007, pp. 435–51

Books (chronological)

Programa de la Cátedra de Elementos de Composición, Barcelona: Cátedra de Elementos de Composición, Monografía 1, Ediciones de la ETSAB, 1972

Ejercicios del Curso de Elementos de Composición 1972–1973, Barcelona: Cátedra de Elementos de Composición, Ediciones de la ETSAB, 1973

Ejercicios del Curso de Elementos de Composición 1973–1974, Barcelona: Cátedra de Elementos de Composición, Ediciones de la ETSAB, 1974

Ejercicios del Curso de Elementos de Composición 1971–1972, Barcelona: Cátedra de Elementos de Composición, Ediciones de la ETSAB, 1975

Ejercicios del Curso de Elementos de Composición 1974–1975, Barcelona: Cátedra de Elementos de Composición, Ediciones de la ETSAB, 1975

La Idea de Arquitectura en Rossi y el Cementerio de Módena, Barcelona: Cátedra de Elementos de Composición, Monografía 4, Ediciones de la ETSAB, 1974 (English version *Oppositions* 5, 1976, pp. 1-30)

Apuntes sobre Pugin, Ruskin y Viollet, Barcelona: Cátedra de Elementos de Composición, Monografía 13, Ediciones de la ETSAB, November 1976 (doctorate course taught in 1975 with Ignasi de Solà-Morales)

Ejercicios del Curso de Elementos de Composición 1975–1976, Barcelona: Cátedra de Elementos de Composición, Ediciones de la ETSAB, 1976

Comentarios sobre dibujos de 20 arquitectos actuales, Barcelona: Cátedra de Elementos de Composición, Monografía 14, Ediciones de la ETSAB, October 1976 (with Juan Antonio Cortés)

Ejercicios del Curso de Elementos de Composición 1976–1977, Barcelona: Cátedra de Elementos de Composición, Ediciones de la ETSAB, 1977

Programas de Curso y Ejercicios de Examen, 1980–1981, 1981–1982, 1982–1983, 1983–1984, Madrid: Cátedra de Composición II, Ediciones de la ETSAM, 1985

Rafael Moneo: Bauen Für Die Stadt. Stuttgart: Verlag Gerd Hatje, 1993

Rafael Moneo: Byggnsader Och Projekt, 1973–1993, Stockholm: Arkitekturmuseet, 1993

The Pritzker Architecture Prize, 1996: Presented to José Rafael Moneo, Los Angeles: Jensen & Walker, 1996

Modern Museum and Swedish Museum of Architecture in Stockholm, Stockholm: Arkitektur Förlag; Raster Förlag, 1998

Rafael Moneo: La Solitudine Degli Edifici e Altri Scriti, Turin: Umberto Allemandi, 1999 (2 vols, ed. Andrea Casiraghi and Daniele Vitale)

Rafael Moneo: De la Fundació a la Catedral de L.A. 1990–2002, Mallorca: Fundació Pilar i Joan Miró a Mallorca, 2002

The Freedom of the Architect (Raoul Wallenberg Lecture), Ann Arbor: University of Michigan, 2002

Theoretical Anxiety and Design Strategies in the Work of Eight Contemporary Architects, Cambridge, Mass.: MIT Press, 2004

Sobre el concepto de arbitrariedad en arquitectura, Madrid: Real Academia de Bellas Artes de San Fernando, 2005 (English version in Flores Caballero, *Rafael Moneo: Writings and Conversations in Peru*)

El edificio del Banco de España, Madrid: Banco de España, 2006

Remarks on 21 Works, New York: The Monacelli Press, 2010

XXXI Pregón Taurino. Sevilla 2011, Seville: Real Maestranza de Caballería, 2011

Unpublished lectures (chronological)

'Gold Medal lecture' 2003, www.architecture.com/go/Architecture/News_2938.html. Royal Institute of British Architects: Royal Gold Medal 2003 presented to Rafael Moneo, London: RIBA, 2003

'New Idea of Space', *On Contemporary Architecture, Session 1*, Cambridge, Mass.: Harvard Graduate School of Design, Spring 2006

'Indifference Towards the Site', *On Contemporary Architecture, Session 4*, Cambridge, Mass.: Harvard Graduate School of Design, Spring 2006

'The Loss of Objecthood and the Death of Organicism', *On Contemporary Architecture, Session 5*, Cambridge, Mass.: Harvard Graduate School of Design, Spring 2006

'Casa da Musica: Rem Koolhaas', *On Contemporary Architecture, Session 9*, Cambridge, Mass.: Harvard Graduate School of Design, Spring 2007

How Difficulties Benefit the Work of the Architect (Kassler Lecture), Princeton, N.J.: Princeton University, 2011

Unpublished manuscripts (chronological)

'Memoria: Concepto. Oposición a la Cátedra de Elementos de Composición en las Escuelas Técnicas Superiores de Arquitectura de Madrid, Barcelona y Sevilla, November 1969', unpublished manuscript

'On Theory', unpublished manuscript presented at the Institute of Architecture and Urban Studies of New York, 1976

We should like to acknowledge the support of Rafael Moneo in this enterprise. He has willingly shared thoughts with us and corrected errors of fact, but he has not sought to exercise any kind of editorial control.

We also thank the following for advice, creative criticism and provocative comments during the writing of this monograph: Nuria Álvarez Lombardero and: Luis Basabe, Nicholas Bullock, Peter Carolin, Javier de Esteban, Enrique de Teresa, Sandra Rush Domínguez, Pedro Feduchi, Edward Ford, Maria Fraile, Fiona Green, Felipe Hernández, Susan James, Gillian Malpass, Fernando Pérez Oyarzun, Ricardo Sánchez Lampreave, Stephen Smith, Emilio Tuñon, Ben Walton. And the Master and Fellows of Jesus College, Cambridge, for financial support and intellectual encouragement.

Naturally the responsibility for errors remains our own.

INDEX